ROMANS

God's Word *for the* Biblically-Inept™ SERIES

Gib Martin

CARTOONS BY
Reverend Fun
(Dennis "Max" Hengeveld)
Dennis is a graphic designer for Gospel Films and the author of *Has Anybody Seen My Locust?* His cartoons can be seen worldwide at www.reverendfun.com.

STARBURST PUBLISHERS®

P. O. Box 4123, Lancaster, Pennsylvania 17604

To schedule author appearances, write:
Author Appearances
Starburst Publishers
P.O. Box 4123
Lancaster, Pennsylvania 17604
(717) 293-0939

www.starburstpublishers.com

CREDITS:
Edited by Larry Richards and Chad Allen
Copyedited by Heather Stroobosscher
Cover design by David Marty Design
Text design and composition by John Reinhardt Book Design
Illustrations by Bruce Burkhart and Melissa A. Burkhart
Cartoons by Dennis "Max" Hengeveld

Unless otherwise noted, or paraphrased by the author, all Scripture quotations are from the New International Version of The Holy Bible.

To the best of its ability, Starburst Publishers® has strived to find the source of all material. If there has been an oversight, please contact us, and we will make any correction deemed necessary in future printings. We also declare that to the best of our knowledge all material (quoted or not) contained herein is accurate, and we shall not be held liable for the same.

First Printing, December 2000

ISBN: 1-892016-27-3
Library of Congress Number 99-69037

Printed in the United States of America

READ THIS PAGE BEFORE YOU READ THIS BOOK . . .

Welcome to the *God's Word for the Biblically-Inept™* series. If you find reading the Bible overwhelming, baffling, and frustrating, then this Revolutionary Commentary™ is for you!

Each page of the series is organized for easy reading with icons, sidebars, and bullets to make the Bible's message easy to understand. *God's Word for the Biblically-Inept™* series includes opinions and insights from Bible experts of all kinds, so you get various opinions on Bible teachings—not just one!

There are more *God's Word for the Biblically-Inept™* titles on the way. The following is a list of available books. (See the following page for purchasing information.) We have assigned each title an abbreviated **title code**. This code along with page numbers is incorporated in the text **throughout the series**, allowing easy reference from one title to another.

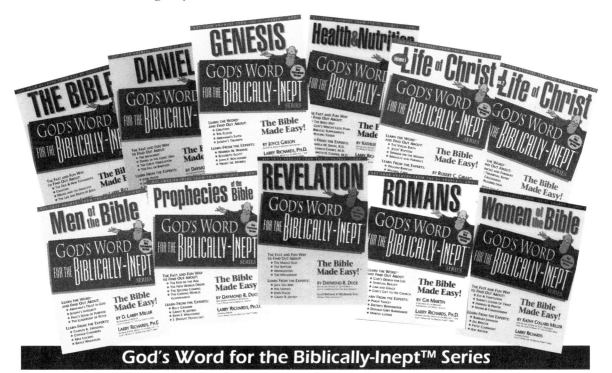

God's Word for the Biblically-Inept™ Series

What's in the Bible for . . .™

From the creators of the *God's Word for the Biblically-Inept™* series comes the innovative *What's in the Bible for . . .*™ series. Scripture has certain things to say to certain people, but without a guide, hunting down *all* of what the Bible has to say to you can be overwhelming. Borrowing the user-friendly format of the *God's Word for the Biblically-Inept™* series, this new series spotlights those passages and themes of Scripture that are relevant to particular groups of people. Whether you're young or old, married or single, male or female, this series will simplify the very important process of applying the Bible to your life.

What's in the Bible for . . .™ Couples *Larry and Kathy Miller*　　**WBFC**
(trade paper) ISBN 1892016028 $16.95

What's in the Bible for . . .™ Women *Georgia Curtis Ling*　　**WBFW**
(trade paper) ISBN 1892016109 $16.95

What's in the Bible for . . .™ Mothers *Judy Bodmer*　　**WBFM**
(trade paper) ISBN 1892016265 $16.95

What's in the Bible for . . .™ Teens *Mark Littleton and Jeanette Gardner Littleton*　**WBFT**
(trade paper) ISBN 1892016052 $16.95

● **Learn more at www.biblicallyinept.com** ●

Purchasing Information
www.starburstpublishers.com

Books are available from your favorite bookstore, either from current stock or special order. To assist bookstores in locating your selection, be sure to give title, author, and ISBN. If unable to purchase from a bookstore, you may order direct from STARBURST PUBLISHERS. When ordering please enclose full payment plus shipping and handling as follows:

Post Office (4th class)	United Parcel Service (UPS)	Canada	Overseas
$3.00 with a purchase of up to $20.00	$5.00 (up to $20.00)	$5.00 (up to $35.00)	$5.00 (up to $25.00)
$4.00 ($20.01–$50.00)	$7.00 ($20.01–$50.00)	15% ($35.01 and up)	20% ($25.01 and up)
8% of purchase price for purchases of $50.01 and up	$12.00 ($50.01 and up)		

Payment in U.S. funds only. Please allow two to four weeks minimum for delivery by USPS (longer for overseas and Canada). Allow two to seven working days for delivery by UPS. Make checks payable to and mail to:

Starburst Publishers®
P.O. Box 4123
Lancaster, PA 17604

Credit card orders may be placed by calling 1-800-441-1456, Mon–Fri, 8:30 A.M. to 5:30 P.M. Eastern Standard Time. Prices are subject to change without notice. Catalogs are available for a 9 x 12 self-addressed envelope with four first-class stamps.

What People Are Saying . . .

"Starburst's success with its *God's Word for the Biblically-Inept* series (100,000 copies sold and counting) may lead the way for other publishers to repackage their own commentaries accordingly, selling them not in seminaries, but at Sam's Clubs."

—*Publisher's Weekly*

"The reader may be *Biblically-Inept* at the beginning, but will be well informed by the end!"

—*Foreword Magazine*

"Congratulations on an outstanding piece of work! I look forward to seeing the entire *Biblically-Inept*™ series. I absolutely love it!"

—Ken Abraham, *best-selling author*

"Fantastic! What a fascinating approach to presenting the book of Revelation. It makes studying Bible prophecy easy, exciting, and interesting for everybody. Good content, great quotes, dynamic graphics. This book has more 'bells and whistles' than anything I've ever seen. It's user-friendly to the max!"

—Dr. Ed Hindson, *Assistant Pastor,*
Rehoboth Baptist Church, and best-selling author

"The Revelation book arrived this morning. I spent a few minutes glancing through it and am confident that you have a winner. The layout— the artwork—the interaction are marvelous. . . . I AM IMPRESSED!"

—Dan Penwell, *Manager, Trade Products,*
Hendrickson Publishers

CHAPTERS AT A GLANCE

PART TWO: God's Forgiveness

PART THREE: Experiencing Grace

PART FOUR: Jews and Gentiles

PART FIVE: A Grace-Filled Church

ILLUSTRATIONS

INTRODUCTION

Welcome to *Romans—God's Word for the Biblically-Inept™*. This volume is part of a series that takes the Bible as it is—the Word of God—and makes it both entertaining and enlightening. If you want learning to be an adventure, you'll appreciate this approach to study. If you have a thirst for the truth, you've just found a cool drink. If you've been looking for a way to enrich your knowledge of God's Word, studying the **apostle** Paul's letter to the Romans is a great way to start.

To Gain Your Confidence

Romans—God's Word for the Biblically-Inept™ keeps God's Word clear and simple and at the same time accurate, thorough, and interesting. It will take us to new spiritual heights in our journey with God. In the thin air of the climb, one's spiritual vision is sharpened, and at the summit we can see more clearly what it means to be a follower of Jesus. So strap on your climbing gear and get ready for this delightful adventure into God's truth!

Why Study Romans?

Romans is a book that helps us understand who God is and who we are in relation to God. If we have a right understanding of these two things, we will know better how to live in such a way that pleases God, brings us fulfillment, and makes a difference in the world around us.

How To Study Romans

There's more than one way to study Romans, but if you're a newcomer to this extraordinary historical writing, I would like to recommend an approach to studying Scripture that has helped many whom I have **mentored** over the years:

Let's Get Started

(Let's Get Started)

apostle: a personal representative of God

(What?)

Romans 1:11 I long to see you so that I may impart to you some spiri-

(Verse of Scripture)

good reasons to study!

KEY POINT

Humility doesn't mean thinking little of yourself, it means thinking nothing of yourself.

(Key Point)

mentored: taught, instructed, guided

Meet Paul

(Meet Paul)

Holy Spirit: the third Person of the Trinity

Grabbed by Grace

(Grabbed by Grace)

IN OTHER LETTERS

(In Other Letters)

Pharisee: one of a sect of Jews who were committed to strict observance of the Old Testament's commandments and their own traditions and interpretations

1. Get acquainted with the writer of the book. In this case, the writer is the apostle Paul and you'll find out more about him a little later under the heading "Paul: Mr. About-Face" and throughout the book with the help of a feature called "Meet Paul."

2. Familiarize yourself with Paul's other letters: 1 and 2 Corinthians, Galatians, Ephesians, Philippians, Colossians, 1 and 2 Thessalonians, 1 and 2 Timothy, Titus, Philemon, and maybe Hebrews.

3. Read through Romans at least once before you begin your study in *Romans—God's Word for the Biblically-Inept™*. This exercise will give you a helpful context for building your understanding.

4. Take time to pray. Invite the **Holy Spirit** to be your teacher and guide. Jesus says that the Spirit *"will guide you into all truth"* (John 16:13).

5. Finally, make journal writing a disciplined habit. This will help you remember what you learn. Here are some possible techniques:
   a. Write down questions that come to mind as you study (for example, the meanings of words with which you are unfamiliar or the names of people and places you want to study in your research later on).
   b. When you come upon the answers to your questions, write them down.
   c. When the Holy Spirit addresses one of your personal needs, make note of it and take a moment to thank God for speaking his will into your heart and mind.
   d. When something you read inspires you in a special way, write a prayer, a poem, or a letter to a special friend, sharing your adventure in God's Word. There is nothing more wonderful than sharing your experience of the God who knows all about you, who loved you enough to send Jesus Christ to share his love with you.

Paul: Mr. About-Face

As a **Pharisee** Paul, whose first name was Saul, believed in the Old Testament prophecies about a Messiah, a great leader who would emerge from the family line of King David. He, like most Jews, believed the Messiah would dethrone Roman rule, impose Old Testament law as national law, and usher in God's new kingdom.

One of Saul's duties as a member of the **Sanhedrin** was to travel around the country and arrest Christians because they were thought to be a serious threat to Judaism. Saul zealously sought to put an end to the exploding work of the Christian church in Jerusalem and all of Judah. We have no record that Paul actually killed Christians, but in Acts 8 we do see him approving of the execution of the Christian disciple, Stephen. The text reveals, "*Saul was there, giving approval to* [Stephen's] *death*" (Acts 8:1).

Not long afterwards Saul was on his way to **Damascus** to imprison Christians when "*suddenly a light from heaven flashed around him. He fell to the ground and heard a voice say to him, 'Saul, Saul, why do you persecute me?' 'Who are you, Lord?' Saul asked. 'I am Jesus, whom you are persecuting,' he replied*" (Acts 9:3–5). This encounter with the risen Christ changed Saul forever. His testimony is recorded three times in the Book of Acts.

Paul spent the rest of his life traveling from city to city spreading the good news that God forgives. At the end of his life he is faithfully serving his Lord in a Roman prison.

Why Use The New International Version (NIV)?

Paul wrote his letter to the Romans in Greek, the common language of the Roman Empire, so every English version of his letter is a translation. There are many good translations available today. This series uses the New International Version (NIV) because it is written in today's language and is easy to read and understand. The NIV accurately expresses the original Bible in clear English while remaining faithful to the thoughts of the original writers.

How To Use *Romans—God's Word For The Biblically-Inept* ™

Sit down with this book and your Bible.

* Start the book at chapter 1.
* As you work through each chapter, read the accompanying verses in your Bible.
* Use the sidebar loaded with icons and helpful information to give you a knowledge boost.
* Answer the Study Questions and review with the Chapter Wrap-Up.
* Then go on to the next chapter. It's simple!

Sanhedrin: *a council that governed the beliefs and lifestyle of the Jews during the time of the Roman Empire*

Damascus: *a city in Syria*

☞ **GO TO:**

Acts 7:54–60;
  1 Corinthians 15:9;
  Philippians 3:6
  (Christian church)

Acts 9:1–31; 22:5–21;
  26:9–20 (three)

Acts 28:17–31 (prison)

(Go To)

(Take It to Heart)

(What Others Are Saying)

Something to Ponder

(Something to Ponder)

Remember This . . .

(Remember This)

CHAPTER WRAP-UP

(Chapter Summary)

This book contains a variety of special features that will help you learn. Here they are again with a brief explanation of each.

Sections and Icons	What's It For?
CHAPTER HIGHLIGHTS	*the most prominent points of the chapter*
Let's Get Started	*a chapter warm-up*
Verse of Scripture	*what you came for—the Bible*
Commentary	*my thoughts on what the verses mean*
GO TO:	*other Bible verses to help you better understand (underlined text)*
What?	*the meaning of a word (bold text)*
KEY POINT	*a major point in the chapter*
Meet Paul	*information about Paul, the man and his beliefs*
Grabbed by Grace	*an explanation of the theme of grace*
IN OTHER LETTERS	*a discussion of how principles in the Book of Romans are in Paul's other letters too*
Take It to Heart	*a practical way to apply Scripture*
What Others Are Saying:	*if you don't believe me, listen to the experts*
Illustrations	*a picture is worth a thousand words*
Something to Ponder	*interesting points to get you thinking*
Remember This . . .	*don't forget this*
Study Questions	*questions to get you discussing, studying, and digging deeper*
CHAPTER WRAP-UP	*the most prominent points revisited*

A Word About Words

There are several interchangeable terms in this book: Scripture, Scriptures, Word, Word of God, and God's Word. All of these mean the same thing and come under the broad heading of the Bible.

The Bible is divided into two sections: the Old Testament and the New Testament. Throughout this commentary I use the words *Old Covenant* and *Old Testament* to mean the same thing, and I use *New Covenant* and *New Testament* to mean the same thing as well.

The word "Lord" in the Old Testament refers to Yahweh, God, whereas in the New Testament it refers to God's Son, Jesus Christ.

One Final Tip

Knowledge of the Bible is not meant to be an end in itself. God wants us to know his Word, but he also wants us to know him. In the same way, Paul wanted his readers to understand what he said, but he also wanted them to have a personal relationship with his Lord.

God, who gave us the Bible, is present with us when we read it. As you read Romans, ask him to help you understand his Word. Ask him to show you his wonderful grace and to help you put your faith in him. You'll be surprised and delighted as he answers your prayer. The Bible will enrich your life!

Bible Quote: This is where you'll read a quote from the Bible.

> **James 1:5** If any of you lacks wisdom, he should ask God, who gives generously to all without finding fault and it will be given to him.

Commentary: This is where you'll read commentary about the biblical quote.

Decisions, Decisions: In Or Out?

James, the brother of Jesus, is writing to the new believers who were scattered about the Roman world (see GWBI, pages 213–214) when they fled from persecution. James knows that godly wisdom is a great gift. He gives a simple plan to get it: if you need wisdom, ask for it. God will give it to us.

Up 'til now we've concentrated on finding the wind for the sails of your drifting marriage and overcoming marital problems. But you may be the reader who is shaking her head, thinking that I just don't understand what you're going through. You can't take the abuse any longer; you've forgiven the **infidelity** time after time; and in order for you and your children to survive, you see no alternative but divorce.

So let me...

husband...
get out a...   ...your
abuse sec...   ...nues,
ing to you; they are also harmful to your children's physical and emotional state.

"What?": When you see a word in bold, go to the sidebar for a definition.

infidelity: sexual unfaithfulness of a spouse

Go To: When you see a word or phrase that's underlined, go to the sidebar for a biblical cross-reference.

☞ **GO TO:**

Psalm 111:10 (source)

When you feel you've depleted all of your options, continue to ask God for wisdom in order to have the knowledge to make the right decisions. Wise women seek God. God is the source of wisdom and wisdom is found in Christ and the Word.

Remember This . . .

Gary Chapman, Ph.D.: Is there hope for women who suffer physical abuse from their husbands? Does reality living offer any genuine hope? I believe the answer to those questions is yes.[6]

Give It Away

You don't have to be a farmer to understand what the Apostle Paul wrote to the Corinthian church (see illustration, page 143). A picture is worth a thousand words, and Paul is painting a master-piece. He reminds us of what any smart farmer knows: in order to produce a bountiful harvest, he has to plan for it.

What Others are Saying:

What Others Are Saying: This is where you'll read what an expert has to say about the subject at hand.

MEN OF POWER: LESSONS IN MIGHT AND MISSTEPS 9

127

Feature with icon in the sidebar: Throughout the book you will see sections of text with corresponding icons in the sidebar. See the chart on page xviii for a description of all the features in this book.

Part One

THE NECESSITY OF FAITH

REVEREND FUN

"They say faith can move mountains . . . How much faith ya got?"

ROMANS 1: A SERVANT'S LONGING

CHAPTER HIGHLIGHTS

- A Divine Appointment
- Commitment and Prayer
- Holy Declaration
- The Human Condition

Let's Get Started

The apostle Paul wrote the Book of Romans in the first century, which was a time of rapid growth for Christianity. Good roads and internal political peace made for swift evangelism throughout the Roman Empire (see illustration, page 4). New churches were founded regularly.

Both biblical and nonreligious history report that many of the founders of the church in the city of Rome were **Jewish Christians**. Some time around A.D. 45 the emperors (first Tiberius and then Claudius) announced an **edict** to expel Jews from **Rome** so the only people left in the Roman church were **Gentiles**. When the edict against the Jews was repealed at the time of Claudius's death, many of the Jews who loved their Roman heritage returned to the city (see Appendix A for a map of the city of Rome).

When they came back, Jewish believers experienced a form of culture shock. The Gentiles gave little regard to many of the traditions and beliefs that the Jews dearly loved. The Roman church, therefore, was in tremendous tension. Paul, a seasoned saint and an expert on church growth, felt their concerns. He knew the Gospel could empower people to stick together despite their differences.

Jewish Christians: *Jews who believed in Jesus*

edict: *a royal command binding on everyone*

Rome: *the capital of the Roman Empire*

Gentiles: *non-Jews, whatever their race or religion*

☞ **GO TO:**

Ephesians 2:14–17; Colossians 3:8–11 (differences)

Meet Paul—In Acts 20 we gain some insight into how Paul arrived at his understanding of truth. The apostle had been in active ministry for a number of years. Prepared to depart from Asia for the next stage of his min-

The dashed lines show the boundaries of the eastern half of the Roman Empire about the time Paul wrote Romans in A.D. 57. The believers who lived in Rome were the recipients of Paul's letter. (For a map of the city of Rome, see Appendix A.)

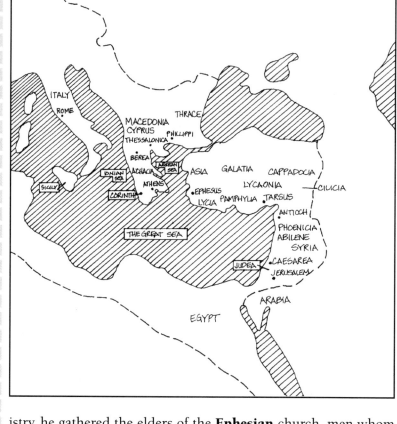

Ephesian: *of the city of Ephesus, in modern Turkey*

☞ **GO TO:**

1 Timothy 4:9–16;
2 Timothy 4:1–8;
Titus 3:1–10
(teaching)

istry, he gathered the elders of the **Ephesian** church, men whom Paul had trained for ministry, so that he could encourage and advise them one last time.

"You know how I lived the whole time I was with you," Paul declared, *"from the first day I came into the province of Asia. I served the Lord with great humility and with tears. . . . For I have not hesitated to proclaim to you the whole will of God"* (Acts 20:18–19, 27).

The phrase *"the whole will of God"* is very important. It probably refers in part to the incompleteness of the Old Testament, foreshadowing what the New Testament reveals in full-orbed beauty. Paul is also pointing out that his <u>teaching</u> is not unbalanced. He doesn't for instance emphasize grace at the expense of responsibility.

Israel emphasized carrying out every detail of the law while neglecting what Jesus thought were the weightier matters (things like caring for sick people and nurturing good heart attitudes). This unbalanced perspective led the Jews to lose sight of God's purposes entirely and drift into legalism, satisfied with externals and unaware that their hearts were far from God. Paul is providing a balanced picture of God's plans and purposes, in which no aspect is emphasized at the expense of another, and with such harmony that the whole can be seen and understood by Jesus' people.

What Others are Saying:

D. Martyn Lloyd-Jones: [Romans] was written as a letter by a great pastor. . . . It is a letter written to a church, and like all New Testament literature it had a very practical aim and end in view. The apostle was concerned to help these Christians in Rome, to build them up and establish them in their most holy faith.[1]

> **Romans 1:1** Paul, a servant of Christ Jesus, called to be an apostle and set apart for the Gospel of God.

Paul@servingJesus.com

what do I build my identity on?

Paul built his identity on being a servant of Jesus. The word "servant" is literally the word for "slave" in that culture, and it means "one who completely belongs to his owner and has no freedom to leave," not that Paul would *want* to leave. He wore this title gladly.

Once Paul was free, God commissioned him personally to be an apostle in the work of the **kingdom** of God. Paul told the Corinthian church, *"For I am the least of the apostles and do not even deserve to be called an apostle, because I persecuted the church of God. But by the grace of God I am what I am, and his grace to me was not without effect"* (1 Corinthians 15:9–10).

The word *apostle* comes from a Greek word meaning "one sent forth." In the historical sense, to be an apostle meant to be sent forth by Jesus Christ to build the church.

Years before Paul penned his letter to the Romans, God gave a man named Ananias a tough assignment. God told Ananias to go see Paul who was staying in the home of a man named Judas and pray for him. All Ananias knew about Paul was that he hated Christians, and Ananias wasn't prepared to be Paul's next victim! But God's command to Ananias was clear: *"Go! This man is my chosen instrument to carry my name before the Gentiles and their kings and before the people of Israel. I will show him how much he must suffer for my name"* (Acts 9:15–16). It's possible Paul learned his first lesson in servanthood from this good man.

☞ **GO TO:**

Galatians 1:10; Titus 1:1 (title)

kingdom: the rule of God

Something to Ponder

☞ **GO TO:**

Acts 1 (Ananias)

Acts 22:3–16; 26:9–18 (instrument)

Something to Ponder

John Chrysostom (A.D. 347–407), a patriarch of Constantinople (A.D. 398–404), was a man of great influence as a preacher, author, and leader. It was reported that he had failing eyesight, so to stay active and theologically accurate, he had Romans read to him twice a week.

Centuries later, John Wesley felt his heart strangely warmed in a little London prayer meeting in Aldersgate where the truths of Romans were being set forth. This experience set Wesley on a path that was to reach out to all of England and across the ocean to America.

What Others are Saying:

epistle: letter

Samuel Taylor Coleridge: [Romans is] the profoundest [*sic*] book in existence.[2]

Martin Luther: The **Epistle** to the Romans is the true masterpiece of the New Testament and the very purest Gospel, which is well worth and deserving that a Christian should not only learn it by heart, word for word, but also that he should daily deal with it as the daily bread of men's souls. It can never be too much or too well read and studied, and the more it is handled the more precious it becomes, and the better it tastes.[3]

F. L. Godet: The Reformation was certainly the work of the epistle to the Romans and that to the Galatians, and it is probable that every great spiritual renovation in the church will always be linked, both in cause and in effect, to a deeper knowledge of this book.[4]

KEY POINT

Paul's servant heart inspired him to live submissively under his Lord's authority.

> **Romans 1:2–4** The Gospel he promised beforehand through his prophets in the Holy Scriptures regarding his Son, who as to his human nature was a descendant of David, and who through the Spirit of holiness was declared with power to be the Son of God by his resurrection from the dead: Jesus Christ our Lord.

Paul's Pocket-Sized Guide To Jesus

Paul began his letter with a brief, yet very complete, account of who Jesus was. He sees an understanding of Christ, as presented in the Bible and revealed through Jesus himself, as the only truth broad enough to consolidate and unify the heart of God's message to humankind. This is why Paul's compact statement of Christ—about his nature, his **lineage**, his **Sonship**, and his resurrection—is Paul's point of departure.

lineage: a person's ancestors

Sonship: Jesus' special relationship with God the Father

On the human side Jesus came through the line of **David**. He was also *"declared with power to be the Son of God."* In this context, declared means "to be determined, to be marked out" with certainty as the Son of God. His divine nature was clearly demonstrated *"by his resurrection from the dead."* He was indeed the long awaited Messiah of Israel and the Savior of humankind (Luke 24:25–27, 45–47).

 Meet Paul—After years of ministering, Paul told the Philippians his reason for living: *"to me, to live is Christ"* (Philippians 1:21). The essence of Paul's life was Christ. His motivation for doing what he did, his goals, the way he treated people around him, everything about him revolved around the person of Jesus. His life was completely wrapped up in the purposes of Christ.

The promise God made to David in the **Davidic Covenant** was an unconditional promise. David would be in the bloodline of the Messiah. The Christ child was a descendant of Nathan, one of David's sons, so the unconditional promise was fulfilled (Luke 1:26–37; 2 Samuel 7:16).

A good example of an **Old Testament** prophecy of the Gospel is found in Acts 8:30–35 where an Ethiopian **eunuch** asks **Philip** who is being referred to in Isaiah 53:7–8. Philip tells him Isaiah is speaking of *"the good news about Jesus."* The eunuch believes immediately and seeks **baptism**.

Francis A. Schaeffer: Paul shows both the human and the divine side of **the Incarnation**. He certainly believed in Christ's deity, but the fact of His being truly divine does not change the fact that Christ was also a true man and came down through the natural line of David.[5]

> **Romans 1:5–6** Through him and for his name's sake, we received grace and apostleship to call people from among all the Gentiles to the obedience that comes from faith. And you also are among those who are called to belong to Jesus Christ.

Called To Christ

The church at Rome was a body of believers made up of both Jews and Gentiles, and Paul's mission was to all nations: *"to call people*

David: King of Israel one thousand years before Jesus' birth and an ancestor of Christ

Davidic Covenant: the promise that the Messiah would be a descendant of David

Old Testament: the first thirty-nine books of the Bible, all written before Christ's birth

eunuch: by the first century, the title of a high government official

Something to Ponder

Philip: a leader of the first Christians in Jerusalem

What Others are Saying:

baptism: sacred ritual involving water, symbolizing membership in God's family and purification from sin

the Incarnation: doctrine that the Son of God became a true human in Jesus

from among all the Gentiles to the obedience that comes from faith." Romans is for everyone.

IN OTHER LETTERS The cross created a level playing field. Each of us can become a child of God through faith in Jesus Christ. Paul reminds the Galatians (see illustration, page 4), *"There is neither Jew nor Greek, slave nor free, male nor female, for you are all one in Christ Jesus. If you belong to Christ, then you are Abraham's seed, and heirs according to the promise"* (Galatians 3:28–29).

The Gospel was the apostle Paul's introduction to grace. In Paul's theological development as a follower of Christ, there was nothing more important to grasp than an understanding of the **grace of God**. He wrote to the Corinthian Church, *"But by the grace of God I am what I am, and His grace toward me did not prove vain; but I labored even more than all of them, yet not I, but the grace of God with me"* (1 Corinthians 15:10 **RSV**). The message of God's grace permeated every aspect of Paul's life and every letter he penned to the churches.

Romans is about something the Bible calls the "New Covenant." Through Moses God had made an agreement—a contract or promise—with the Jewish people. This contract, also called the **Mosaic law**, was the "Old Covenant." Through Moses God promised to bless his people if they obeyed him, and to punish them if they disobeyed. Jesus introduced a "New Covenant." The New Covenant was predicted by the prophet Jeremiah, who said it would not be like the Old Covenant. God's people had not been able to keep the Old Covenant, and suffered many troubles. With the New Covenant God said he would change people from within, to make them truly good. Romans is about the New Covenant, and key words are righteousness and grace.

> **Romans 1:7** To all in Rome who are loved by God and called to be **saints**: Grace and peace to you from God our Father and from the Lord Jesus Christ.

From A God's-Eye View

As the epistle opens, we are introduced to God's view of the believers in Rome. Paul begins with a greeting, which acknowledges

---

Grabbed by Grace

grace of God: *kindness and love shown by God to people who do not deserve it*

RSV: *the Revised Standard Version of the Bible*

Something to Ponder

☞ **GO TO:**

Acts 26 (life)

Mosaic law: *the Ten Commandments and the other laws that God gave to Moses as standards of righteousness*

saints: *people who trust in Jesus as their Savior*

---

that these people have a special place in God's heart. Paul's Roman brothers and sisters were not called to be apostles, as he had been called, but to be "saints," a word that was commonly used for believers back then. The words *apostle* and *saint* both carry the idea of being "set apart," or called to holiness.

Linguistic scholar W. E. Vine says, "This sainthood is not an attainment; it is a state into which God in grace calls men."[6] Saints are deeply loved and share in God's life and mission. Paul's greeting demonstrates his recognition that all believers are members of one body, God's family.

Prior to this, Paul had completed a number of missionary journeys in the eastern Mediterranean region, quite a distance from Rome. He had been planting churches in a number of major metropolitan centers throughout southern and western Asia Minor (present-day Turkey, Greece, and Albania). The Roman Empire indirectly helped to spread the Gospel. Travel throughout the region was fairly easy by the day's standards. Roads were good, language was unified, and people were free to travel without fear (see illustration below).

Rome was heavy on Paul's heart, but he wouldn't be able to visit the city until the second stage of his church-planting agenda. Though Paul deeply wanted to spend time with these believers, he planned to do so later on his way to Spain.

☞ **GO TO:**

1 Peter 1:15–16; Ephesians 1:1–2 (sainthood)

☞ **GO TO:**

Romans 15:24, 28 (Spain)

Symbol of the Roman Empire

Among other ways they unified the region, the Romans used an eagle, shown here on a ball, as a symbol for the Roman Empire.

finished work: salvation through Christ's death on the cross

Something to Ponder

Why is this here?

Lamb of God: Jesus, referring to his death as a sacrifice for our sins

What Others are Saying:

Paul longed to go to Rome both to meet the saints there and to minister to them, but due to other responsibilities, he was prevented from doing so. This letter was his way of serving the believers in Rome even while he was physically absent from them. A letter is still a wonderful way to encourage a friend, build a relationship, and serve the kingdom of God. When was the last time you wrote to your friend who lives on the other side of the world? Remember, a letter is a missionary visit in printed form.

Dr. Francis A. Schaeffer thoughtfully reminds us, "Everything depends upon the **finished work** of Jesus Christ."[7] This is the divine power behind God's work of grace. God has no alternative plan. The Gospel of Jesus Christ is God's concluding message to a needy, sinful world. Paul discerned that his major mission was to plant the seeds of the Gospel as far and wide as the Spirit would lead him. He saw it as God's answer to our enslavement to sin, to self, and to Satan. In Christ Jesus, God had entered history as *"the **Lamb of God**, who takes away the sin of the world"* (John 1:29).

Saint Augustine: Here again [in Romans 1:7] Paul has emphasized God's grace rather than the saint's merit, for he does not say "to those loving God" but rather "to God's beloved."[8]

> **Romans 1:8a** First, I thank my God through Jesus Christ for all of you . . .

The First Item On Paul's Agenda

Having taken care of the "From" and "To" parts of his letter, Paul lingers for awhile in introductory matters before getting into his main concern. Why? It appears Paul just couldn't help but express how much he cared about his listeners. Like a boy who can't wait to show his mother the finger painting he did in school, Paul can't resist showing his gratitude. "I thank GOD for you!" he says.

The Bible tells us we ought always to pray and not lose heart. The disciples asked Jesus to teach them to pray because they saw how much he valued prayer. We too ought to ask God to teach us how to pray.

One of the best signs of a right understanding of grace is a

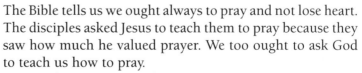

desire to pray—not prayer on the run, but deep, thoughtful prayer on your knees, in your bedroom, in your study, or with a few close friends. It is a privilege we are to take advantage of daily.

Paul wanted to rescue the Romans from their bondage to the <u>law</u> and lead them into an understanding of grace through **faith**. Paul's prayers were not performances of **piety** to impress people; they were evidence of the fire in his soul.

☞ **GO TO:**

Galatians 4:1–7;
Romans 6:14 (law)

Remember This . . .

Adolf Schlatter: For Paul all that God does obligates him to give thanks, because God is "his God" . . . his capacity to give thanks is the work of Jesus in him; he is giving thanks "through him."[9]

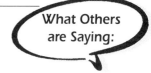

What Others are Saying:

> **Romans 1:8b** . . . because your faith is being reported all over the world.

faith: *trust in and reliance on God and his Word*

piety: *devoutness*

World-Class Faith

Here we see the object of Paul's passion: spreading the Gospel. He doesn't say, "I thank God for you because of all the nice stuff you sent me last Christmas," or anything like that. He thanks God for them because he was thrilled that word of their faith was spreading. He goes so far as to use the exaggeration, *"all over the world."* When we consider how much of "the world" was unknown to Paul, a contemporary equivalent to this statement might be, "I thank God for you because your faith is spreading all over the universe!" He was exaggerating, of course, much like the fisherman who gets really excited about his catch and says, "It was the size of Texas!"

People might get bent out of shape if you say the Bible includes exaggeration. They may think you mean, "The Bible is full of inaccuracies so you can't really trust it." As long as you're clear about the *kind* of exaggeration you're talking about, arguments over this matter should be few.

There are basically two types of exaggeration. One is the Texas-sized fish exaggeration mentioned above, which is also known as hyperbole (pronounced HI-PER-BULL-EE). Hyperbole is used strictly for effect and would never deceive anyone. No one, for example, would really believe you if

Something to Ponder

you said you had a "mile-high ice cream cone." The other kind of exaggeration takes facts and distorts them in such a way that people can be deceived. Pretend a driver was backing up in your local K-Mart's parking lot and barely bumped into you. You would be using the second kind of exaggeration if you told a police officer that the other driver was speeding at 100 miles per hour. This kind of exaggeration is more accurately called lying. The Bible does not lie to us, but here and there you will find the use of hyperbole, which, incidentally, makes for fun reading!

What Others are Saying:

John F. Walvoord and Roy B. Zuck: Paul made a practice of beginning his letters with a word of thanks to God, a specific prayer, and a personal message to the recipients. For the Romans he rejoiced that news of their faith had spread all over the world, a hyperbole, meaning throughout the Roman Empire.[10]

> **Romans 1:9–10** God, whom I serve with my whole heart in preaching the gospel of his Son, is my witness how constantly I remember you in my prayers at all times; and I pray that now at last by God's will the way may be opened for me to come to you.

Don't Doubt

The only time Paul used the phrase *"God is my witness"* is when there might have been some reason for his listeners to doubt him. So, why wouldn't the Romans have believed that Paul prayed fervently for them? Well, if an acquaintance wrote you a Christmas card that said, "I pray for you always," wouldn't you assume they were just being nice and didn't really expect to be taken literally? Most of the Roman Christians did not even know Paul, so hearing him say he prayed for them all the time would have been odd to them. Now, imagine if the above-mentioned acquaintance said this instead: "I pray for you all the time, and I'm not just saying that. I really mean it!" You might be a little more convinced. This is similar to what Paul was doing with his *"God is my witness"* statement.

Also, Paul was about to leave for Jerusalem when he wrote this letter, but had not yet visited Rome. He may have thought the Roman Christians would think he didn't care as much about them as he did about the Christians in Jerusalem. He was doing his best to quell such suspicions.

He then told the Roman Christians that he was praying God would open the way for him to visit them. Paul did not rely on his own will but on God, *"both to will and to do for His good pleasure"* (Philippians 2:13 **NKJV**). Fortunately, God eventually answered Paul's prayer in the affirmative. Acts 18–28 gives an account of how Paul made it to Rome.

NKJV: the New King James Version of the Bible

Pelagius: Paul does not find the way **propitious** unless the will of God who knows all things has directed him to a place where he might reap some fruit. For example, we read in Acts that, although he wanted to go to one place, he was directed to another.[11]

What Others are Saying:

William S. Plumer: Like other things, journeys are prosperous or adverse, as the Lord **vouchsafes** or withholds his favor and blessing. . . . And we should acknowledge his hand in the [most common] affairs of life.[12]

propitious: favorable

vouchsafes: grants

Meet Paul—What Paul says concerning his prayer life is evidence of his religious roots. As a former Pharisee, Paul would have been used to a prayer ritual. As a devout Jew, he might have spent several hours a day in prayer, as many did in conjunction with the morning and evening offerings in the **Temple**.

Temple: where Jews went to pray, worship, and offer sacrifices

Prayer

Prayer is learned, just as speaking is learned. We learn a few words and our parents praise us, even applaud us. Then we begin to build sentences. So it is with prayer.

Prayer is our method of communication with God. Jesus, our **high priest** (see illustration, page 14) and mediator, hears the prayers of all believers and delivers them to the Father. We pray because we have a Father who will consider our requests and answer them according to his divine will.

The Holy Spirit empowers the believer's prayer life. When the Word of God exhorts us to *"pray in the Spirit"* (Ephesians 6:18), it points us to the reality that God's Spirit lives in us and prays through us.

God helps us further by providing the Psalms as our prayer book. The Psalms act as a tutorial, showing us the purpose of prayer, the intimacy of prayer, and the potential of a life bathed in prayer. Paul often quoted the Psalms in his letters.

☞ **GO TO:**

Hebrews 4:14–16; Hebrews 2:17 (high priest)

Romans 3:9–18; Romans 15:9, 11 (Psalms)

high priest: chief person who represents believers before God

Romans 1:11–13 I long to see you so that I may impart to you some spiritual gift to make you strong— that is, that you and I may be mutually encouraged by each other's faith. I do not want you to be unaware, brothers, that I planned many times to come to you (but have been prevented from doing so until now) in order that I might have a harvest among you, just as I have had among the other Gentiles.

It's Been Way Too Long

In order to interpret this passage accurately, we need to step out of our technological age, with its ability to provide up-to-the-second worldwide communication, and into the apostle's sandals. When Paul wrote, *"I long to see you,"* he meant he had a yearning that could not be fully satisfied apart from a face-to-face visit. He tells them he wants to give them "a spiritual gift," but as soon as he says this he humbly asserts that encouragement would flow in both directions.

Jesus taught his disciples, *"From everyone who has been given much, much will be demanded; and from the one who has been entrusted with much, much more will be asked"* (Luke 12:48b). Paul had been given much. The apostle held himself accountable to share his spiritual wealth with the people of God as well as with the **pagans**—an expression of humility, not pride.

Remember This . . .

Dietrich Bonhoeffer, *writing in prison during World War II:*

What Others are Saying:

Who am I? They often tell me
I stepped from my cell's confinement
Calmly, cheerfully, firmly,
Like a squire from his country house.
Who am I? They often tell me
I used to speak to my warders
Freely and friendly and clearly,
As though it were mine to command.
Who am I? They also tell me
I bore my days of misfortune
Equably, smilingly, proudly,
Like one accustomed to win.

KEY POINT

Humility doesn't mean thinking little of yourself, it means thinking nothing of yourself.

Am I then really all that which other men tell of?
Or am I only what I myself know of myself?
Restless and longing and sick, like a bird in a cage,
Struggling for breath, as though hands were compressing my throat,
Yearning for colours, for flowers, for the voices of birds,
Thirsting for words of kindness, for neighbourliness,
Tossing in expectation of great events,
Powerlessly trembling for friends at infinite distance,
Weary and empty at praying, at thinking, at making,
Faint, and ready to say farewell to it all?

Who am I? This or the other?
Am I one person today and tomorrow another?
Am I both at once? A hypocrite before others,
And before myself a contemptibly woebegone weakling?

Or is something within me still like a beaten army,
Fleeing in disorder from victory already achieved?
Who am I? They mock me, these lonely questions of mine.
Whoever I am, Thou knowest, O God, I am Thine![13]

Mother Teresa:
Give the world the best you have,
    and it may never be enough;
Give the world the best you've got anyway.

You see, in the final analysis,
    it is between you and God;
It was never between you and them anyway.[14]

Francis A. Schaeffer: Paul is not distant or aloof from the people he writes to. . . . He knows that such maturity will bring sweet and wonderful fellowship between himself and the Romans. He expects to receive a blessing from them as well as giving one to them. This is surely true among Christians always . . . the blessings run in both directions.[15]

> **Romans 1:14–15** I am obligated both to Greeks and non-Greeks, both to the wise and the foolish. That is why I am so eager to preach the gospel also to you who are at Rome.

Paul, The Eager Beaver

covenant: formal, binding agreement or promise

Paul explains his **covenant** responsibilities: *"I am obligated,"* or as it is translated in the King James Version, *"I am debtor."* A debtor is a person under obligation. Why does Paul consider himself a debtor? For the same reason all Christians are debtors. When we were saved, we were simultaneously called to be *"Christ's ambassadors, as though God were making his appeal through us"* (2 Corinthians 5:20). Having been **reconciled** to God, God is calling each one of us to be ministers of reconciliation.

reconciled: restored to harmony with God

Paul's calling, like ours, was universal. He was indeed obligated to Greeks and to non-Greeks (non-Jewish people), to the wise and the foolish. He was, as are we, called by God to lay aside all prejudices, all judgments, and all slander. He is boldly affirming that God is for all people, everywhere, regardless of gender, race, or nationality.

☞ **GO TO:**

1 Corinthians 9:19–27 (all people)

Like fish that swim upstream, Paul went against a culture that was full of prejudice, hatred, and abuse. The Greeks considered themselves wise and the world foolish barbarians. The Jews looked upon the Gentiles as unclean and therefore dangerous.

Paul considered himself a debtor to both Jews and Greeks. He thought of himself as obligated to do <u>good</u> to all people, which eventually brought <u>hostility</u> from many directions.

 Meet Paul—Paul was eager to preach the Gospel in Rome or wherever else the Lord took him, regardless of the cost. He was ready to mobilize, to do whatever was required to accomplish God's bidding in this world-famous city, but neither fame nor money motivated Paul; his central concern <u>was always the glory of God</u>.

When you give your life to the Lord, there is a cost. Jesus warned his **disciples**, *"If the world hates you, keep in mind that it hated me first. If you belonged to the world, it would love you as its own. As it is, you do not belong to the world, but I have chosen you out of the world. That is why the world hates you. Remember the words I have spoken to you: 'No servant is greater than his master'"* (John 15:18–20). We ought to remember and be encouraged by the truth that if the world hates us, it is because the world is ignorant of Christ's love.

> **Romans 1:16** I am not **ashamed** of the gospel, because it is the power of God for the salvation of everyone who believes: first for the Jew, then for the Gentile.

Shout It From The Housetops

Paul wants to establish clearly in the hearts of his recipients that he is not in any way *"ashamed of the gospel,"* not even in the capital city of the Roman Empire.

He explains why: *"because it is the power of God for the salvation of everyone who believes."* The word *power* speaks of God's quenchless energy to transform all believing human beings into citizens of the kingdom of Christ. This <u>transformation</u> begins with the <u>new birth</u> and continues day after day, year after year until we finally meet Jesus face-to-face.

Note also that Paul says *"first for the Jew, then for the Gentile."*

Something to Ponder

☞ **GO TO:**

2 Corinthians 10:31–32; 1 Peter 4:11 (good)

2 Corinthians 6:3–10 (hostility)

Take It to Heart

disciples: *committed first followers of Jesus*

world: *society, culture*

ashamed: *concerned others will think less of me*

☞ **GO TO:**

2 Corinthians 3:17–18; John 14:1–7; Revelation 21:1–4; 1 John 3:1–3 (transformation)

John 3 (new birth)

This statement reflects Paul's basic strategy in all of his missionary journeys. When Paul arrived in a new city, he went first to the Jewish synagogues. He did this not only because Jews were there, but because God-fearing Gentiles were there, people who were interested in the Jewish view of God and in Jewish moral teachings. Out of this group he formed a core of leaders around whom he would build a church.

Locating True North

A compass is an instrument used for showing direction. Its swinging magnetic needle, which always points north, can keep you from going in the wrong direction. A compass is an excellent tool when you're lost.

The Gospel is the Christian's compass (see illustration, page 19). If we live the Gospel, if we love the Gospel, if we continue to trust the Gospel, it will eventually lead us home. That is God's New Covenant promise: *"Never will I leave you; never will I forsake you"* (Hebrews 13:5). Now *that* is Good News.

Return to this starting point frequently, letting it do the work of a compass, pointing you to the true "North."

What Others are Saying:

Apollinaris of Laodicea: Paul says that even if, in the very largest cities, the preacher of the cross of Christ will be mocked by the ignorant, he is not to be ashamed. For if the Son of God bore the shame of the cross on our behalf, how could it not be out of place for us to be ashamed at the Lord's suffering for us?[16]

Karl Barth: The Gospel is not a truth among other truths. Rather, it sets a question-mark against all truths. . . . Anxiety concerning the victory of the Gospel—that is, Christian Apologetics—is meaningless, because the Gospel is the victory by which the world is overcome. By the Gospel the whole concrete world is dissolved and established. . . . God does not need us. Indeed, if He were not God, He would be ashamed of us. We, at any rate, cannot be ashamed of Him.[17]

> **Romans 1:17** For in the gospel a righteousness from God is revealed, a righteousness that is by faith from first to last, just as it is written: "The righteous will live by faith."

Compass

A compass is an excellent metaphor for the Gospel.

☞ **GO TO:**

Genesis 1:3 (the Fall)

Righteousness From God

Here we are brought to our predicament. Because of **the Fall**, our relationship with God has been fatally damaged and needs to be reconciled (see GWGN, pages 37–48). The Gospel is God's way of extending his grace, love, and **mercy**—his only way of restoring our souls. It is through this restoration that we receive absolute righteousness from God.

the Fall: Adam and Eve's disobedience, which corrupted human nature

mercy: compassion for the needy that moves one to help

faith: trust in God's promise of salvation

Because we do not deserve this wonderful gift, and can do nothing to earn it, God elects to offer it to his fallen creation through the gift of **faith**, hence the phrase, *"a righteousness that is by faith."* We gain eternal life and a relationship with our Creator, and it costs us nothing.

To show the Christians in Rome that this is not some new, upstart doctrine, Paul quotes a famous Old Testament passage from Habakkuk 2:4: *"The righteous will live by . . . faith."* Note the unity of the message between the Old and New Testaments.

☞ **GO TO:**

Galatians 3:11, Hebrews 10:38 (faith)

What Others are Saying:

D. Martyn Lloyd-Jones: "The just shall live by faith". . . is the theme of this Epistle to the Romans; it says that God in His infinite wisdom, and in His infinite love and mercy and compassion, has found a way to save the unrighteous and to make them righteous, and the way is that He gives to us, that He imputes to us, the righteousness of His own Son, our blessed Lord and Saviour Jesus Christ. Now that is the heart of the Gospel.[18]

> **Romans 1:18–20** The wrath of God is being revealed from heaven against all the godlessness and wickedness of men who suppress the truth by their wickedness, since what may be known about God is plain to them, because God has made it plain to them. For since the creation of the world God's invisible qualities—his eternal power and divine nature—have been clearly seen, being understood from what has been made, so that men are without excuse.

The Great Devastation

Paul moves in verse 18 to a point that is critical to understanding his argument. He is making a historical statement, referring back to what happened in Genesis when humankind fell, but what he says is true on a psychological level as well so it is certainly relevant today.

suppress: to push down in one's consciousness, to ignore

He uses the word "**suppress**" to describe what people in their wickedness do with truth. If people suppress the truth, obviously they have some knowledge of the truth. We know about truth because God has built within us a recognition of himself. That's why Paul says, *"God has made it plain to them."*

How do we recognize God? Through creation. Psalm 19 says, *"The heavens declare the glory of God; the skies proclaim the work of his hands. Day after day they pour forth speech; night after night they display knowledge."* The psalmist is expressing in poetry the same truth that Paul expressed in his letter to the Romans. Creation shouts to us that God exists, and we hear those shouts. We may try to ignore them, but we hear them nonetheless.

The Wrath Of God

☞ **GO TO:**

2 Thessalonians 1:5–10; Revelation 20:11–15 (wrath of God)

In my nearly forty years of ministry, preaching, and counseling, I have come to agree wholeheartedly with Karl Barth when he says, "Indeed, [judgment] is the fact most characteristic of our life."[19] Our sinfulness and all the atrocity that results from it has stirred the wrath of God. A holy God must of necessity reject all that is unholy. His wrath is a display of that rejection.

> **Romans 1:21–25** For although they knew God, they neither glorified him as God nor gave thanks to him, but their thinking became futile and their foolish hearts were darkened. Although they claimed to be wise, they became fools and exchanged the glory of the immortal God for images made like mortal man and birds and animals and reptiles.
>
> Therefore God gave them over in the sinful desires of their hearts to sexual impurity for the degrading of their bodies with one another. They exchanged the truth of God for a lie, and worshiped and served created things rather than the Creator—who is forever praised. Amen.

What Were We Thinking?

Paul points out that despite the knowledge of God people received through creation, they did not act on it. They did not give him glory, nor thank him. Their minds were clouded and their hearts were darkened. They began worshiping idols instead of God.

As mentioned before, this is true historically, but it is true psychologically as well. People who reject God become futile in their thinking and their hearts become clouded. They begin to set other things in place of God.

God turns people who reject him over to their sinful desires to reap the **retribution** of choosing to live in sin and for sinful pleasure. God judges sin in part by allowing it to run its course. Yet, it is the resulting sense of darkness that often opens our hearts to God's holy light. Therefore, we see that there is both grace and mercy in the midst of **judgment**.

retribution: repayment

judgment: assessing penalties for wrongdoing

IN OTHER LETTERS Paul says similar things in many of his letters. For example, he tells the Ephesian church that they are not to live any longer as the Gentile world "*in the futility of their thinking. They are darkened in their understanding and separated from the life of God because of the ignorance that is in them due to the hardening of their hearts*" (Ephesians 4:17–18). Note Paul's mention of the mind and the heart here, which he mentions in Romans too. He says their understanding is darkened as a result of the state of their hearts.

Karl Barth: The more the unbroken man marches along his road secure of himself, the more surely does he make a fool of himself, the more certainly do that mortality and that manner of life which are built upon a forgetting of the abyss, upon forgetting of men's true home, turn out to be a lie.[20]

Adolf Schlatter: The individual does not save himself from the powers that urge him to sin by a new resolution or a new idea. He is saved by him who lives and works for all . . . as the bringer of grace, takes the place of the law. The believer is saved through the message of Christ which reveals God's righteousness, rather than his wrath.[21]

shameful lusts: evil desires

> **Romans 1:26–27** Because of this, God gave them over to **shameful lusts**. Even their women exchanged natural relations for unnatural ones. In the same way the men also abandoned natural relations with women and were inflamed with lust for one another. Men committed indecent acts with other men, and received in themselves the due penalty for their perversion.

☞ **GO TO:**

Leviticus 18:22
(indecent acts)

Take Two

We come to the second *"God gave them over"* statement; the first was back in verse 24. This time Paul says God gave them over to immorality, sexual immorality. They exchanged the truth of God for a lie and then exchanged natural sexuality for unnatural sexuality.

☞ **GO TO:**

Romans 1:25 (lie)

Instead of using the normal Greek words for "men" and "women," he uses the words for "males" and "females." Ironically, humans (men and women) are the only species that engage in homosexuality. It does not exist in the animal kingdom.

Remember This . . .

It's important to understand that depraved behavior always begins with a lie, and Satan is the father of lies. When we choose darkness over light, we exchange God's truth for Satan's lie. While Adam and Eve were in paradise—a sinless environment—they believed Satan's lie and in so believing became liars themselves (see GWGN, pages 37–45).

Pelagius: Once lust is unbridled, it knows no limits. In the order of nature, those who forget God did not understand themselves either.[22]

Francis A. Schaeffer: With a realism we see throughout the Bible, Paul addresses the issue of male (and female) homosexuality. Religious people don't always like to deal with the reality of such things, but the Bible never covers up reality. It deals with humanity just the way it is.[23]

What Others are Saying:

> **Romans 1:28–32** Furthermore, since they did not think it worthwhile to retain the knowledge of God, he gave them over to a depraved mind, to do what ought not to be done. They have become filled with every kind of **wickedness**, **evil**, **greed** and **depravity**. They are full of envy, murder, strife, deceit and malice. They are gossips, slanderers, God-haters, insolent, arrogant and boastful; they invent ways of doing evil; they disobey their parents; they are senseless, faithless, heartless, ruthless. Although they know God's righteous decree that those who do such things deserve death, they not only continue to do these very things but also approve of those who practice them.

wickedness: the exact opposite of righteousness

evil: vile

greed: a constant urge to acquire more

depravity: a state of internal evil

Like A Pig In Its Wallow

what do you think?

This is a statement of judgment. God didn't just let people be depraved. God, as an act of judgment, caused them to be depraved. The fact that people become *"filled with every kind of wickedness, evil, greed and depravity"* is evidence that they have rejected God. Here, Paul is demonstrating the existence of sin and the reality that human righteousness does not exist.

Imagine a boy and a girl who are walking down a road together. Imagine their hands brush and eventually they find themselves holding hands. This happens because there is an attraction between them.

Now imagine the same girl is ironing her clothes before going out with the boy and her hand touches the hot iron. She jerks it away. The fact that she jerks her hand away shows antagonism, not attraction.

Paul is saying human beings prove they are lost because they jerk away from God when they come into contact with him. Human beings are sinners and are not righteous, no matter what they pretend.

Something to Ponder

doesn't mean irredeemable

KEY POINT

People are not righteous because they have rejected God.

perma-jerk vs. occasional rebellious-jerk

Study Questions

1. How did God confirm Paul's apostolic office? *By appearing to Paul*
2. On what or whom did Paul build his identity? *as Jesus' slave*
3. According to Paul, how was Jesus' divine nature confirmed? *resurrection*
4. Paul presents a worldview that is both comprehensive and built on the authority of the Bible as the Word of God. What was his key to being able to accomplish this?
5. Why was Paul not ashamed of the Gospel of Jesus Christ? *It is the means of salvation*
6. Paul gives the world a picture of the destruction of the human soul. Is this simply Paul's judgment, or is it God's word to man to alert us concerning his wrath?

CHAPTER WRAP-UP

- Romans introduces us to Paul, the apostle. His call and commitment to the Gospel of God deeply influence both the substance and the tone of his message. (Romans 1:1–7)

- Paul holds prayer as a key to a faith that is fresh and continues to unfold as he serves Jesus Christ. Having received God's forgiveness, Paul longs to share God's love and purpose with the world. (Romans 1:8–15)

- The Gospel was Paul's deepest motivation for ministry. He knew it was God's way of reaching a world lost in darkness and evil. He knew God's power to overcome evil was centered in the Gospel message. (Romans 1:16–17)

- Paul speaks plainly about the wrath of God, a subject that many seek to ignore, but love motivates the true disciple of Christ to speak the whole counsel of God. Due to men's wickedness they began to suppress the truth. So God gave them over to wickedness to receive in themselves the due penalty of their sin. (Romans 1:18–32)

ROMANS 2: JUDGMENTALISM AND HYPOCRISY

CHAPTER HIGHLIGHTS

- Stomping Out Judgmentalism
- God's Kindness
- God's Wrath
- No Favorites
- Sin Is Universal
- Jewish Hypocrisy
- Outward Sign, Inward Reality

Let's Get Started

Jesus taught that looking down on people, no matter who they are, is wrong. This is because Jesus knew that everyone is in the same boat. We've all sinned. *We all* fall short of the glory of God. We may be tempted to say, "Oh yes, but *her* sin is much worse than *my* sin," but when it comes to what we deserve, it is only by the grace of God that any of us escapes death.

In chapter 2 Paul addresses those who may be tempted to look down on others. More specifically, he is addressing those who after reading the first chapter's description of humanity's indecency might quickly react with, "That's awful! People who do those things are terrible!"

Let's see what he says.

KEY POINT

Looking down on anyone is wrong.

(1) Read Ch. together
(2) Summarize in 1-2 sentences
(3) Questions & comments on specific verses.

> **Romans 2:1–2** You, therefore, have no excuse, you who pass judgment on someone else, for at whatever point you judge the other, you are condemning yourself, because you who pass judgment do the same things. Now we know that God's judgment against those who do such things is based on truth.

thinking someone else is sinful and you're not is not truth

And That Goes For You Too

Judgmental people obviously have the capacity to distinguish between right and wrong, but here's the snag. If you have the ability to distinguish between right and wrong, and then you do wrong, you don't have an excuse.

Today, Paul might say something like this: "You're like a silly fool with ketchup stains all over his shirt who points out a little spot on his friend's shirt." Note the similarities between what Paul said here and what Jesus said in the gospel of Luke: *"How can you say to your brother, 'Brother, let me take the speck out of your eye,' when you yourself fail to see the plank in your own eye? You hypocrite, first take the plank out of your eye, and then you will see clearly to remove the speck from your brother's eye"* (Luke 6:42).

Paul then points out that judgmental people do not make judgments based on truth. If they did, they would see their own faults! God's judgments, however, are based on truth and therefore only he has the right to judge.

Something to Ponder

Some believe Jesus' plank-in-your-eye statement was meant to be taken humorously. Perhaps you'll understand why if you imagine a man with an enormous pillar sticking out of his eye reaching over to remove a little piece of dirt from another fellow's eye. It's a picture of ridiculousness.

> **Romans 2:3–4** So when you, a mere man, pass judgment on them and yet do the same things, do you think you will escape God's judgment? Or do you show contempt for the riches of his kindness, tolerance and patience, not realizing that God's kindness leads you toward repentance?

Kindness With A Sharp Edge

Those whose habit is to judge others have an additional habit of ignoring their own faults. Paul asks the question, *"Do you think you will escape God's judgment?"* Paul is implying, as Jesus did, that people should practice what they preach. Rather, ponder God's *"kindness, tolerance and patience,"* says the apostle, and keep in mind that *"God's kindness leads you toward repentance."* That's why God does not immediately punish people for sinning; he is holding back his wrath so that people will have an opportunity to repent.

What we ought to do with our moral capacity is exercise it against ourselves. This will enable us to see our great need for God and for repentance. It will also create within us a deep thankfulness to God, for he has chosen to love us despite the inescapable reality that, next to his holiness, we are despicable.

Matthew Henry: What method God takes to bring sinners to repentance. He leads them, not drives them like beasts, allures them; and it is goodness that leads, bands of love. The consideration of the goodness of God, his common goodness to all, should be effectual to bring us all to repentance.[1]

Meet Paul—Let's remember Paul had done plenty of faultfinding in his time. He was a zealous persecutor of Christians who imprisoned them and approved of their punishment, which in the case of <u>Stephen</u> was death. Surely he would have looked down on Christians. But by the time he wrote his letter to the Romans, Paul was a changed man. One possible reason for why Paul was so passionate about stomping out judgmentalism in his Roman brothers and sisters is that he had been confronted with the reality of his own judgmentalism not long before.

☞ **GO TO:**

Acts 7:54–60 (Stephen)

> **Romans 2:5–6** But because of your stubbornness and your **unrepentant heart**, you are storing up wrath against yourself for the day of God's wrath, when his righteous judgment will be revealed. God "will give to each person according to what he has done."

unrepentant: unwilling to admit guilt, to seek forgiveness, or to change

heart: seat of motivation, character

Wake Up!

Paul uses some harsh language in an attempt to shock his listeners out of their complacency. He wants them to take this matter of looking down on others very seriously. Imagine Billy Graham walked up to you and said, "Because of the way you're living, you are filling a massive reservoir full of molten rock, sewage, and nuclear waste that will be poured out on you in the not too distant future." What would you do? Would you run in the opposite direction as fast as you could? Would you stomp on Mr. Graham's toe? Would you grab his knees and beg him to save you? You could react any number of different ways, but one thing I doubt you would do is yawn, as if he had just told you two plus two equals four. Harsh language has a way of getting people's attention, and Paul desperately wanted the attention of his readers.

Because you are judgmental, said Paul, you are, as water flowing into a dam, storing up divine wrath against yourselves. He reminds his listeners that divine wrath is nothing less than getting what they deserve.

Remember This . . .

We must realize that *"Nothing in all creation is <u>hidden</u> from God's sight"* (Hebrews 4:13). This is an awesome and freeing truth when understood properly. God is seeking to remove all pretense, all hypocrisy, and all evil from the lives of those who choose to believe in him. He is not snooping, as some suggest; rather, he is discipling us, <u>training</u> us in righteousness. He is committed to being our heavenly Father. He disciplines us for our own good.

Something to Ponder

When on the road, we are aware of many warnings. Stop. Proceed With Caution. No Right Turn. Warnings are a form of grace to protect ourselves and others. Warnings are useless if we ignore them. But if we heed them, they can save our lives.

What Others are Saying:

Matthew Henry: The wrath of God is not like our wrath, a heat and passion; but it is a righteous judgment, his will to punish sin. This righteous judgment of God is now many times concealed in the prosperity of sinners, but shortly it will be manifested before all the world.[2]

☞ **GO TO:**

Hebrews 4:12 (hidden)

Hebrews 12:11–12 (training)

Martin Luther: The sum and substance of this letter is: to pull down, to pluck up and to destroy all wisdom and righteousness of the flesh (i.e., of whatever importance they may be in the sight of men and even in our own eyes), no matter how heartily and sincerely they may be practiced, and to implant, establish, and make large the reality of sin (however unconscious we may be of its existence).[3]

> **Romans 2:7–8** To those who by persistence in doing good seek glory, honor and immortality, he will give eternal life. But for those who are self-seeking and who reject the truth and follow evil, there will be wrath and anger.

"Look Ma, No Crystal Ball"

Paul didn't need a crystal ball to tell the future. He knew from Jesus and his disciples that those who sought after and followed God would enjoy eternal peace. He also knew that those who rejected the truth and followed evil would experience eternal anguish. Paul was not exaggerating. He was delivering a sobering description of the way things really are. And guess what? If he were to sit with you over a cup of coffee today and say the same thing, his description would still be absolutely true. Those whose hope is in God will receive eternal life. Those who reject truth and follow evil will experience the wrath of God.

What Is Eternal Life?

Christians usually think of "eternal life" in one of two ways. They either equate it with heaven, thinking heaven is a place of paradise to which Christians go after death, or they think of it as *everlasting* life—life that continues forever. Both of these ideas have some validity, but by themselves, they give an incomplete picture of what biblical "eternal life" is.

First, we should remember that eternal life is a gift from God and comes through Jesus Christ. It's not something we earn or will ever deserve. Secondly, eternal life starts from the moment a person turns to Christ. It does not start at death. If you are a Christian, you have eternal life right now. *"God has given us eternal life, and the life is in his Son. He who has the Son has life; he who does not have the Son of God does not have life"* (1 John 5:11b–12). Thirdly, we should consider the question, How does "eternal life" look? It looks like obedience to God. It looks like following Jesus by loving the people around you. It looks like helping people who are less fortunate than you. It looks like bringing healing where there is pain, order where there is chaos. All of these things are a part of eternal life, which will have its fulfillment in boundless fellowship with God forever.

> **Romans 2:9–11** There will be trouble and distress for every human being who does evil: first for the Jew, then for the Gentile; but glory, honor and peace for everyone who does good: first for the Jew, then for the Gentile. For God does not show **favoritism**.

[Eternal] life is in His Son

favoritism: showing partiality or respect

A Long Line Called History

Paul says there will be *"glory, honor and peace for everyone who does good."* If we took this verse out of context, we might conclude it means that the good works of following the law will get people into heaven, but in chapter 3 we'll hear Paul say, *"Therefore no one will be declared righteous in [God's] sight by observing the law; rather, through the law we become conscious of sin"* (Romans 3:20). Is Paul contradicting himself? No, in the first verse above he is saying glory, honor, and peace await those whose lives are filled with the natural outcome of turning to Jesus—good works. In the second verse he is making it clear that no one can be saved by the law alone.

What about this *"first for the Jew, then for the Gentile"* language? He said it back in chapter 1, too. Why does Paul keep saying this? To understand why, you need to think about God the same way Paul thought about him. To Paul, God was the Person who made a covenant with Israel (the Jewish nation) way back in Genesis. God said things to Israel like, *"Obey me and do everything I command you, and you will be my people, and I will be your God"* (Jeremiah 11:4). That's an awesome statement when you consider God could have chosen whatever people he wanted to choose.

The Jews did not obey God, however, so about two thousand years after God made his first covenant he sent Jesus to set things straight. God said, *"Everyone who calls on the name of the Lord will be saved"* (Romans 10:13). This was the New Covenant. With Jesus the gospel floodgates swung wide open to Gentiles and prostitutes and thieves and slaves and everybody. So, when Paul says, *"first for the Jew, then for the Gentile,"* he's giving a *chronological* description of how God laid the groundwork for saving the human race.

Something to Ponder

sin: *violation of the standards*

law: *Ten Commandments and other laws that God gave to Moses*

☞ **GO TO:**

Galatians 2:17–21 (law)

The Gospel shows no favoritism. The word favoritism comes from two Greek words, one meaning "to receive" and the other meaning "to face." We are to see people as God sees them, not as we want to see them. He sees their value, their worth. In showing no favoritism, God is demonstrating how to exercise grace and not judgment. We are called to serve others, not to sort them.

Favoritism is both an Old and a New Covenant truth. In Leviticus 19:15 God exhorts, *"Do not pervert justice; do not show partiality to the poor or favoritism to the great, but judge your neighbor fairly."* In this context, judge means to treat them as you would be treated. Or as Jesus put it, *"Love your neighbor as yourself"* (Matthew 22:39).

Romans 2:12–15 All who **sin** apart from the **law** will also perish apart from the law, and all who sin under the law will be judged by the law. For it is not those who hear the law who are righteous in God's sight, but it is those who obey the law who will be declared righteous. (Indeed, when Gentiles, who do not have the law, do by nature things required by the law, they are a law for themselves, even though they do not have the law, since they show that the requirements of the law are written on their hearts, their **consciences** also bearing witness, and their thoughts now accusing, now even defending them.)

Everyone sins-whether they have the law or not and sin is sin

conscience: *an internal awareness of right and wrong*

Face The Facts

Whether you've sinned does not depend on whether you know the law, said Paul. Some Jews of his day thought because they had the privilege of knowing the law, and kept it partially, they were righteous. Paul says to think again. Merely hearing the law isn't enough, you must *do* the law, and doing it partially won't wash either. You must do it perfectly because God is perfect. Of course, Paul knew it was impossible for the Jews to keep the law perfectly.

Though the Gentiles did not have Mosaic law, they did have conscience. Paul speaks of their consciences as *"now accusing, now even defending"* them. In other words, when they did something wrong, they felt guilty, but they made excuses. Both of these things, feeling guilty and defending themsleves, are proof that they had violated their consciences. If the Gentiles hadn't violated their consciences, they wouldn't have felt guilty. If they hadn't violated their consciences, they wouldn't have had any need for excuses. Paul is pointing out that people are condemned apart from God's law because they know they have violated their own standards, much less God's.

Paul is saying both Jew and Gentile, the first who knows the law and the second who doesn't, have the same problem. Both deserve condemnation because both are aware they are sinners.

> *KEY POINT*
>
> Every one of us is a sinner because every one of us has failed to live up to our own standards, let alone God's.

Every culture in the world has some notion of right and wrong. Though the particularities of law and custom may differ from one place to another, no culture should be considered to have a totally different morality. No culture, for example, admires a man who backstabs all the people who have been kindest to him. No country praises a soldier who turns tail in the middle of battle. In some cultures, you may be allowed to have more than one wife, but no culture says you can have any woman you want any time you want her. Every culture has some idea of right and wrong.

Pre/extra-marital sex in U.S. - does our culture really say it is o.k.?

Something to Ponder

It is not sufficient to *know* well, nor to *promise* well, but as our text says, it's important that we *do* well. God wants us to rely on the fact that he is just and that justice will be done. Our obedience or our disobedience, each in its own way, reveals the secrets of our hearts—secrets on which God will pronounce his righteous judgment. For the Christian, law and conscience are used by the Holy Spirit to confront any disobedience that leads us away from God's will.

> **Romans 2:16** This will take place on the day when God will judge men's secrets through Jesus Christ, as my gospel declares.

Say When

This verse is referring back to verses 12 and 13 where Paul explained how people would be judged. Paul is letting his readers know there will come a judgment day. "It's coming," he says. "And you'd better be ready." Think of Arnold's famous line, "I'll be back," and you'll get some idea of what Paul is trying to communicate. It's not a matter of if, it's a matter of when.

Note two more things. First, for some reason Paul places special importance on "men's secrets" here, as if he wanted to underscore the truth that we can run, but we can't hide from God. Secondly, our acts will pass through the filter of Jesus Christ on the way to judgment. If you have put your faith in Christ, God will forgive them because Jesus paid the price of punishment for you. If not, you will be punished accordingly.

We walk with a God who is really present, a God who encourages that which is righteous and confronts that which is evil or wrong.

So many places God says you'll be judged by your actions, yet we know faith saves - good way to state it.

Jew: *a descendant of Abraham, Isaac, and Jacob*

law: *here, the whole Old Testament revelation*

pretty harsh

> **Romans 2:17–24** Now you, if you call yourself a **Jew**; if you rely on the **law** and brag about your relationship to God; if you know his will and approve of what is superior because you are instructed by the law; if you are convinced that you are a guide for the blind, a light for those who are in the dark, an instructor of the foolish, a teacher of infants, because you have in the law the embodiment of knowledge and truth—you, then, who teach others, do you not teach yourself? You who

> preach against stealing, do you steal? You who say that people should not commit adultery, do you commit adultery? You who abhor idols, do you rob temples? You who brag about the law, do you dishonor God by breaking the law? As it is written: "God's name is blasphemed among the Gentiles because of you."

Look At The Man In The Mirror

Paul turns his attention to the Jew. Jews of his day had a great deal of confidence because they knew more about moral matters than the rest of humankind. They knew more because God chose to give them the law before he gave it to anyone else. Futhermore, Jews believed that in the law they had the embodiment of all knowledge and truth. This is understandable when you consider who gave them the law. God himself inscribed the tablets with the Ten Commandments, and he did so specifically for the Jews. It's no wonder they thought they were hot stuff!

The problem was this: though the Jews had the law, they didn't keep it. Paul points out the Jews' hypocrisy by asking a series of questions. He wants the Jews to look at themselves for who they really are. The Jews were breaking the same law of which they were so proud.

Something to Ponder

Do you think Paul was being too harsh on the Jews? Consider this: in the first century the rabbis had decided that the prohibition against aldultery and the sentence of stoning adulterers should be disregarded because there were so many adulteries. There was so much adultery going around, the rabbis decided they couldn't do anything about it.

Remember This . . .

In case we're tempted to think, "Oh, those nasty first-century Jews. How *could* they!" we would do well to remember the skeletons lurking in our own closets. Remember, Paul said God will judge the secrets of *all* humankind. His words are just as true for us as they were for Jews of the first century.

Probably very hard for Jews to hear

Romans 2:25–26 Circumcision has value if you observe the law, but if you break the law, you have become as though you had not been circumcised. If those who are not circumcised keep the law's requirements, will they not be regarded as though they were circumcised?

circumcision: *cutting off the foreskin of the penis; a physical sign of one's identity as a Jew, set apart to God*

Counterfeit Righteousness

Imagine a friend presents you with a Jaguar XJR for your birthday (I know it's hard, but try). With a 370 horsepower engine, this car is reported to do 0 to 60 miles per hour in 5.4 seconds. Naturally, you want to look at the engine. You want to take in the sight and pay respect where respect is due. You slide into the leather seat and pop the hood. You walk to the front of the car, smiling, letting your finger glide over the shiny hood. You lift it up, and to your astonishment, there's nothing inside! What looked good on the outside was actually a sham.

Circumcision was an outward sign of a covenant relationship with God. In the context of that covenant relationship with God, God's people were called to walk with, worship, and obey him. Just as a fancy Jaguar with no engine is a terrible disappointment, Paul told the Jews circumcision without obedience was meaningless.

circumcision must be inward not merely outward same as an empty baptism

Meet Paul—Paul had to part ways with his fellow Jews on the topic of circumcision. For the Jew, circumcision *was* the covenant, but Paul believed what Scripture taught. Circumcision was *the sign* of the covenant. This difference is significant. God, through Abraham (see GWMB, pages 13–28) and then Moses, was creating a people from whom the Messiah would be born. Circumcision was affirmation that the covenant continued from generation to generation. It had no power to save.

Paul's view of circumcision was that it had value, but it could not bring **justification** to a sinner. It was never intended to.

Why does Paul choose to focus so much attention on the Jews? Paul's focus on the Jewish people is due to God's choice to make the Jews his vehicle of revelation. It is from the Jews that God brought forth the Messiah who is our only source of true righteousness. *"Salvation is from the Jews,"* Jesus said (John 4:22). Through the Jews the living God and true spirituality were revealed in the person of Jesus.

We struggle with similar issues in churches today. Many people practice the rituals of the faith (**baptism**, **communion**, recitation of formal prayers) because they know about God, but their hearts are unchanged. In this way, God's name is blasphemed throughout the world.

justification: *legal standing as innocent before God*

baptism: *a sacred Christian rite involving water*

communion: *a sacred Christian rite involving consecrated bread and wine*

Something to Ponder

Remember This . . .

> **Romans 2:27** The one who is not circumcised physically and yet obeys the law will condemn you who, even though you have the written code and circumcision, are a lawbreaker.

Left Behind

Tim LaHaye and Jerry Jenkins probably weren't thinking of Romans 2:27 when they started work on their popular *Left Behind* series, but the title is a good description of where Paul thought the Jews would be if Gentiles who didn't have the law obeyed it better than the Jews who did. The Jews would be left behind.

It's bad enough to get beat, but to get beat by someone whom you think is inferior to you is like getting a humble pie thrown in your face. It just doesn't get any more humiliating. Paul left no room for the Jews to be boastful.

> **Romans 2:28–29** A man is not a Jew if he is only one outwardly, nor is circumcision merely outward and physical. No, a man is a Jew if he is one inwardly; and circumcision is **circumcision of the heart**, by the Spirit, not by the written code. Such a man's praise is not from men, but from God.

How would you feel if you were a Jew reading this?

circumcision of the heart: *spiritual commitment to God, in contrast to mere physical descent from Abraham*

messianic mission: *Christ's mission to save individuals and establish God's rule*

Godliness Is An Internal Affair

With these verses Paul wraps up his discussion of law and circumcision. The Jews tended to place unwarranted confidence in both. Merely knowing the law wasn't enough to be in God's favor. Circumcision by itself did not have power to save.

God was concerned with the heart. Paul wasn't forbidding circumcision—an ancient Jewish covenantal rite—but was interested in establishing its purpose in the greater light of God's **messianic mission**. Its purpose had been polluted, and as a result the God who had appointed it was being misrepresented.

There are two kinds of pride: good pride and evil pride. While good pride appreciates the beauty or meaning of something, evil pride is arrogant. People who wrestle with evil pride think they're <u>better than others</u> or that they have some unique advantage.

The Jews used the law in an unlawful manner. They

☞ **GO TO:**

Isaiah 9:6–7; 57 (messianic mission)

Luke 18:9–14 (better than others)

Something to Ponder

thought that if you knew the law, you were saved, but in fact, the law is not **salvific**. The grace of the law is that it enables us to see ourselves as God sees us—needy, sinful, and in need of salvation.

What Others are Saying:

Francis A. Schaeffer: External rites, whether those of Judaism or of **Christendom** are meaningless unless there is a circumcision of the heart, unless God has touched the person's heart and there is a reality to his or her faith . . . to live lives that are a scandal in the sight of nonbelievers, to profess a faith that means nothing in our inward parts, this surely places us under God's wrath.[4]

Study Questions

1. Why is God concerned about judgmentalism?
2. How does God's kindness bring us to repentance?
3. What did Paul mean when he said judgmental people were storing up wrath for themselves?
4. What does it mean that God shows no favoritism?
5. What is meant by the statement, *"the requirements of the law are written on their hearts"*? (Romans 2:15)

Handwritten notes in margin:

1. It causes false pride and it is based on a lie — that they are sinful and I'm not

e-mail
Cott Buddy retreat

2. It makes me take a good look at myself in comparison Ex: Dad's sweetness w/ Jacob last night was in contrast to my impatience

3. Judgmental people are usually unrepentant — don't see their own sin, see no need to forgiveness ∴ wrath is coming

4. A sinner is a sinner

5. People know right & wrong through their conscience — whether it is a written code or not

CHAPTER WRAP-UP

- When we pass judgment on someone else we have three fingers pointing back at ourselves. Their sins are our sins, only in different expressions. (Romans 2:1–2)

- We all need to think on God's kindness. If God, who is completely holy and the source of our righteousness, is kind toward our sinful race, surely we, who share in that sin, need to follow God's example. (Romans 2:3–4)

- If man fails to repent and remains stubborn, he is storing up wrath for the day of judgment. (Romans 2:5–6)

- Paul reminds the church that God shows no favoritism. If we do evil, we store up wrath; if we seek glory and honor, God will give eternal life. (Romans 2:7–11)

- Both Jews and Gentiles are sinners. The Jews violate God's law, and the Gentiles violate their consciences. (Romans 2:12–16)

- The Jews were hypocritical in that though they had the law, they did not keep it. (Romans 2:17–24)

- Outward signs are nothing without inward realities. Truly being a part of God's family depends on obedience and devotion to God. (Romans 2:25–29)

Part Two

GOD'S FORGIVENESS

REVEREND FUN

ROMANS 3: IN SEARCH OF RIGHTEOUSNESS

CHAPTER HIGHLIGHTS

- God's Faithfulness
- Deserving Condemnation
- Silence before God
- The Sacrifice of Christ
- No Boasting

Let's Get Started

In the everydayness of life, we tend to forget the enormity of the universe. But in our forgetfulness we also forget the One who created it, whose power and glory are awesome. The November 20, 1995 issue of *Time* magazine gave us a stunning display of activity in the Eagle Nebula through pictures that were taken from the Hubble Space Telescope. This Nebula is some seven thousand light years from earth, which is more than four hundred million times as far away as our sun.

In a similar way, the Jews in the everydayness of their religion got caught up in the activity of religion, while the wonder, grace, and beauty of a relationship with God got pushed aside. Somewhere in their distant past they chose outward ritual over a personal relationship with God. Judaism became a religion of law, void of God's grace. They thought of God as only their God, not the God of the whole world.

> **Romans 3:1–2** What advantage, then, is there in being a Jew, or what value is there in circumcision? Much in every way! First of all, they have been entrusted with the very words of God.

The Jewish Advantage

Paul, once limited by his own Jewish outlook, knew his Jewish readers would ask this question. It would have been a valid question to raise after reading what Paul had written in the first two chapters. If the Jews and Gentiles stood on a level playing field, then what advantage was it to be a Jew?

Paul's response was a positive one: *"Much in every way!"* In Paul's view, being the appointed guardians of God's Word was the chief advantage of being a Jew. They could know the will of God, and they had access to the God whose will it was!

Torah: the law and the whole Jewish way of life

Eusebius of Emesa: When Paul says "to begin with," he does not go on to list a second or third item. He means rather that what he begins with is comprehensive of all good things. For what could be better than to believe the words of God?[1]

James R. Edwards: If **Torah** was the pride of the Jews, their response to it was disappointing. Torah was not a possession to be hoarded but a gift which entailed a responsibility. Calvin believed the Jews were first to be the depositories of Torah and then the dispensers of it. But in this they failed.[2]

> **Romans 3:3–4a** What if some did not have faith? Will their lack of faith nullify God's faithfulness? Not at all!

A Heart That's True

circumcised: when the foreskin of the penis has been removed

In chapter 2 Paul pointed out that though all Jews were **circumcised** outwardly, only some had circumcised hearts. In other words, only some of the Jews were faithful to God. Upon hearing this, a Jew might very well ask, "So, does that mean God was unfaithful to the Jews who are not faithful?"

KJV: the King James Version of the Bible

Paul's answer is one of the strongest expressions used in the New Testament to express disagreement: *"Not at all!"* In the **KJV**, this phrase is always translated, *"God forbid."* What Paul is saying is that if a certain Jew is not faithful to God, that's not God's fault. God never stopped being faithful. Choosing not to follow God is the fault of the person who makes that choice.

interpretation: understanding

A true faith is dependent on a true **interpretation** of the Word. The Jews' faithfulness (whatever degree of faithfulness they had) to the Old Covenant tended to lead them into further unbelief in Christ. This is also true in the Christian faith today. A wrong interpretation of Scripture leads people down many a blind alley. We need to handle God's Word with great care and prayer.

Remember This . . .

D. Martyn Lloyd–Jones: When the New Testament is talking about faith it is talking about something special, something new: 'By grace are ye saved through faith, and that not of yourselves; it is the gift of God.' All men have not faith, says the Scriptures. This is something that is only to be found in a Christian.[3]

> **What Others are Saying:**

> **Romans 3:4b** Let God be true, and every man a liar. As it is written: "So that you may be proved right when you speak and prevail when you judge."

Let God Be True

Paul says if ever there is wickedness, it does not come from God. God always proves true to his promises. To prove his point, Paul quotes a Psalm in which David confesses his sin. To understand this quote, we need to look at what precedes and follows it in scripture. Here is Psalm 51:3–5:

> *"For I know my transgressions, and my sin is always before me.*
>
> *"Against you, you only, have I sinned and done what is evil in your sight, so that you are proved right when you speak and justified when you judge.*
>
> *"Surely I was sinful at birth, sinful from the time my mother conceived me."*

David came face-to-face with his own sin, and Paul hoped the Jews would come face-to-face with theirs.

Meet Paul—Paul faced his sin on the Damascus Road (see illustration, page 42). He was commissioned by the **Sanhedrin** of Jerusalem to go to Damascus and round up the Christians there. They were to be imprisoned and await sentencing in Jerusalem. Near Damascus, Jesus appeared to Paul (who was then known as Saul) and asked why Paul was persecuting him. Paul was confronted with the terrible mistakes of his past. The experience dramatically changed his life forever, for from that moment on, Paul was a missionary for Christ.

☞ **GO TO:**

Acts 22:6–10 (Damascus Road)

Sanhedrin: *a council of seventy-one members who governed the Jewish faith and lifestyle during the time of the Roman Empire*

> **What Others are Saying:**

Apollinaris of Laodicea: Let it be agreed, Paul says, that God is faithful and true in every case, whereas men have been judged as unfaithful and untrue, so that God by his goodness may conquer the self-righteousness of men by bestowing his own righteousness upon them.[4]

The Damascus Road

This map shows the location and route of the Damascus Road from Jerusalem to Damascus. On this road Paul heard God's voice, saw a blinding light, and was converted to Christianity.

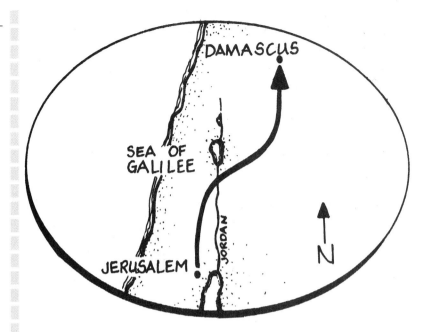

KEY POINT

The Word of God becomes active when grasped by faith.

Romans 3:5–8 But if our unrighteousness brings out God's righteousness more clearly, what shall we say? That God is unjust in bringing his wrath on us? (I am using a human argument.) Certainly not! If that were so, how could God judge the world? Someone might argue, "If my falsehood enhances God's truthfulness and so increases his glory, why am I still condemned as a sinner?" Why not say—as we are being slanderously reported as saying and as some claim that we say— "Let us do evil that good may result"? Their condemnation is deserved.

A Dumb Question

Teachers often encourage their students to learn by telling them there are no dumb questions, but Paul had to draw the line somewhere. The question Paul is addressing might be rephrased to read something like this: "If the darkness of my sin makes the brightness of God's holiness a little brighter, then shouldn't I sin all the more?" The ridiculousness of such a question is self-evident. God's holiness cannot be brightened. It would be like trying to make completeness more complete, perfection more perfect, or wholeness more whole.

Paul answers the question by drawing from the nature and the attributes of God himself. Because God will judge the world, he cannot be unjust. It is only inadvertently that sin ever brings glory to God. God came to save sinners and he found just ways to accomplish this extraordinary task without changing his character in any way.

The statement *"Let us do evil that good may result"* comes from hearts that are so contradictory to God, Paul says, *"their condemnation is deserved."* A person with such a heart has made up his or her mind to be evil.

 **GO TO:**

Romans 3:21–26
(just ways)

Sir Robert Anderson: The Gospel brings peace to the sinner, not because it makes light of sin, or lowers the inexorable claims of Divine perfection, but because it tells how Christ has made it possible for an absolutely righteous and thrice Holy God to pardon and save absolutely sinful and evil men.[5]

What Others are Saying:

KEY POINT

God's nature does not change.

> **Romans 3:9** What shall we conclude then? Are we any better? Not at all! We have already made the charge that Jews and Gentiles alike are all under sin.

Who's The Better Sinner?

Paul addressed questions that he knew would surface from either the Jews or the **Greeks**. These are sensitive topics due to the cultural differences. Paul is trying throughout this entire epistle to neutralize any ethnic division. It is sin that keeps us from God, not race. Paul also points out that sinfulness is something we all have in common.

Greeks: similar to the term Gentile, indicating all non-Jews

Sin is real. It is continuously present because of our fallen nature and Satan's activity. The law can diagnose our sinfulness and the moral illness it produces, but it has no power to cure it. Rather, it makes us more miserable, showing us what is wrong but offering no solutions. We want to escape the law and its clutches, but apart from the intervening grace of God, we lack the power to make the escape.

In the final analysis there is no difference between the Jews and the Gentiles; we're all sinners in need of salvation. However, it was through the Jews that God sent the Messiah. Through the Jewish race he brought forth a Savior for the whole world, Jew and Gentile alike.

Remember This . . .

Total depravity is the human lot and no one escapes the effects of sin.

total depravity: the doctrine that anything human beings do is tainted by sin and cannot contribute to salvation

> **Romans 3:10–18** As it is written: "There is no one righteous, not even one; there is no one who understands, no one who seeks God. All have turned away, they have together become worthless; there is no one who does good, not even one. Their throats are open graves; their tongues practice deceit. The poison of vipers is on their lips. Their mouths are full of cursing and bitterness. Their feet are swift to shed blood; ruin and misery mark their ways, and the way of peace they do not know. There is no fear of God before their eyes."

Paul The Bible Thumper

Up to this point, Paul has demonstrated by argument that all have sinned, both Jew and Gentile. Now he proves his point by using Scripture. The Jews acknowledged that God is present in his revelation, and Scripture is God's revelation. This therefore would have been the ultimate evidence to his readers. Scripture itself says there is no one righteous.

What we learn from this is that while we can reason with the most acute logic and demonstrate with the most persuasive arguments, that which actually *proves* is Scripture. It is the final word on any matter. Why? Because Scripture is from God.

☞ **GO TO:**

2 Timothy 3:16 (from God)

"all scripture is God-breathed..."

"The law's purpose is to silence us before God." No boasting!

> **Romans 3:19–20** Now we know that whatever the law says, it says to those who are under the law, so that every mouth may be silenced and the whole world held accountable to God. Therefore no one will be declared righteous in his sight by observing the law; rather, through the law we become conscious of sin.

All Rise, Justice Yahweh Is Taking The Bench

Paul sets the stage for a courtroom scene in which people stand before God as Judge. When the law is presented, detailing the right way to live, the people immediately realize they have not done so. They are silent. They have absolutely nothing to say in their defense.

Secondly, Paul makes sure his listeners understand that the law is not going to make anyone righteous. The law's intended purpose is not to save us but to show us our need for salvation. The law can in this way lead us to faith. This is how law and faith work with instead of oppose each other.

We might wonder why the Jews had such a hard time abandoning their trust in the law. To understand why, it may help to look at Acts 17, which is about Paul's visit to Athens, a city of **pagans** in his time. The apostle preached that it was obvious the Athenians were very religious because of all the idols around town, but he told them it was also obvious they had not heard about God, the one God, the God of the universe. When they heard this, *"some of them sneered, but others said, 'We want to hear you again on this subject.'"*

If it was this difficult for people to give up their trust in petty idols, imagine how much more difficult it would have been for the Jews to give up their trust in a holy law that they knew came from God and on the fulfillment of which rested all their hopes for both present and eternal peace.

God gave the <u>Ten Commandments</u> both to reveal his righteousness and to confront sin (see GWBI, pages 28–30). Take time to read the words and teachings of the Ten Commandments and see if they make you conscious of sin, your own and the sin you observe in the world.

Saint Augustine: Let us distinguish the following four states of human existence: before the law, under the law, under grace and at rest. Before the law we follow the lust of the flesh. Under the law we are dragged along by it. Under grace we neither follow it nor are dragged along by it. At rest (in glory, after the resurrection) there is no lust of the flesh.[6]

Karl Barth: If all the great outstanding figures in history, whose judgments are worthy of serious consideration, if all the prophets, Psalmists, philosophers, fathers of the Church, Reformers, poets, artists were asked their opinion, would one of them assert that men were good, or even capable of good? Is the doctrine of original sin merely one doctrine among many? Is it not rather, according to its fundamental meaning . . . the doctrine which emerges from all honest study of history? Is it not the doctrine which, in the last resort, underlies the whole teaching of history? Is it possible for us to adopt a 'different point of view' from that of the Bible, Augustine, and the Reformers? What then does history teach about the things which men do or do not do?[7]

Something to Ponder

pagans: *people who worshiped the multiple gods of Greek mythology*

☞ **GO TO:**

Exodus 20:1–17; Deuteronomy 5:6–22 (Ten Commandments)

Take It to Heart

What Others are Saying:

KEY POINT

The law did not create sin; it revealed it.

> **Romans 3:21–24** But now a righteousness from God, apart from law, has been made known, to which the Law and **the Prophets** testify. This righteousness from *(of)* God comes through faith in Jesus Christ to all who believe. There is no difference, for all have sinned and fall short of the **glory** of God, and are justified freely by his grace through the redemption that came by Christ Jesus.

"Free Grace! Get Your Free Grace Here!"

Note how Paul begins this section: *"But now."* What do you mean "But now," Paul? You've just demonstrated with reason and proved with Scripture that we're all a bunch of guilty sinners who deserve only God's wrath. What on earth could you say that would give us hope?

Indeed there is hope. Paul announces the good news that a righteousness we could *never* obtain through the law has been made available by a different means. Faith in Jesus Christ will give us the righteousness we need to be saved from our sins. Since all have sinned, it is obvious the only hope for any of us is to have righteousness credited to our account by someone who does have that righteousness. Jesus did just that, and this righteousness is available to anyone who puts his or her trust not in oneself, not in the law, but in Jesus Christ.

When Paul says *"there is no difference,"* he means that when it comes to the fact of sin, both Jews and Gentiles are guilty. When it comes to who falls short of the glory of God, all of us have, regardless of who has committed greater or lesser sins. If we visited a prison, we would find people who were there for lesser crimes than others, but we would find no innocent people!

What Others are Saying:

Brennan Manning: The Good News of the Gospel of Grace cries out: we are all, equally, privileged but unentitled beggars at the door of God's mercy.[8]

> **Romans 3:25–26** God presented him as a sacrifice of atonement, through faith in his blood. He did this to demonstrate his justice, because in his forbearance he had left the sins committed beforehand unpunished— he did it to demonstrate his justice at the present time, so as to be just and the one who justifies those who have faith in Jesus.

Paid In Full

God had a score to settle. His justice had not yet been satisfied. He either had to condemn us for our sins or make the costliest sacrifice ever. Because he loved us (we don't know why), God made the sacrifice of Christ, which did not merely cover our sins but satisfied all the requirements of justice. It paid the penalty in full. This kind of sacrifice is known as propitiation (PRO-PI-SHEE-AY-SHUN).

propitiation – payment in full

Propitiation was necessary not only for our own sins of the past, present, and future, but it was also necessary for all sin from the beginning of history. When Paul says *"because in his forbearance he had left the sins committed beforehand unpunished,"* he is pointing out that up to the death of Christ, God had let the sins of humankind go unpunished, which would have been contrary to his nature if he had not eventually presented the sacrifice of Christ. God punished everybody's sins on the crucifixion cross. He did not show favoritism to anyone. He let Christ serve as the propitiation so that people who had faith in him could be justly forgiven.

We ought to reflect on the costliness of God's sacrifice. Jesus took on the pain of sin, which was the absence of God. We have no idea what this would be like because God loved us so much he couldn't live without us. We've done nothing that he should love us. He just does.

Take It to Heart

Redemption is a costly matter. It cost the Son of God his life. The Old Covenant prefigured in its sacrificial system of worship and redemption the need for blood redemption. Jesus, called "the Lamb of God," became God's ultimate sacrifice. He was made sin for us. This was God's predetermined plan of grace for the entire human race.

Something to Ponder

Matthew Henry: It is by his grace. And to make it the more emphatic, he says it is 'freely by his grace'. It comes freely to us, but Christ bought it, and paid dearly for it.[9]

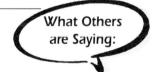

What Others are Saying:

Francis A. Schaeffer: In a way, this phrase [*"so as to be just and the one who justifies those who have faith in Jesus"*], and the verses that surround it constitute the center of the whole Bible, for they answer the most profound of all questions: How can God remain the absolutely just ruler of the universe, and yet justify me, an ungodly sinner?[10]

Romans 3:27–31 Where, then, is boasting? It is excluded. On what principle? On that of observing the law? No, but on that of faith. For we maintain that a man is **justified** by faith apart from observing the law. Is God the God of Jews only? Is he not the God of Gentiles too? Yes, of Gentiles too, since there is only one God, who will justify the circumcised by faith and the uncircumcised through that same faith. Do we, then, nullify the law by this faith? Not at all! Rather, we **uphold** the law.

God's The Only One With Bragger's Rights

Paul is mainly talking to the Jews here because we know from verses in Romans 2:17 and 2:23 that the Jews had a tendency to boast. He says that because righteousness comes through faith, not from ourselves, boasting is eliminated.

The Jews believed that salvation came from observation of the law, so when Paul said it came through faith, Jews might very well have asked, "Well, okaaaay, but what good is the law then?" Paul anticipated this question and answered that, far from nullifying the law, Christians upheld the law because they put it in its rightful place. Law was intended to shut peoples' boastful mouths before God and to demonstrate the utter necessity of faith. The law was *not* a way of salvation as had been perceived within Judaism.

What Others are Saying:

Larry Richards: The death Jesus died must not be trivialized. It was a costly death, a death in which the Son took our sins upon Himself and experienced the full weight of the Father's wrath against unrighteousness. Only that kind of death could have met the demands God's nature imposed upon Him. Only that kind of death could have won us the freedom which we now have in Him.[11]

Study Questions

1. Did the Jews have an advantage over the Gentiles?
2. Why does our unrighteousness cause God to judge the world?
3. How is it that no one is righteous?
4. How does the law make us conscious of sin?
5. Why is there no boasting?

1. They had the words of God in the Law
2. An unrighteous God cannot stand unrighteousness - there must be punishment or forgiveness in order for justice to be had. Like in a trial if guilty there must be a consequence
3. We can't make ourselves sinless.
4. Shows how we can't keep the law; need a Savior
5. All sinners - regardless of background

GOD'S WORD FOR THE BIBLICALLY-INEPT

- There is nothing in this world system—political, religious, or academic—that will nullify God's faithfulness. Absolutely nothing! (Romans 3:1–3)

- Jew or Gentile, with the law or with conscience, we all deserve condemnation. (Romans 3:9–18)

- The law's purpose is to silence us before God. The law brings us to a knowledge of our need for salvation. (Romans 3:19–20)

- Jesus was God's propitiation. This means that God's justice is fully satisfied by the blood of Jesus Christ. Christ's death is the greatest proof of our need for righteousness. God's way is the only way for sinners to be declared righteous. (Romans 3:22–26)

- We have no room to boast because it is only by faith in Christ that we are saved. The rightful place of the law is to show us our need for salvation. It is not, nor was it ever intended to be, a way of salvation. (Romans 3:27–31)

ROMANS 4: ABE'S FAITH

CHAPTER HIGHLIGHTS

- Abraham's Faith
- Wages vs. Gifts
- Forgiven and Justified

Let's Get Started

We often make light of sin. We say, "Well, after all, I'm only human," or we tell others who rebuke us, "Quit being so self-righteous!"

Why do we have this lax attitude toward sin and its devastating consequences? In Jesus' conversation with a Pharisee named <u>Nicodemus</u> (see GWLC, pages 111–116), who came to Jesus one night to discuss spiritual matters, Jesus reminded this educated man, *"This is the verdict: Light has come into the world, but men loved darkness instead of light because their deeds were evil"* (John 3:19).

In chapter 4 we move into one of the most exciting discussions of faith and its extraordinary importance in both initiating the experience of salvation and its continuing work in **sanctification**. Indeed, *"without faith it is impossible to please God"* (Hebrews 11:6).

> **Romans 4:1–2** What then shall we say that Abraham, our forefather, discovered in this matter? If, in fact, Abraham was **justified** by works, he had something to boast about—but not before God.

First Affidavit: Our Forefather Abraham

Knowing that the Jews loved to boast of Abraham as their father, Paul suggested going back to the story of Abraham to see what it said about justification (see GWGN, pages 129–131).

☞ **GO TO:**

John 3:1–16
(Nicodemus)

2 Corinthians 3:17–18;
Romans 8:11
(sanctification)

sanctification: to become righteous in character and practice

justified: declared righteous by God

Note that if Abraham had been justified by works—and by the way nothing could have been further from the truth—he would have had the right to boast only before people, not before God. God is under any circumstance our master. We are his creatures. Our rightful place, our happiest place is beneath him.

> **Romans 4:3** What does the Scripture say? "Abraham believed God, and it was credited to him as righteousness."

Inspecting Scripture

Paul asked a loaded question and put the ball in the Jews' court: *"What does the Scripture say?"* He then took them back to Genesis 15:6. The moment Abraham took God at his word, God declared him righteous. Abraham did not do anything to earn this declaration. He simply believed. This is the doctrine of justification through faith.

Abraham's faith counted him as righteous long before he was circumcised and long before God had given the law to Israel. This would have been further evidence to the Jews they were placing unwarranted confidence in the wrong things because if circumcision and the law were the means to righteousness, then how was Abraham who had neither considered righteous?

☞ **GO TO:**

Ephesians 2:8–9
(through faith)

whole point is Paul's argument

What Others are Saying:

James D. G. Dunn: Abraham's faith was a firm confidence in God as the one who determines the future according to what he has promised.[1]

Meet Paul—If you've ever been on a debate team, you would have been glad for a teammate like Paul. He was a master at crafting persuasive arguments. Paul's use of the scriptural account of Abraham, for example, to demonstrate that righteousness comes only by faith was nothing short of brilliant when you consider who Paul's readers were. Not only did the Jews reverence Scripture to a fault, Abraham was the founder of their race. Jews thought so much of Abraham, they kept meticulous records to prove they were his descendants. When Paul jabbed with Scripture and landed an uppercut with Abraham, the Jews would have been down for the count.

Matthew Henry: Here the apostle proves that Abraham was justified not by works, but by faith. He appeals to the case of Abraham their father, and puts his own name to the relation, being a Hebrew of the Hebrews: *Abraham our Father.*[2]

Saint Augustine: Since Abraham without the law obtained glory not by the works of the law (as if he would fulfill the law in his own strength), since the law had not yet been given, the glory belongs to God, not to him. For he was justified not by his own merit, as if by works, but by the grace of God through faith.[3]

Charles R. Swindoll: Justification is the sovereign act of God whereby He declares righteous the believing sinner—while he is still in a sinning state. Even though Abraham (after believing and being justified) would continue to sin from time to time, God heard Abraham when he said, "I believe . . . I believe You." And God credited divine righteousness to his account.[4]

Paul said that grace was something Abraham *"discovered"* (Romans 4:1). What an exciting word. Faith in God is a discovery. **Conversion** has a characteristic of ecstasy about it. Like Abraham, we discover it is by grace and not by our works. When we believe, God credits our spiritual account with (his) righteousness. *"righteousness of God"*

Grabbed by Grace

> **Romans 4:4** Now when a man works, his wages are not credited to him as a gift, but as an obligation.

Paychecks Don't Come In Fancy Paper

Paul is making a clear distinction between gifts and wages. Using the analogy of working for wages, Paul again is confronting potential deceptions in this matter of godly faith. If a man works for a certain wage and at the end of the day or week goes to his employer to get his paycheck, is it a gift or is it wages due? Obviously he is receiving what is due to him. A paycheck is not a gift. This is something you have rightly earned. But we cannot rightly earn our salvation.

If we attempt in any way to apply our works to our salvation, then the truth of the Gospel is defiled. There is only one work that we can count on, and that is the work of Christ on the cross! What saves is faith in him.

What Others are Saying:

Charles R. Swindoll: But with God the economy is altogether different. There is no wage relationship with God. Spiritually speaking, you and I haven't earned anything but death. Like it or not, we are absolutely bankrupt, without eternal hope, without spiritual merit.[5]

Take It to Heart

It is true, good works will not get you to heaven, but that doesn't mean they aren't important. Scripture is clear that faith without works is as good as no faith at all. "Okay," you may answer, "but what kinds of works should I be doing?" That's an excellent question.

There are many different ways to serve God. Start by asking God to show you how he wants to use you. Next, be on the lookout. If you keep your eyes and ears open, God will indeed show you how to do your part in his world. He may want you to babysit. He may want you to feed the hungry or shelter the homeless. He may want you to take special action to get rid of a sin with which you've been struggling. He may want you to be with a friend who is sad. No matter how he uses you, one thing's for certain: If you ask God to put you to work, he will.

☞ **GO TO:**

Matthew 25:31–46;
Galatians 6:1–6
(good works)

> **Romans 4:5–8** However, to the man who does not work but trusts God who justifies the wicked, his faith is credited as righteousness. David says the same thing when he speaks of the blessedness of the man to whom God credits righteousness apart from works: "Blessed are they whose transgressions are forgiven, whose sins are covered. Blessed is the man whose sin the Lord will never count against him."

Second Affidavit: Our Forefather David

David: the famous king of Israel who ruled from 1010–970 B.C.

Now Paul brings his second powerful witness: **David** (see GWBI, pages 60–67). He reminds the people in Rome that David speaks of this same truth. Faith saves apart from the law. Those who oppose this great truth say we must satisfy the justice of God by our works. Here again we find God crediting righteousness to a Jewish forefather apart from his spiritual accomplishments.

David was profoundly blessed with the knowledge of his forgiveness. That is what justification does; it assures us we are forgiven. David repeatedly put the concept and his feelings about it into songs and prayers.

 GO TO:

Psalm 32:1–2; Psalm 103:12 (justification)

Justification was a great part of the battle for truth that the men and women of the **Reformation** had to confront. Luther, Calvin, Melanchthon, Zwingli, and many other faithful servants of the Lord changed the course of history in their battle for this truth. Paul was their primary mentor in this struggle for reform.

Something to Ponder

Francis A. Schaeffer: The basis of salvation by grace is the finished work of Jesus Christ. The instrument is our faith. Nothing else is allowed.[6]

What Others are Saying:

The Divine Verdict

Picture yourself standing before God in heaven's great courtroom. God looks around and says there is *"No one righteous, not even one"* (Romans 3:10). What do you say in your defense? Nothing, you're speechless. You know the Judge has spoken true.

Your heart begins racing, but wait. A chair creaks. Who's that? A lawyer takes his place between you and the Judge. He looks at you with burning love in his eyes. He faces the Judge.

"May it please the court, Father. The defendant has put his faith not in himself, not in the law, not in riches," he says confidently. "The defendant, whom I love, has put his faith in me."

"Very well," the Judge says to you. "On the basis of your faith in my Son, Jesus Christ, I hereby pronounce you NOT GUILTY."

Reformation: a movement in the sixteenth century led by Martin Luther that resulted in the establishment of the Protestant Church

Augustine reminds us that "God gave by grace, because he gave to sinners so that by faith they might live justly, that is, do good works."[7] Paul saw the underpinning of God's justification as grace—undiluted, unadulterated grace.

Grabbed by Grace

Larry Richards: To "justify" is to declare righteous as a judicial act. But God does more than this for us. He acts in our lives to actually *make* us righteous.[8]

What Others are Saying:

What is this "impossible" the "Law" (handwritten)

Martin Luther: It is foolish and absurd to say: God has obligated us to possess grace and thus to do the impossible. I excuse our most faithful God. He is innocent of this imposture. He has not done this. He has not obligated us to possess grace, but he has obligated us to fulfill the Law, in order that he might give this grace to those of us who have been humbled and who implore his grace.[9]

> **Romans 4:9–11a** Is this blessedness only for the circumcised, or also for the uncircumcised? We have been saying that Abraham's faith was credited to him as righteousness. Under what circumstances was it credited? Was it after he was circumcised, or before? It was not after, but before! And he received the sign of circumcision, a seal of the righteousness that he had by faith while he was still uncircumcised.

translate to baptism? (handwritten)

A Righteous Brother

The Jews put their trust in the outward sign of circumcision, ignoring that Abraham's faith was credited to him as righteousness fourteen or fifteen years *before* he was circumcised. Circumcision was merely a sign, to Abraham and to the world, that Abraham had been set apart for God.

Today baptism serves a similar function to that which circumcision served in Abraham's day. Baptism is a sign that those baptized belong to Christ, not the world. As with first-century Jews and circumcision, people sometimes place too much trust in baptism. Some people think baptism will get them into heaven, but this is not true. Faith is the only thing that can do that. Baptism is only a sign and apart from faith it means nothing.

but who the sign a Jew was not a Jew (handwritten)

father: spiritual ancestor

> **Romans 4:11b–12** So then, he is the **father** of all who believe but have not been circumcised, in order that righteousness might be credited to them. And he is also the father of the circumcised who not only are circumcised but who also walk in the footsteps of the faith that our father Abraham had before he was circumcised.

God Of All

Paul argues that Abraham is the father of all who believe, regardless of ethnicity. This supports the words of our Lord at his ascension (see GWLC2, pages 279–283). He told the eleven disciples, *"Therefore go and make disciples of all nations, baptizing them in the name of the Father and of the Son and of the Holy Spirit, and teaching them to obey everything I have commanded you"* (Matthew 28:19–20).

As baptism follows conversion as a sign of union with and commitment to Jesus Christ, so with Abraham circumcision followed as an outward sign of the righteousness that had been credited to his account. Abraham was uncircumcised at the time he was justified, so uncircumcision was not a **barrier** to the Gentiles, as some of them feared.

Seems very straight-forward here

barrier: *reason to exclude*

What Others are Saying:

John Piper: The faith of Abraham was a faith in the promise of God to make him the father of many nations. This faith glorified God because it called attention to all the resources of God that would be required to fulfill it. Abraham was too old to have children, and Sarah was barren. Not only that: how do you turn a son or two into "many nations" which God said Abraham would be the Father of? It all seemed totally impossible. Therefore Abraham's faith glorified God by being fully assured that he could and would do the impossible.[10]

Matthew Henry: In [Abraham] commenced a much clearer and fuller dispensation of the covenant of grace than any that had been before **extant**; and therefore he is called the father of all that believe.[11]

extant: *in existence*

James R. Edwards: Since Abraham was justified *before* he was circumcised, his circumcision was a "sign" of righteousness, not a cause of it. Whereas Judaism came to regard circumcision as a good work, as something *achieved*, Paul refers to it as something received [Romans 4:11]. Judaism emphasized the doer of the act; Paul emphasizes the Giver of the sign.[12]

> **Romans 4:13–15** It was not through law that Abraham and his offspring received the promise that he would be heir of the world, but through the righteousness that comes by faith. For if those who live by law are heirs, faith has no value and the promise is worthless, because law brings wrath. And where there is no law there is no transgression.

Heir Of The World

One night the word of the Lord came to Abraham. God took him outside and said, *"Look up at the heavens and count the stars . . . so shall your offspring be"* (Genesis 15:5). God promised Abraham that he would be *"heir of the world."* In other words, Abraham would be the father of all believers. Paul points out that this would not happen through Abraham's observance of the law. In fact, Abraham <u>disobeyed God</u> several times. It would happen through Abraham's faith.

He further points out that because no one can keep the law, the law brings wrath. Many of the Jews treasured their law highly. The idea that the law brought wrath was probably completely foreign to them.

☞ **GO TO:**

Genesis 12:1–4, 10–20; 20 (disobeyed God)

> **Romans 4:16–17** Therefore, the promise comes by faith, so that it may be by grace and may be guaranteed to all Abraham's offspring—not only to those who are **of the law** but also to those who are of the faith of Abraham. He is the father of us all. As it is written: "I have made you a father of many nations." He is our father in the sight of God, in whom he believed—the God who gives life to the dead and calls things that are not as though they were.

of the law: Jews

The Purpose Of Promise

<u>Promise</u> is one of the great spiritual terms used throughout Scripture. The promises of God open the path of faith to fallen and finite people, which in turn opens the door to the grace of God. Promise, by nature, requires faith on behalf of the one to whom the promise is given, while at the same time it exalts the sovereign nature of the One who makes the promise. God chose this as a way to give us sinners a sure way to enter his kingdom.

Because Abraham was made to be the *"father of many nations"* (Genesis 17:5), and this according to promise, he has become *"the father of us all."* This makes both Jews and Gentiles heirs of promise. This great truth had escaped Paul when he was still Saul the Pharisee. Without a doubt, this is why he was so capable of tracing all the implications of this most essential doctrine.

☞ **GO TO:**

Deuteronomy 9:28; 10:9; 1 Kings 9:5; Hebrews 10:23 (promise)

What Others are Saying:

John Piper: He says, "If those who are of the Law are heirs, faith is made void and the promise is nullified" [Romans 4:14]. In other words, the "promise" of God's grace was meant to be received by "faith," not earned by what he calls, "Being of the Law"—a phrase that probably implies relying on our religious culture or morality rather than on God's grace.[13]

> **Romans 4:18–22** Against all hope, Abraham in hope believed and so became the father of many nations, just as it had been said to him, "So shall your offspring be." Without weakening in his faith, he faced the fact that his body was as good as dead—since he was about a hundred years old—and that Sarah's womb was also **dead**. Yet he did not waver through unbelief regarding the promise of God, but was strengthened in his faith and gave glory to God, being fully persuaded that God had power to do what he had promised. This is why "it was credited to him as righteousness."

dead: beyond the normal age for bearing children

The Very First Promise Keeper

From a human perspective, God's promise that he would have a son and inherit the world looked impossible. Abraham was a hundred years old (*"his body was as good as dead"*) and Sarah, his wife, was beyond childbearing years, yet Abraham did not allow unbelief to rob him of the promise God had made to him. Rather, he chose to believe that God, who came to him unsolicited, would keep his word.

KEY POINT

A dead womb, like a dead life, cannot produce anything.

> When God makes a promise, we ought to focus on the truth that God never lies and that he is capable of doing whatever he wants to do. Though *we* may be limited by our circumstances and the natural world, God is not.

Remember This . . .

> **Romans 4:23–25** The words "it was credited to him" were written not for him alone, but also for us, to whom God will credit righteousness—for us who believe in him who raised Jesus our Lord from the dead. He was delivered over to death for our sins and was raised to life for our justification.

For Me? Thank You!

Did you know Genesis was written for you? "It was!" said Paul. The assurance that Abraham's faith equaled righteousness is as much for us as it was for Abraham. Just as God credited Abraham's faith to him as righteousness, he will credit our faith to us as righeousness.

Jesus suffered the unspeakable for our sins. He endured being forsaken by his Father. If he had not done this, God would have forsaken us forever. Not only are we saved from the penalty of our sin, but also Christ's resurrection gives us an entirely new position before God. If we are in Christ, we are <u>new creations</u>.

☞ **GO TO:**

Galatians 6:15
(new creations)

**Something
to Ponder**

Abraham's faith transcends time, reminding us that *"the words 'it was credited to him' were written not for him alone, but also for us, to whom God will credit righteousness."*

What does this reveal to every believer today? That the faith we embrace is not just for us, but for the world we are called to love and serve in Christ's name. God dropped a pebble of truth into the pool of Abraham's heart and the ringlets reach out to us and further and further and further.

IN OTHER LETTERS

In Galatians Paul gives more details for us to ponder. He writes, *"Now you, brothers, like Isaac, are children of promise. At that time the son born in the ordinary way* [Ishmael] *persecuted the son born by the power of the Spirit* [Isaac]. *It is the same now"* (Galatians 4:28–29). The message here is that just as Christians are like Isaac, who had a supernatural birth, instead of like Ishmael, Christians can expect their experiences to be like that of Isaac. Specifically, just as Isaac was persecuted by his half brother Ishmael, Christians can expect to be persecuted by their half brothers—unbelieving religious people like the Pharisees and religious leaders of Jesus' day, the fanatically religious Judaizers of Paul's day, and the unbelieving members and leaders of churches in our own day.

**What Others
are Saying:**

John Calvin: It becomes more clear now why and how his faith brought righteousness to Abraham: it was because he depended on the Word of God, and did not reject the grace that God promised. This relationship between faith and the Word is to be continually maintained and committed to memory.[14]

Theodoret of Cyr: Abraham believed against the hope of nature but in the hope of the promise of God.[15]

John Chrysostom: Abraham trusted God even though God gave him no proof, nor even a sign. Rather, there were only mere words promising things which by nature were impossible.[16]

Francis A. Schaeffer: As if to emphasize that Abraham's faith was not just "faith in faith," Paul spells out the specific promise of God that Abraham believed: "So shall thy seed be."[17]

Study Questions

1. What one word summarizes Abraham's life and why? *Faith*
2. Did circumcision precede or follow the promise given to Abraham? Why is this order significant? *Follow - justification came because of his faith not circum*
3. Why did Abraham believe he would have a son when he and his wife were beyond the age of having children? *- faith in God keeping His promises*
4. Why is righteousness such an important matter for us? For God? *We must be righteous to be in fellowship w/him. Our righteousness reflects God's character to others*

CHAPTER WRAP-UP

- Paul pointed out to the Roman Christians that it was Abraham's faith that was credited to him as righteous, not his observance of the law. (Romans 4:1–3)

- Wages are not a gift, but what a person deserves for his or her labor. Grace is a gift that we can do nothing to earn. David wrote poems and songs about the blessing of being forgiven. (Romans 4:4–8)

- Faith and grace, forgiveness and justification are couplets that help explain the vastness of God's love and his matchless plan. (Romans 4:9–25)

ROMANS 5: THE BENEFITS OF BELONGING TO CHRIST

CHAPTER HIGHLIGHTS

- God's Path to Peace
- Proof of God's Love
- God's Love Keeps Going
- No More Wrath
- Grace Is Bigger Than Sin

Let's Get Started

As we begin this chapter, it is good to keep in mind Paul is not writing a theological textbook, even though at times it surely seems that way. There is definite order to the letter. There is a progression of thought and serious theological content throughout. Paul's purpose for writing is apparent, chapter by chapter: He wants to proclaim the grace of God in Jesus Christ.

As a missionary and teacher, this proclamation is in agreement with the materials he taught in Galatia, Pontius, Phrygia, Cilicia, and Asia (all provinces in Asia Minor). Paul spent years studying the **Old Covenant** while he was discovering what life is like under the **New Covenant**. Paul's faith and the truth he presents is grounded in Scripture and in spiritual reality.

Paul lived, as we do, amidst the tension between how life is and how it ought to be. Thus, his teaching is very practical. He uses spiritual insight, doctrines, history, and examples, all with the desire to encourage his readers and help make their lives more fruitful in the work of the kingdom of God.

As he leaves the discussion of sin and justification in chapters 1–4, he moves to topics that deal more with spiritual growth now that the believer has an understanding of sin and the need for righteousness.

Paul doesn't present a glorified view of the **Christian walk**, quite the opposite. He was in touch with the influences of **the world**, **the flesh**, and **the demonic**, and he faced each one in Christ's grace and power.

Old Covenant: Moses' law

New Covenant: the Gospel

Christian walk: the Christian way of life

the world: aspects of culture and society that oppose Christianity

the flesh: one's own tendencies toward evil

the demonic: supernatural evil

> **Romans 5:1–2** Therefore, since we have been justified through faith, we have peace with God through our Lord Jesus Christ, through whom we have gained access by faith into this grace in which we now stand. And we rejoice in the hope of the glory of God.

Therefore—What's It There For?

My seminary professor, Dr. Howard Hendricks, always instructed us, "When you see a 'therefore,' be sure to answer the question, 'What's it there for?'" That has been good counsel to follow. Here, in Romans 5, Paul begins with "therefore." Paul's *therefore* serves to remind us of the journey we have just made through chapters 1–4 where Paul mapped out God's road to freedom from sin and the gift of righteousness through faith for the sinner. He now proceeds on the assumption that his readers have an understanding of justification by faith and indeed that this justification is a reality in his life as well as in the lives of his readers.

Because we are justified by faith, we are at peace with God. Washed continually in grace, no longer are we God's enemies. We are God's friends, just like <u>Abraham</u> was. No longer should we fear the wrath of God. We should look for the blessings of God. Jesus has introduced us to his Father, and the Father loves us. Futhermore, because we are completely justified by faith in Jesus, we can look forward to a time when we will enjoy the full presence of Almighty God. We have hope. No matter what happens here on earth, we know that everything will turn out alright in the end.

☞ **GO TO:**

Isaiah 41:8 (Abraham)

John 4:23–24 (worship)

Take It to Heart

Justification, peace, and access ought to motivate us to <u>worship</u> and praise. *"We rejoice in the hope of the glory of God."* God knows how to repair a broken vessel and make it useful once again. Why do we rejoice? We believe that now our worship will truly bring glory to God. Our faith has been renewed. Our hope has been restored. Let's praise him!

Something to Ponder

In chapter 5 Paul gives several benefits of justification.

- We have access to God and his grace (Romans 5:2).
- We have (present tense) absolute salvation (Romans 5:10).
- We have reconciliation (Romans 5:11).
- We have the capacity to live a righteous life (Romans 5:17).

- We have life itself (Romans 5:18).
- We have eternal life (Romans 5:21).
- We don't have to try to create peace because God has granted us peace through Christ. (Romans 10:11)

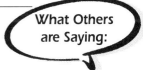
What Others are Saying:

John Calvin: Peace, therefore, means serenity of conscience, which originates from the awareness of having God reconciled to oneself. This serenity is possessed neither by the Pharisee, who is inflated by a false confidence in his work, nor by the senseless sinner, who, since he is intoxicated with the pleasure of his vices, feels no lack of peace . . . a dull conscience implies a departure from God.[1]

KEY POINT

The King has given us access to the grace of God. Let us stand in awe!

> **Romans 5:3–5** Not only so, but we also rejoice in our sufferings, because we know that suffering produces perseverance; perseverance, character; and character, hope. And hope does not disappoint us, because God has poured out his love into our hearts by the Holy Spirit, whom he has given us.

But Wait, There's More

After talking about the good things that come from being justified by faith, Paul goes on to add another benefit that may seem strange when we first hear of it. He says we now rejoice in our sufferings. Notice that he does not say we rejoice *at* our sufferings. We don't like to suffer, and we shouldn't. What Paul is saying, however, is that now our sufferings have meaning and purpose. Our sufferings are leading us somewhere.

Paul says that suffering produces perseverance. Perseverance is the ability to continue onward in the face of hard times. If we are persevering people, we don't give up. We push forward. Paul then says perseverance produces character. By facing trials and working through them, God is molding us into better people. We give up bad habits, for example, and replace them with good ones. Lastly, Paul says character produces hope. When we look back on the process through which God has brought us and realize that we are still in this process, we have a firm basis for hope. We know that just as he has brought us through trials of the past, he will bring us through trials of the future, and this will continue, because he loves us, until the very end when we will enjoy his presence forever.

☞ **GO TO:**

Psalm 116:8–11;
   Romans 8:17–27;
   2 Corinthians 4:7–12;
   James 1:2–4
   (sufferings)

uncertainty of job situation (suffering?) if so → perseverance → character (woman of faith, looking at good of now), hope (He will provide a place to work)

Something to Ponder

Joni Eareckson Tada was seventeen, full of life and hope, when she dived into the Chesapeake Bay, struck a submerged rock, and instantly became a quadriplegic. Twenty-eight years following the accident, an interview in *Leadership Magazine* records these words spoken by Tada: "Pain and suffering have purpose. . . . I get impatient with people who want to get all their needs met. . . . With my disability, some days are easier than others. But for me, life is always difficult. These are issues I must face every single morning. Every morning somebody has to give me a bath in bed, dress me, lift me into a wheel chair, comb my hair, brush my teeth, fix my breakfast, cut up my food, feed me. . . . I have to turn them, by the grace of God, into something that has meaning and purpose."[2]

Take It to Heart

When we are in the throes of suffering, we are so busy hurting, sometimes it can be difficult to see any purpose in it. Often it is not until afterwards that we can look back and see that God had a reason for the suffering. He was pushing us to a higher level. He was sculpting us to look more like Jesus. We will not reach perfection before we die, but God means to bring us as far as he can. We will reduce the pain we experience if while we suffer we can somehow remember that suffering has purpose.

Some Christian martyrs actually sang praises to God while burning in the flames of their persecutors. How did they do this? They had a remarkably clear understanding of the truth that suffering has purpose.

KEY POINT

Suffering has purpose.

 Meet Paul—Paul was not unaccustomed to suffering himself. In 2 Corinthians 11:23–29, he recounts:

- Five times I received from the Jews the forty lashes minus one.
- Three times I was beaten with rods.
- Once I was stoned.
- Three times I was shipwrecked.
- I spent a night and a day in the open sea.
- I have been constantly on the move.
- I have been in danger from rivers, bandits, countrymen, and Gentiles.
- I have been in danger in the city, country, and sea.
- I have been in danger from false brothers.

- I have gone without sleep and food.
- I have been cold and naked.

What Others are Saying:

Charles R. Swindoll: Paul viewed his circumstances as having cleared the way 'for the greater progress of the gospel' of Christ to be released.[3]

Francis A. Schaeffer: This [*"hope does not disappoint us"*] takes us all the way back to our theme verses, where Paul says that he is *"not ashamed of the gospel of Christ"* (Romans 1:16) . . . he is proud of the Gospel because of the great hope it has given him; it is a hope that has not disappointed him, and therefore a hope of which he need never be ashamed.[4]

Dietrich Bonhoeffer: So the Christian, too, belongs not in the seclusion of a cloistered life but in the thick of foes.[5]

what does this have to do w/ the discussion

> **Romans 5:6–8** You see, at just the right time, when we were still powerless, Christ died for the ungodly. Very rarely will anyone die for a righteous man, though for a good man someone might possibly dare to die. But God demonstrates his own **love** for us in this: While we were still sinners, Christ died for us.

love: commitment to act on another's benefit

Loving The Ugly Duckling

We were completely powerless to do what was right when Jesus died for us. Few, if any, will die for a good man, though someone might. God's love, however, is so gracious that he died for us when we were still sinners. He did not wait for us to clean up our acts. He died for the *ungodly*.

Our experience of God's love is subjective, but there is an objectiveness to God's love as well. That Jesus died for us when we were sinners is unmistakable proof that God loves us. You can stake your life on it.

KEY POINT

Where you find love, you find God; when you find love, you find God.

What Others are Saying:

Philip Yancey: Jesus said God is like a shepherd who leaves ninety-nine sheep inside the fence to hunt frantically for one stray; like a father who can't stop thinking about his rebellious ingrate of a son though he has another who is respectful and obedient; like a rich host who opens the doors of the banquet hall to a menagerie of bag-ladies and bums. God loves people not as a race or species, but rather just as you and I love them: one at a time. We *matter* to God. Jesus said that angels rejoice when a single sinner repents. A solitary act on this speck of a planet reverberates throughout the cosmos.[6]

What Others are Saying:

Frederick Buechner: Love: the first stage is to believe that there is only one kind of love. The middle stage is to believe that there are many kinds of love and that the Greeks had a different word for each of them. The last stage is to believe that there is only one kind of love . . . of all powers, love is the most powerful and the most powerless. It is the most powerful because it alone can conquer that final and most impregnable stronghold which is the human heart. It is the most powerless because it can do nothing except by consent. To say that love is God is romantic idealism. To say that God is love is either the last straw or the ultimate truth.[7]

blood: *a symbol of Jesus' death*

reconciled: *brought into harmony with God*

if saved thru His death; how much > thru His resurrecti

Romans 5:9–11 Since we have now been justified by his **blood**, how much more shall we be saved from God's wrath through him! For if, when we were God's enemies, we were **reconciled** to him through the death of his Son, how much more, having been reconciled, shall we be saved through his life! Not only is this so, but we also rejoice in God through our Lord Jesus Christ, through whom we have now received reconciliation.

Celebrate Good Times, Come On!

We were busy hating God—spitting on him, throwing dirt in his face, kicking him—while he was busy taking our sin upon his own back and dying for us, so Paul asks a simple question. If that's how God treated us when we were his enemies, don't you think he'll be good to us now that we are his own? Of course he is! God *has done* that which is difficult (loving one's enemies), of course he *will* do that which is easy (loving one's friends).

Christ's death reconciled us to God, Christ's resurrection ensures that we will live new lives in him. We are new creations!

Lastly, Paul writes that we will praise God. What a change from three chapters ago! In chapter 2, we were standing guilty and silent before a holy Judge. Now through our Lord Jesus Christ, we are praising God who used to be our Judge! We need not, indeed we cannot, do anything to earn this reconciliation. The reconciliation is done. All we have to do is receive it.

What Others are Saying:

Philip Yancey: Unavoidably, we transfer to God feelings and reactions that come from our human parents. George Bernard Shaw had difficulty with God because his father had been a scoundrel, an absentee father who cared mostly about cricket and pubs. Likewise, C. S. Lewis struggled to overcome the imprint left by his own father, a harsh man who would resort to quoting Cicero to his children when scolding them. When his mother died, Lewis said, it felt as if Atlantis had broken off and left him stranded on a tiny island. After studying at a public school led by a cruel headmaster who was later certified insane and committed to an institution, Lewis had to overcome the impact of these male figures to find a way to love God.[8]

Take It to Heart

Our reconciliation is established on the foundation of Christ's finished work and now, right now, we are being saved by our risen Savior. His fellowship, his counsel, and his gift of presence flow from the promise of the Word. With the exercise of our gifts and the recognition of our call, God receives glory from our lives.

obedience brings glory
good works

What Others are Saying:

John Calvin: The sum of the whole is that if Christ has attained righteousness for sinners by His death, He will much more protect them from destruction when they are justified. It would not have been enough for Christ to have once procured salvation for us, were He not to maintain it safe and secure to the end. This is what the apostle now asserts, declaring that we have no need to fear that Christ will terminate the bestowal of His grace upon us before we come to our appointed end.[9]

Yes, but...

> **Romans 5:12–14** Therefore, just as sin entered the world through one man, and **death** through sin, and in this way death came to all men, because all sinned— for before the law was given, sin was in the world. But sin is not taken into account when there is no law. Nevertheless, death reigned from the time of Adam to the time of Moses, even over those who did not sin by breaking a command, as did Adam, who was a pattern of the one to come.

death: both biological and spiritual

Sin has always been even before the law came

Wanted: A New Covenant

depraved: *morally corrupt*

☞ **GO TO:**

Genesis 3 (the Fall)

Luke 3:38; Romans 5:14; 1 Corinthians 15:22, 45; 1 Timothy 2:13–14 (Genesis account)

There was no sin in the Garden of Eden. It was a perfect environment, and Adam and Eve were free to live in perfect happiness, having fellowship with God and with each other. They were capable of perfect obedience. How long they enjoyed this state of grace is unknown.

Paul explains the sequence of events at the point where sin entered their experience as the consequence of their action. This is what we refer to as the Fall, the historical event when Adam and Eve sinned and death, both spiritual and physical, became a part of human experience (see GWGN, pages 37–47). This is also referred to as original sin—original because it was the very first.

Paul says *"death came to all men, because all sinned."* This means that we are **depraved** from birth. The entrance of sin into life on this planet created an immediate need for a new approach to God who knew no sin. Here God began to make a way for sinners to be received into his holy kingdom through a covenant of grace.

God's Plan: The "Reign of Grace" through Christ

The Two Men	Adam (verse 14)	Christ (verse 14)
The Two Acts	Adam—one trespass: verses 12, 15, 17–19	Christ—one righteous act (on the cross): verse 18
The Two Results	By Adam—Condemnation, guilt, death: verses 15–16, 18–19	By Christ—Justification, life, kingship: verses 17–19
The Two Differences	*In degree* (verse 15): The grace of God by Christ abounds beyond the sin of the creature, Adam.	*In type* (verse 16): One sin, by Adam—condemnation and reign of death. Many sins on Christ—justification and "reigning in life" for those accepting God's grace by him.
The Two Kings	Sin—reigning through death: verse 17	Grace—reigning through righteousness: verse 21
The Two Contrasted States	Condemned people, slaves of death, by Adam	Justified people, reigning in life, by Christ

SOURCE: William R. Newell, *Romans Verse by Verse* (Chicago: Moody Press, 1938), 176.

Something to Ponder

It is good to take note that Paul believed the Genesis account. He makes a number of references to it in this and other epistles. He didn't consider the Genesis account to be a myth containing some amount of truth. Rather, Paul, like Jesus in the Gospel accounts, treated the account of the Fall as fact.

The generations between Adam and Moses had no written law, but there was still death during this time because people willfully violated their God-given consciences. The Old Testament does give us several accounts of people who lived godly lives beyond the Fall. These are examples of the grace of God at work in the midst of human evil.

Grabbed by Grace

What Others are Saying:

Origen: The death which entered through sin is without doubt that death which the prophet speaks when he says: "The soul which sins shall surely die" [Ezekiel 18:4].[10]

Mark Driscoll: To be under law means to operate under a covenant of works. The law demands of us how we should live, but does not give us the power to achieve its demands. . . . To be under grace means to operate under a covenant of blessing. Grace empowers us to live a life free of sin and free to God. Therefore, to be under grace means that we would not continue in habitual sin because we have been freed from the impossible task of living up to the law by our own efforts.[11]

> **Romans 5:15–17** But the gift is not like the trespass. For if the many died by the trespass of the **one man**, how much more did God's grace and the gift that came by the grace of the one man, Jesus Christ, overflow to the many! Again, the gift of God is not like the result of the one man's sin: The judgment followed one sin and brought condemnation, but the gift followed many trespasses and brought justification. For if, by the trespass of the one man, death reigned through that one man, how much more will those who receive God's abundant provision of grace and of the gift of righteousness reign in life through the one man, Jesus Christ.

one man: Adam

Adam's 1 sin → judgment
Jesus taking on many sins → justification

beautiful

Grace Is On The House

"The gift is not like the trespass" in that while sin made us all black with sin, God's grace is more than enough to wash the blackness away until we gleam with the bright holiness of God. To put it simply, God's grace is bigger than sin, and the final results of grace will be far beyond the results of sin.

Paul is seeking to show that the sin of the one man, Adam, brought all people into condemnation. But God's grace is sufficient to overcome that condemnation. While sin destroys lives, grace helps us to live full lives—lives of abundant blessing. God's gift of life through Jesus Christ eradicates the consequences of sin.

Eight times in Romans 5:15–17, Paul speaks of *grace* and *the gift*:

Grabbed by Grace

- *the gift* is not like the trespass (verse 15)
- God's *grace* (verse 15)
- *the gift* (verse 15)
- the *grace* of one man (verse 15)
- *the gift* of God (verse 16)
- *the gift* followed by many trespasses (verse 16)
- God's abundant provision of *grace* (verse 17)
- *the gift* of righteousness (verse 17)

Paul was stumbling over himself to make certain his readers understood they didn't have to do anything to have their sins forgiven except receive through faith in Jesus Christ the reconciliation that had already been made.

What Others are Saying:

Francis A. Schaeffer: Just as in the Old Testament a brother raised up seed to his brother who had died childless (Deuteronomy 25:5–6) so, with humanity having died in the sin of Adam, Christ came to raise up a real, living humanity. The man who raised up seed for his dead brother under Old Testament law was called a kinsman redeemer. Christ is the true kinsman redeemer. He raised up a seed to God.[12]

John Chrysostom: If a Jew should ask you: How was the world saved by the power of the one Christ? you can answer him and say: How was the world damned by the one disobedient Adam? Nevertheless, grace and sin are not equal, and neither are death and life nor God and the devil.[13]

Martin Luther: For God has arranged to remove through Christ whatever the devil brought in through Adam. And it was the devil who brought in sin and death. Therefore God brought about the death of death and the sin of sin, the poison of poison, the captivity of captivity. As he says through Hosea: "O Death, I will be your death; O Hell, I will be your bite" [Hosea 13:14].[14]

> **Romans 5:18–21** Consequently, just as the result of one trespass was condemnation for all men, so also the result of one act of righteousness was justification that brings life for all men. For just as through the disobedience of the one man the many were made sinners, so also through the obedience of the one man the many will be made righteous.
>
> The law was added so that the trespass might increase. But where sin increased, grace increased all the more, so that, just as sin reigned in death, so also grace might reign through righteousness to bring eternal life through Jesus Christ our Lord.

[handwritten margin note: Thru Adam's sin - death / Thru Jesus obedience - life]

One Part Sin, Five Bezillion Parts Grace

Here Paul offers concluding statements on the nature of the Fall and the condemnation it brought upon humanity. What one man's sin brought upon the entire human race is mind boggling.

Paul reviews the consequences of Adam's sin and Jesus' gift of life for all who believe. He addresses the following: trespass, condemnation, righteousness, justification, life, sin, grace, death, obedience, and law. Paul explains how all of these work together to point us once again to Jesus Christ.

When Paul says, *"The law was added so that the trespass might increase,"* he's saying the more clearly we see what's right, the more things we discover are wrong. Furthermore, the more people realize they are sinners and are dead, the more aware they become of the penalty from which God saved them.

Paul's emphasis is on life, not death. Those in Jesus Christ past, present, and future are not dead, but alive! Grace abounds for those whose hearts are anchored in Christ Jesus as Lord and Savior. At great cost, Jesus paid our debt of sin. His grace abounds to all who believe.

☞ **GO TO:**

Matthew 6:33
(grace abounds)

Study Questions

1. Peace is a wonderful grace of God. How do we find peace?
2. Why would we rejoice in suffering?
3. What is unmistakable proof that God loves us?
4. What does Paul mean when he says, *"The gift is not like the trespass"* (Romans 5:15)?
5. Why was the law added?

- Being justified by faith brings peace, access to God, hope for heaven, and purpose for our suffering. (Romans 5:1–5)

- Christ died for us when we were sinners, which is unmistakable proof of God's love. (Romans 5:6–8)

- If Christ loved us when we were sinners, he will of course continue to love us after we have become his own. (Romans 5:9–11)

- God knew that sin would enter the world, but he had a plan to put the world right. In Christ Jesus, God's grace abounds. (Romans 5:15–19)

- The law showed us more clearly what righteousness is so that we might also see more clearly what the breadth of sin is. God's grace is bigger than sin. (Romans 5:20–21)

Part Three

EXPERIENCING GRACE

REVEREND FUN

"He's getting cranky again . . . Stay hidden until he comes over and then we'll jump him."

ROMANS 6: A LIFE-OR-DEATH SITUATION

CHAPTER HIGHLIGHTS

- A Brand New Life
- United: A Permanent Relationship
- Sin Is No Longer Our Master
- Three Verbs
- Two Outcomes

Let's Get Started

If you've flown on airplanes much at all, you've probably had the experience of circling the airport, either because the field is too busy for the plane to land or because there's a problem in the tower that necessitates a temporary delay. As we come to Paul's discourse in Romans 6, we get the feeling that he's been circling the runway for some time and is about to prepare for landing.

At this point in the apostle's discussion, he makes a major transition. In Romans 1:18–3:20 Paul establishes a need for righteousness. In Romans 3:21–4:25 he explains how God justifies sinners. He uses Abraham as an example of what it means to be **justified by faith**.

Then in Romans 5 Paul describes some of the results of justification: we have peace with God, through faith we have access to Jesus, and we are able to rejoice in the truth that our suffering has purpose. He concludes this chapter by reflecting on the entrance of sin into human experience and on the consequences of that tragic moment in history. Grace steps in and reveals both the love and the power of God. This is the good news.

Finally, Paul explains how Jesus, God's second Adam, became salvation for us. Here we see the wonderful coming together of faith and grace, righteousness and justification, bringing *"eternal life through Jesus Christ our Lord"* (Romans 5:21).

In Romans 6 Paul makes the point that righteousness is not only a matter of how God sees us through faith in Jesus Christ.

justified by faith:
declared innocent by God through trust in Jesus

KEY POINT

Righteousness is something we should experience.

Righteousness is also something we should experience. Let's see how his discussion unfolds.

I like that!

> **Romans 6:1–2** What shall we say, then? Shall we go on sinning so that grace may increase? By no means! We died to sin; how can we live in it any longer?

There's No Winning In Sinning

We have learned God's grace is enough to justify us. That's the good news of the Gospel, but the question remains: *"Shall we go on sinning so that grace may increase?"* This might at first appear like a foolish question, but Paul's been around the block a few times. He had preached this message on several occasions, and he knew how difficult it was to walk a sinless path, despite God's grace and mercy.

Some misinformed people were tempted to give up all self-control. They reasoned that since God forgave all their sins, the more they sinned, the more grace God would give them. If one measure of grace was good, they figured they could get a double measure by being even more sinful.

Paul's reply to his question is, *"By no means!"* (or *"God forbid"* in the KJV). It is an exclamation of the highest degree in Jewish thought—not shock, but disgust. The phrase is used when truth is being trashed. When Paul speaks of being dead to sin, he is expressing how powerful God's righteousness can be for those who believe and walk in it.

> **Romans 6:3–4** Or don't you know that all of us who were baptized into Christ Jesus were baptized into his death? We were therefore buried with him through baptism into death in order that, just as Christ was raised from the dead through the glory of the Father, we too may live a new life.

A Second Definition For Baptism

I don't think they are mutually exclusive. Why wouldn't water baptism be the way to union?

Paul uses some difficult language here. What does it mean to be *"baptized into Christ Jesus"*? When we hear the word baptism, we normally think of water baptism, but here, Paul is using the word in a different way. He's using baptism as a metaphor for when one person is united with another person or other people. Remember when God used Moses to part the Red Sea, and all the Israelites were saved? In 1 Corinthians 10, Paul refers to this event by saying the Israelites were *"baptized into Moses,"* which is to say they were united to Moses like never before. They recognized his leadership and their dependence on him. In the same way, we are *"baptized into Christ Jesus."* We are united to Jesus. The identity of Jesus is inseparably linked with our own identities.

That's why Paul says we are *"baptized into his death."* What he means is that we are so perfectly united to Christ that his death becomes our death, not in the physical sense but in the spiritual sense. In other words, Christ's death was the death of our sin. It was the death of our old relationship with Adam, the essence of which was sin.

☞ **GO TO:**

John 14–16 (union)

Something to Ponder

It is interesting to note that although Jesus emphasized the importance of following him throughout his ministry, he never talked about <u>union</u> with himself until his crucifixion was near.

Two Types of Baptism

References to Water Baptism	References to Spiritual Baptism
Mark 16:16	Matthew 3:11
John 4:2	Mark 1:8
Acts 2:38–41	Luke 3:16
Acts 8:12–16	John 1:26, 33
Acts 9:18	Acts 2:38–39
Acts 10:47–48	Acts 8:16
Acts 16:15, 33	Acts 11:16
Acts 18:8	Romans 6:3–4
Acts 19:5	1 Corinthians 10:2
Acts 22:16	1 Corinthians 12:13
1 Corinthians 1:13–17	Galatians 3:27
Hebrews 6:2	Ephesians 4:5
1 Peter 3:21	Colossians 2:12
	1 Peter 3:21

Romans 6:5 If we have been united with him like this in his death, we will certainly also be united with him in his resurrection.

Ed McMahon, Eat Your Heart Out

Imagine someone transferred a million dollars into your checking account. Imagine it's sitting there right now, just waiting to be used. What do you do? Assuming you wouldn't give it all away, you would instantly have a new lifestyle. You would probably drive a different car, live in a different place. You would go on more vacations. There's one thing a million dollars can't do for you, though, and that is change your spiritual condition, but what if there was such a thing as a million dollars for the soul? What if someone could give you something that would instantly change the condition of your spirit? What would it be like? Would you walk around with warm fuzzies all the time? Would you be "above" all the trials of the world?

Paul says that we are not only united with Christ in his death, we are united with Christ in his resurrection. We too have new life. A new relationship has been born between us and Christ, the essence of which is life. We may not be completely at peace all the time, but we do know that God is always with us, that trials have a purpose, and that one day we'll enjoy the paradise of the full presence of God.

What Others are Saying:

James R. Edwards: God's grace is indeed freedom, but freedom *from* sin, not freedom *for* it—whoever sees in grace a pretext to get away with as much as possible is simply showing contempt for Christ who died for sin. The freedom created by grace leads not to license but to obedience. Obedience honors God's boundless love and responds to that love in the freedom which love creates.[1]

Something to Ponder

It is the Holy Spirit, not water, who joins a person to Christ. This is the dynamic work of the <u>Gospel</u>. Water is an outward sign, practiced as an ordinance or sacrament, of one's profession of faith. This has been a doctrine in the church since its inception.

When adult Christians decide to be baptized, it is not a **work of righteousness**. Rather, it is, or should be, their response to a God who loved them and was willing to take on their sin. Baptism is also an act of Christian obedience. It is our affirmation that we have believed and want to follow in Christ's footsteps.

☞ **GO TO:**

John 1:12–13 (Gospel)

all true the argument

work of righteousness: something we do that makes us better or gains merit with God

is in it's necessity for Salvation

No longer are we slaves to sin. We are now servants of Christ. We have become part of a new priestly order. Spirituallyspeaking, we are in paradise. If we were to act as if we were in spiritual paradise, how would our lives be different? Would we worry as much as we do? Would we get angry as often as we do? Would we look to the needs of others more often? Would we be more deliberate in how we live our lives?

Take It to Heart

Spiritual realms

IN OTHER LETTERS

Paul takes up this same discussion in his letter to the Galatians. He writes to the people in the churches of Galatia, a Roman province where Paul went on his first missionary journey (see illustration below), reminding them of this very essential matter: *"You are all sons of God through faith in Christ Jesus, for all of you who were baptized into Christ have clothed yourself with Christ"* (Galatians 3:26–29). Paul's message is consistent. We are united with Christ.

united identified

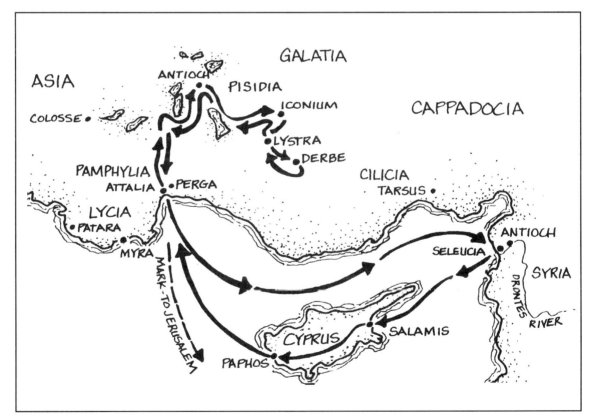

Paul's First Missionary Journey

This map shows the route Paul took through Galatia on his first missionary journey.

old self: *our sinful nature*

John Chrysostom: Being dead to sin means not obeying it any-more. Baptism has made us dead to sin once and for all, but we must strive to maintain this state of affairs, so that however many commands sin may give us, we no longer obey it but remain un-moved by it, as a corpse does.[2]

> **Romans 6:6–7** For we know that our **old self** was cru-cified with him so that the body of sin might be done away with, that we should no longer be slaves to sin—because anyone who has died has been freed from sin.

Follow The New Captain

What Paul is saying in these verses may be best illustrated with a story.

Once there was a crew of sailors whose captain was insane. For a long time the crew obeyed the man because, insane or not, he was their captain. There was only one problem. The insane captain's leadership often brought disaster.

One night the crew came very close to death because the captain led the crew into a frightening storm. On the following morning the first mate went around to each of the men and explained they no longer needed to pay attention to the insane captain. He was now so crazy that he wouldn't know the differ-ence. The first mate became their new captain, and the crew eventually learned to ignore the old captain when he shouted orders. They did only what their new captain commanded. The wise leadership of the new captain brought joy and wealth to all the crew.

This story illustrates what our union with Christ is like. The old captain is our "old self," from whom we used to take all our orders and to whom we need no longer pay attention. The new captain is Christ, whose leadership will bring us abun-dant life.

Paul wants the believer to see that the *"body of sin"* has truly been done away with. As Jesus' death and resurrection were his-torical facts, so the believer's death and resurrection in Christ are rooted in objective truth.

*Then why do I
feel i act so
sinful*

Sometimes it takes a lot to convince ourselves that we are *"freed from sin."* After all, sin is still evident both in us and around us. This is one reason why faith is so important. Paul tells us that faith (in our freedom from sin) must come first; then we will see the results. It doesn't work the other way around. We can't wait to be convinced that we are free and then have faith that we are. That's not the way God set things up. He says to have faith, and the rest will come.

Be convinced that Christ has freed me from sin

John Chrysostom: Paul does not say that we have been cruci-fied but we have been crucified *with him,* thus linking baptism with the cross. . . . You are dead not in the sense that you have been obliterated but in the sense that you now live without sin.[3]

What Others are Saying:

maybe w/o eternal consequences of sin?

> **Romans 6:8–10** Now if we died with Christ, we be-lieve that we will also live with him. For we know that since Christ was raised from the dead, he cannot die again; death no longer has mastery over him. The death he died, he died to sin once for all; but the life he lives, he lives to God.

*died to sin
lives to God
We have a new leader*

Knowing's Half The Battle

Here Paul begins using a series of three active verbs that we can think of as three steps to overcoming sin. The first verb is to *know.* Paul says *"we know"* that Jesus rose from the dead, he cannot die again, and therefore death has no mastery over him. This is the first step in overcoming sin—*knowing* that Christ died to sin and lives for God.

Oswald Chambers: To become one with Jesus Christ, a person must be willing not only to give up sin, but also to surrender his whole way of looking at things. . . . No one experiences complete sanctification without going through a "white funeral"—the burial of the old life. . . . You cannot die or go to your funeral in a mood of excitement. Death means you stop being.[4]

What Others are Saying:

- does this mean we'll mourn our old life/ nature?

> **Romans 6:11–14** In the same way, count yourselves dead to sin but alive to God in Christ Jesus. Therefore do not let sin reign in your mortal body so that you obey its evil desires. Do not offer the parts of your body to sin, as instruments of wickedness, but rather offer

dead to sin, no longer alive to God / respond to sin.

> yourselves to God, as those who have been brought from death to life; and offer the parts of your body to him as instruments of righteousness. For sin shall not be your master, because you are not under law, but under grace.

Take It As True

Here are the second and third steps to overcoming sin. In the same way we *know* death has no mastery over Christ, we ought to *take it as true* that we are no longer in slavery to sin because we are joined with Christ in his death through the power of the Holy Spirit. The King James Version uses the verb *reckon*. We ought to reckon ourselves dead to sin. Paul is saying, "Make up your minds that sin does not have power over you."

The third and final step in overcoming sin is to *yield* to God. We should not offer our bodies to sin. We should offer them to God. It is not a matter of doing nothing. It is a matter of doing the right thing.

God is stronger than sin, fact

We are God's truth

Children: We are stronger than sin

Something to Ponder

Jesus is both our example of a life that is fully surrendered to the will of God and the one who enables us to walk in that same surrender. It is our faith that makes the connection. Faith overrules our own will and allows us to abide in God's will. Ultimately, there is only one will that is holy: God's.

IN OTHER LETTERS Paul reminded the Galatians, *"Do not be deceived: God cannot be mocked. A man reaps what he sows. The one who sows to please his sinful nature, from that nature will reap destruction; the one who sows to please the Spirit, from the Spirit will reap eternal life"* (Galatians 6:7–8). People may breathe a sigh of relief after doing something wrong, thinking, "Great! I didn't get caught," but the reality is there is no such thing as not getting caught. There is no avoiding the destructive consequences of sin. Sometimes they come immediately, sometimes they come later, but they do come.

We have to live in these bodies the rest of our lives on earth. Just as Jesus carries scars on his hands and feet, sin, even when confessed and forgiven and cleansed by his blood, often leaves an indelible mark. One day we will look upon Christ's scars and realize we participated in putting them there.

Paul entreats, *"Do not offer the parts of your body to sin, as instruments of wickedness, but rather offer yourself to God, as those who have been brought from death to life."* This is a faith offer. Your body will fight against a righteous walk with God until it is brought into submission to God's will. This means we have to choose, carefully, what we look upon, what (and how) we touch, what we listen to, and, if we are overcome with the sin of gluttony (see GWHN, pages 227– 230), we need to watch what we taste and smell.

Remember This . . .

it's a sinful nature that wants more than it needs.

✗ I must hate sin because my ✗ God hates sin in order to overcome it

---

Francis A. Schaeffer: As Christians we have the possibility of living by faith, on the basis of the blood and in the power of the Spirit. Therefore, it isn't necessary that sin should have dominion over us. As Paul will say later, ". . . that the righteousness of the law might be fulfilled in us, who walk not after the flesh, but after the Spirit" [Romans 8:4] . . . we are under grace. The finished work of Christ and the indwelling of the Spirit are ours. It is possible for us to yield to the power of Christ.[5]

What Others are Saying:

Martin Luther: Nothing lives to God, however, except that which lives eternally and spiritually, because God is eternal and a spirit, before whom nothing counts except what is spiritual and eternal; but the flesh and temporal things are nothing to Him.[6]

I think earthly things matter to God in the eternal results they bring e.g. beauty of earth → thinking of God ⇒ praising/ belief in God

---

Dietrich Bonhoeffer: Baptismal death means justification from sin. The sinner must die that he may be delivered from his sin (Romans 6; Colossians 2). Sin has no further claim on him, for death's demand has been met, and its account settled. Justification from sin can only happen through death. Forgiveness of sin does not mean that sin is overlooked and forgotten, it means a real death on the part of the sinner and his separation from sin.[7]

forgiveness of sin is 2 way covenant - God forgives & we die to our allegiance to it "new captain"

> **Romans 6:15–18** What then? Shall we sin because we are not under law but under grace? By no means! Don't you know that when you offer yourselves to someone to obey him as slaves, you are slaves to the one whom you obey—whether you are slaves to sin, which leads to death, or to obedience, which leads to righteousness? But thanks be to God that, though you used to be slaves to sin, you wholeheartedly obeyed the form of teaching to which you were entrusted. You have been set free from sin and have become slaves to righteousness.

Whose Slave Are You?

Paul wants it to be understood that being under grace in no way lessens the <u>righteous demands</u> of the law. If anything, grace becomes more demanding.

In the Roman Empire people became slaves a number of different ways. One way was to be born into a slave family, another was to be captured in battle, and still another was to be forced into slavery if one's nation was taken over. One final way was if an otherwise free person went into another's household and acted as a slave. Under Roman rule, if a person did this, he or she was a slave. The idea was, "A man is as he does."

Paul says if you act as a slave to sin by doing sinful things, you *are* a slave to sin. If you act as a slave to God by doing good things, you are a slave to God.

Note there are only two options. Slavery to sin or slavery to God. There is no such thing as not having a master. We all have a master. The question is, Which one? The way we act is a demonstration of our choice.

Paul keeps bringing grace into his discussion with the church in Rome. He knows that while the law reveals sin, grace brings healing to the sinner. While the law points out our sins and weaknesses, grace points up to our Savior and his strength. We are *"under grace."* It's our umbrella to protect us from the spiritual turmoil that surrounds us. If we fail to grasp the significance of the grace of God in Christ Jesus, we will always be in bondage to sin.

☞ **GO TO:**

Matthew 5:17
(righteous demands)

A man is as he does – am I God's slave or Satan's. God's instrument or Satan's for righteousness or evil

Grabbed by Grace

Our struggle is not with the law, nor with grace; our struggle is with sin. The law drags us out into the light, exposing our sin, and grace leads us to the Cross where our sin is paid for and done away with.

Remember
This . . .

As believers we have changed masters; once we were slaves to sin, finding no way out, but now we are servants of righteousness. Paul states it more definitively: you *"have become slaves to righteousness."* The following hymn illustrates what sweet captivity this is:

Something
to Ponder

> *Wonderful grace of Jesus, greater than all my sin;*
> *How shall my tongue describe it, where shall its praise*
>   *begin?*
> *Taking away my burden, setting my spirit free,*
> *For the wonderful grace of Jesus reaches me.*
> —Haldor Lillenas[8]

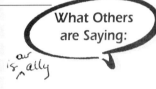

What Others
are Saying:

Martin Luther: But temptation becomes a servant when we resist it, because it then produces a hatred of iniquity and a love of righteousness.[9]

view temptation as the enemy - righteousness is our ally

John Calvin: *"And being set free from sin."* The meaning is that it is absurd for anyone to continue in bondage after he has gained his freedom. He ought to maintain the state of freedom which he has received. It is not fitting, therefore, for believers to be brought again under the dominion of sin, from which they have been set at liberty by Christ.[10]

> **Romans 6:19** I put this in human terms because you are weak in your natural selves. Just as you used to offer the parts of your body in slavery to impurity and to ever-increasing wickedness, so now offer them in slavery to righteousness leading to holiness.

Key point.
You will have a master - who will you choose

Speaking Your Language

When Paul says, *"I put this in human terms,"* what he's saying is this: "I'm using this slavery analogy because slavery is something you're familiar with." Slavery would have been an effective reference point because slaves were a major economic asset in first-century Rome. A large percentage of the professionals, including teachers and doctors, were slaves. The Roman church would have known all about slavery—its advantages and disadvantages, its binding nature, and how to avoid or enter into it.

> **Romans 6:20–23** When you were slaves to sin, you were free from the control of righteousness. What benefit did you reap at that time from the things you are now ashamed of? Those things result in death! But now that you have been set **free from sin** and have become slaves to God, the benefit you reap leads to holiness, and the result is eternal life. For the wages of sin is death, but the gift of God is eternal life in Christ Jesus our Lord.

free from sin: *free from sin's power, not its presence*

What's In It For Me?

Paul goes on to discuss what results from servitude to either master. Here is what sin offers:

- Slavery to impurity (6:19)
- Ever-increasing wickedness (6:19)
- Slavery to sin (6:20)
- Shame (6:21)
- Death (6:21, 23)

holiness: *true inner goodness of character; God-likeness*

Paul reminds believers that God's righteousness leads to **holiness**. To understand real holiness, we need to look at Jesus in the Gospels. His is a holiness that fits the plan and purposes of God. He wasn't self-righteous. Rather, his piety led to charity, kindness, compassion, service, mercy, tenderness, and forgiveness. His purity led to devotion to his Father. His compassion enabled him to reach out to the poor, the needy, and the religious. His tenderness led him to stop and talk with the children, to make them a real part of the kingdom of God.

Holiness is not an escape from the world, it's the godly way to enter the world—to glorify God and to be a blessing to others. The apostle Peter understood holiness after years of missing the mark. He wrote in his first epistle, *"But just as he who called you is holy, so be holy in all you do; for it is <u>written</u>: 'Be holy, because I am holy'"* (1 Peter 1:15–16). Holiness means separation from all that is sinful and consecration to all that is holy. It requires our total person to be set apart for God.

☞ **GO TO:**

Leviticus 19:2 (written)

Charles Hodge: The leading doctrine of this section, and of the whole gospel, in reference to sanctification, is, that grace, instead of leading to the indulgence of sin, is essential to the exercise of holiness. So long as we are under the influence of a self-righteous or legal spirit, the motive and the aim of all good works are wrong or defective.[11]

they will all be for our benefit not someone else's

Study Questions

1. Does sin cause grace to abound?
2. What does it mean to be baptized into Christ's death?
3. What does it mean to *"be united with* [Christ] *in his resurrection"*?
4. We have been united with Christ in his resurrection. How does that free us from sin?
5. Since we have been set free from sin, how is it that so many Christians live in sin?

CHAPTER WRAP-UP

- Paul speaks about death and life. Because we have been baptized in Christ, we now share his identity and rejoice in hope. (Romans 6:1–4)

- We have been identified and united with Christ in his death, burial, and resurrection. Through the exercise of faith we receive the benefits that accompany this great work of grace on behalf of humanity. (Romans 6:5–7)

- Because of the resurrection, sin is no longer our master. By faith, we can count ourselves *"dead to sin and alive to God in Christ."* (Romans 6:8–11)

- In addition to knowing that we are joined with Christ in his death and resurrection, we need to take this as true and choose to obey God. In this way, we will demonstrate who our master is. A man is as he does. (Romans 6:12–14)

- We must choose between two masters, sin or God. The result of sin is death, and the reward of God is righteousness and eternal life (Romans 6:15–23)

ROMANS 7: THE TENSION OF TWO NATURES

CHAPTER HIGHLIGHTS

- Freedom by Death
- Two Natures
- The Goodness of the Law
- The Badness of Sin
- Vexed and Bewildered
- Deliverance and Thanksgiving

Let's Get Started

Paul's writings are the key that enables the church to unlock the gospel message. We have seen from the first six chapters how precious the Gospel is to Paul. It is easy for us to forget how good God is and to put conditions on his grace—especially conditions that we apply to others.

As a committed Pharisee, Paul was well schooled in the law, which included the Ten Commandments as well as other God-given laws. There were laws that guided temple worship, laws about what to eat and what not to eat, laws surrounding childbirth, laws related to various infections and diseases, and laws that set moral standards.

While the law was never intended to bring about salvation, the law was holy in that it was an expression of God's character. The law helped people recognize their need for salvation.

> **Romans 7:1–3** Do you not know, brothers—for I am speaking to men who know the law—that the law has authority over a man only as long as he lives? For example, by law a married woman is bound to her husband as long as he is alive, but if her husband dies, she is released from the law of marriage. So then, if she marries another man while her husband is still alive, she is called an adulteress. But if her husband dies, she is released from that law and is not an adulteress, even though she marries another man.

Death Unlocks The Shackles

As chapter 7 opens, Paul is answering a question that his Jewish readers would have been sure to ask: How can we be legally freed from the law? Paul answers this question by using marriage as an illustration. The law binds a wife to her husband for as long as the man lives and no longer.

Paul uses the marriage covenant as a lens to sharpen our vision. It is an apt analogy. Here's Paul's rationale:

- The law has authority over people for as long as they live.
- Only death can break or end that authority (as death ends marriage).
- All attempts to circumvent the law's authority lead to a violation.
- Death frees one from the law.
- Jesus died to the law in order that the law would be dead to us, and we to the law.

Take It to Heart

reign: control, authority

It takes discernment to know when we are under the law or just being obedient on the basis of our faith. If we are still under the rule of law, trying to obey the law instead of being submissive to the law of Christ, we are still under the **reign** of sin. Remember that the power of sin resides in the power of the law. It is Jesus Christ who fulfilled the just requirements of the law and, in so doing, broke the power of sin.

Dying to the law does not mean practicing lawlessness. It means discovering the joy and freedom of following the Lawgiver, for the Lawgiver revealed himself in the person of Jesus.

Remember This . . .

God did for us, in the death of his Son, what we could not do for ourselves. We would still be under law—every precept, every command, every ordinance—if we had not *"died to the law through the body of Christ, that* [we] *might belong to another"* (Romans 7:4). By the grace of God, we belong to Jesus, our Savior, Mediator, High Priest, and Lord.

What Others are Saying:

William Barclay: When a man rules his life by union with Christ he rules it not by obedience to a written code of law which may actually awaken the desires of sin, but by an allegiance to Jesus Christ within his spirit and his heart. Not law, but love, is the motive of his life: and the inspiration of love can make him able to do what the restraint of law was powerless to help him do.[1]

> **Romans 7:4–6** So, my brothers, you also died to the law through the body of Christ, that you might belong to another, to him who was raised from the dead, in order that we might bear fruit to God. For when we were controlled by the sinful nature, the sinful passions aroused by the law were at work in our bodies, so that we bore fruit for death. But now, by dying to what once bound us, we have been released from the law so that we serve in the new way of the Spirit, and not in the old way of the written code.

Rotten Fruit

When we relate to God through the law by trying our hardest to do what's right, all that happens is the old nature is stimulated by the law to produce fruit that is contrary to God, *"fruit for death,"* Paul calls it.

Here's an example. Let's say a man makes up his mind to stop taking the Lord's name in vain. Let's say he succeeds, but now he looks down on everyone around him who does take the Lord's name in vain, and he also becomes very proud of his own accomplishment. The man succeeds in not taking the Lord's name in vain, but he becomes judgmental and prideful in the process. This is the way of the old nature. One step forward, two steps back.

The way of the new nature is different. The new nature looks to God for guidance, not the law. You might say, "Well, okay, but didn't the law come from God?" The answer is yes, but the law is not meant to be a guide for our lives. If you're an apprentice in carpentry and the master carpenter gives you a box of tools, will you use the hammer to tighten screws? Of course not! Every tool has its purpose.

The law's purpose is to show us how much we need the Holy Spirit to guide us. To use the carpentry analogy again, when we compare our work to the work of the master carpenter, we see how far we have to go. We are therefore motivated to listen and learn from the master. In the same way, the law shows us how much we need to listen to God.

KEY POINT

Look to God for guidance, not to the law.

Two Natures and Their Outcomes

Nature	Stimulated by . . .	To Produce . . .
Old Nature	The law	Fruit for death
New Nature	The Holy Spirit	Fruit for God

KEY POINT

Fruit is produced in both the old and the new natures. Whoever we are in union with will determine the kind of fruit we bear.

— think marriage, friendships, etc.

Something to Ponder

It was the apostle James who wrote, *"As the body without the spirit is dead, so faith without deeds is dead"* (James 2:26). This is what Paul means when he speaks of being controlled by the old nature, bearing *"fruit for death."* When the Holy Spirit indwells our body, in accord with the teaching of the New Covenant, we will *"bear fruit to God."*

What Others are Saying:

Matthew Henry: Good works are the children of the new nature . . . there is no fruit brought forth to God till we are married to Christ. This distinguishes the good works of believers from the good works of hypocrites and self-justifiers, that they are done in union with Christ.[2]

Take It to Heart

Christ's purpose is unswerving: He came to fulfill the divine will and to make known the glory of God. This is a guide for believers in our service for the kingdom of God. Paul spells it out plainly to the Corinthians: *"So whether you eat or drink or whatever you do, do it all for the glory of God. . . . For I am not seeking my own good but the good of many"* (1 Corinthians 10:31, 33). To glorify God is to reveal, by word and by life, what God is like. We are called upon by the Spirit of God to reflect the Person whose life we possess. We are to *"do it all for the glory of God."* God's expectations are of the highest order because he has given us his greatest good: the very life of his Son.

☞ **GO TO:**

John 5:40; 8:50; 17:5; Colossians 1:27; 2 Peter 1:3 (glory)

What Others are Saying:

Adolf Schlatter: As long as [Jesus Christ] had a body, he was under the law (Galatians 4:4), and there would have been no liberation from the law, if the judgment of death had not been carried out in his body. All those who belong to him are included in what Jesus did. His divine, powerful love renders his association complete and effective for all.[3]

William S. Plumer: The legal spirit is a great enemy of the gospel. Legal repentance is wholly diverse from evangelical sorrow for sin. Mount Sinai is far from Mount Calvary. It was Joshua, not Moses, that let Israel into Canaan . . . great is the mystery of godliness.[4]

> **Romans 7:7–8** What shall we say, then? Is the law sin? Certainly not! Indeed I would not have known what sin was except through the law. For I would not have known what coveting really was if the law had not said, "Do not covet." But sin, seizing the opportunity afforded by the commandment, produced in me every kind of covetous desire. For apart from law, sin is dead.

Magnifying Our Sin

Sin is used several times in verses 7–12. In these verses it is referring not to an act of sin, but to the sin principle, the powerful force within us that stays relatively quiet until we are told we should not do certain things (the law). *"Do not covet"* is one example. Then sin wells up within us. The surest way to lose flowers from your garden bed is to post a sign that reads, "Don't Pick the Flowers." If sin is allowed to run its full course, it eventually destroys us.

The apostle knew his discussion of the law would raise a number of questions in his readers' minds. For example, because our *"sinful passions"* are *"aroused by the law"* (Romans 7:5), is the law not wicked?

Paul responds, *"Certainly not!"* The issue at hand is our awareness of sin, which is created by the law. The law does not cause sin, it identifies sin. The law acts like a magnifying glass; it helps us see our sin in large, bold type. God's commandments make it clear to us that we prefer to follow our own will instead of his.

Adolf Schlatter, a professor in theology at Tubingen University in the late nineteenth and early twentieth centuries, brings clarity to what the apostle communicated. He writes, "The law gives rise, not to sin, but to the knowledge of sin, which is non-existent without the law."[5]

It is because of this law-provoked inclination toward sin that Paul tells the believers in Rome to look carefully at *"the new way of the Spirit, and not in the old way of the written code"* (Romans 7:6). Paul had learned that we must be dead to the law before we can truly lay hold of Christ.

How do we do that?

Something to Ponder

covetousness: *a desire for the possessions of others*

Covetousness is a sin that shows up early in childhood. It's a sign for parents to begin praying for the salvation of their child. The flame of covetousness cannot be beaten away with a rod, but it can be enveloped and consumed in the fire of God's blessing. The way to stop coveting is to realize how much we have in Christ. We torture ourselves thinking, "If only," while the infinite joy of God sits neglected under our noses.

Paul's Different Uses For "Law"

Paul used the word *law* in three different ways, as follows:

1. The Old Testament and its commandments
2. The principle of the sin nature (we act against that which God says is right)
3. The principle of the new nature (we follow God)

context: *the textual setting of a word that can shed light on its meaning*

The way to discern which definition Paul is using is by looking at the **context** of the word. For example, when Paul says in 7:21, *"So I find this* law *at work: When I want to do good, evil is right there with me,"* we know from the context that Paul is not talking about the Old Testament and its commandments or the principle of the new nature. He's talking about the principle of the sin nature.

Martin Luther: The real difference between the old and the new law is this, that the old law says to those who are proud in their own righteousness: "You must have Christ and His Spirit"; the new law says to those who humbly admit their spiritual poverty and seek Christ: "Behold, here is Christ and His Spirit." Therefore, they who interpret the term "Gospel" as something else than "the good news" do not understand the Gospel, as those people do who have turned the Gospel into a law rather than grace have made Christ a Moses for us.[6]

Douglas J. Moo: God's work in Christ, mediated by the Spirit, is what overcomes the inability of the law, weakened by the flesh, and liberates the believer from the *"law of sin and death."*[7]

> **Romans 7:9–11** Once I was alive apart from law; but when the commandment came, sin sprang to life and I died. I found that the very commandment that was intended to bring life actually brought death. For sin, seizing the opportunity afforded by the commandment, deceived me, and through the commandment put me to death.

he realized just how sinful he was when compared w/ Christ.

Commandment And Conviction

When Paul says he was *"alive apart from the law,"* he is referring to a time in his life when he assumed that he was fulfilling God's commandments. Before his conversion Paul was, like other Pharisees, proud of his commitment to keep God's rules and observe his rituals. But the Pharisees focused on outward things. As long as they seemed to keep the commandments and remained ceremonially clean, they believed they were right with God. During this time in his life Paul was unaware of the sin within him.

Sometime after his conversion, however, Paul realized he was sinful (*"the commandment came"*). He was so intensely convicted that he likened the experience to death.

Paul did not see the condemnation of the law until he came face-to-face with Jesus. It was in the light of his grace and kindness that this hostile, angry man was brought to his knees. Until that point, Paul considered himself *"alive apart from the law"* (Romans 7:9). Once Paul was in the presence of true righteousness, he was <u>convicted</u> like never before.

How are the commandments *"intended to bring life"*? They confront people with their need for righteousness. People are then called to turn to the Lawgiver, and to seek mercy and forgiveness. Upon receiving God's grace, life expands in the heart of the believer to the point of breaking open and doing away with the shell of the old self.

Remember This . . .

☞ **GO TO:**

Romans 7:13 (convicted)

> **Romans 7:12** So then, the law is holy, and the commandment is holy, righteous and good.

Don't Fault The Law

After arguing for the goodness of the law at length, Paul concludes his thesis by making it absolutely clear that the law is holy, righteous, and good. Paul wanted to dispel any remaining false notions concerning the law. He therefore gives it his highest commendation.

Saint Augustine: Man needed to be shown the foulness of his malady. Against his wickedness not even a holy and good commandment could avail; by it the wickedness was increased rather than diminished.[8]

William S. Plumer: The moral law is unto life among unsinning angels. It was unto life to our first parents till they ate the forbidden fruit . . . but every man, who has had conviction of sin, has, like Paul, found the law to be unto death, that is to condemnation, to the death of legal hope, and to the arousing of wicked principles in the soul into lively action. The law, rightly used, **conduces** to holiness and happiness; broken or misused, it conduces only sin and misery.[9]

conduces: leads to

The law gives life only to the sinless

> **Romans 7:13** Did that which is good, then, become death to me? By no means! But in order that sin might be recognized as sin, it produced death in me through what was good, so that through the commandment sin might become utterly sinful.

Shows I am sinful & I am w/o Christ.

Law vs. Sin

Paul finds himself in front of a question that he had not fully pondered: *"Did that which is good, then, become death to me?"* Is that possible? What was the relationship between the law and **death**? Having concluded the commandment not to covet, which Paul used to represent the whole law, was *"holy righteous, and good,"* was it possible the law produced death in him?

death: spiritual and physical

Paul concludes, *"By no means!"* It's not the law that produces death in individuals; it's sin. He concludes that sin uses that which is *"good"* (the law) as an instrument to produce death in a person. This happens because we cannot keep the standard of God's righteousness.

Paul concludes that because sin uses the law to bring death, sin reveals itself as truly despicable. The law triumphs: it fully exposes sin for the evil thing it is.

> **Romans 7:14–16** We know that the law is spiritual; but I am unspiritual, sold as a slave to sin. I do not understand what I do. For what I want to do I do not do, but what I hate I do. And if I do what I do not want to do, I agree that the law is good.

Bewitched, Bothered, And Bewildered

Paul switches to the present tense here, whereas before he was using the past tense. He is obviously referring to his present struggles with sin, which daily try to gain control of his life.

Paul wonders why he can't control the advance of sin within him. He has the right attitude—he wants to do what is right and good. Yet, he still wallows in the mud that consumes his heart and soul. He believes in God, but wonders where God is.

Herein we see the conflict, the step that most, if not all, resist in some manner. Paul discovers that there is a difference between what he wants to do and what he actually does. He is *"sold as a slave to sin."* He has no capital, no assets to buy himself out of the slave market.

He can readily agree that the law is good, but the law is powerless to change him on the inside. It's unable to give him the resources he needs to fulfill the demands of the law, the very same law that is considered good.

> When Paul says the law is spiritual, he's referring to the source of the law, which is God, who is <u>Spirit</u>. When he says he is unspiritual, he is contrasting himself with the nature of the law. The law was pure, but he was full of sin.

> The **sanctification** process is fraught with conflict. Sin and death have been an integral part of Paul's discussion since the middle of chapter 5.

> Paul does not retreat from life's conflicts. Rather, he puts himself squarely in life's path. We will never find answers by hiding from the difficulties of life. Paul searched diligently for the will of God as well as the ways of God. He wanted his life, and the lives of those he was responsible to teach, to express what it means to live for the glory of God. We are called to do likewise.

sanctification: to become righteous in character and practice

☞ **GO TO:**

John 4:24 (Spirit)

2 Corinthians 3:17–18; Romans 8:11 (sanctification)

Something to Ponder

Remember This . . .

Take It to Heart

Kenneth L. Barker and John R. Kohlenberger III: From this point on to the end of the chapter, the personal emphasis continues and with increased intensity. The powerful forces of law and sin are depicted as producing a struggle that ends in a confession of despair, relieved only by the awareness that in Jesus Christ there is deliverance.[10]

John F. Walvoord and Roy B. Zuck: Understanding the conflict in personal sanctification involves seeing the relationship between a believer and his indwelling sin . . . in relating his personal experience in 7:14–25 Paul consistently used the present tense whereas he had used the **imperfect and aorist** tenses. Obviously he was describing his present conflict as a Christian with indwelling sin and its continuing efforts to control his daily life.[11]

imperfect and aorist:
*two Greek tenses which
when used together place
an action in the past*

> **Romans 7:17–20** As it is, it is no longer I myself who do it, but it is sin living in me. I know that nothing good lives in me, that is, in my sinful nature. For I have the desire to do what is good, but I cannot carry it out. For what I do is not the good I want to do; no, the evil I do not want to do—this I keep on doing. Now if I do what I do not want to do, it is no longer I who do it, but it is sin living in me that does it.

A Noble Struggle

After debunking the idea that the law is sin or that the law brings death, Paul addresses the question, Does the believer struggle with the law too? He answers by sharing from his own experience as a believer trying to keep the law.

Larry Richards writes a paraphrase that highlights the key points of Paul's argument. The paraphrase starts at verse 15: "I don't understand my own actions. I don't do what I want—I do the very thing I hate. Because I don't want to do the things I do, it's clear that I agree that what the law says is good and right. I'm that much in harmony with God. But somehow I'm not in control of my own actions! Some sinful force within takes over and acts through my body."[12] A change was underway, but Paul was still struggling.

Just because we struggle with sin doesn't mean we are not Christians. It takes self-control and diligence to overcome the temptations that the world around us presents. Christ fought and won the final battle over sin, but we need to apply that victory to daily life. Satan loves to whisper to us, saying we deserve this or that and making evil look like a reward. Often we find a set of rigid rules easier to follow than examining and changing our wrong attitudes and motives. In chapter 8 Paul will give us some very valuable information about how to overcome sin.

Take It to Heart

Earlier Paul said his sinful nature could not save him and neither could the law, though in itself the law is holy and righteous and good. Paul then explains that even with a new nature, **his will** could not save him. Here Paul says the *"sin living in* [him]*"* is responsible for his doing evil. In this way, Paul avoids Satan's false promise of **sinless perfection**.

Remember This . . .

Martin Luther: Therefore sin remains in the spiritual man for the exercise of grace, for the humbling of pride, for the repression of presumptuousness.[13]

What Others are Saying:

William S. Plumer: Here then it is conceded that the language of Romans 7:14–25 is appropriate to the case of Christians; that all Christians have a contest like that here described; and that the matter is of a very weighty character—a matter of universal Christian experience, than which nothing is to us more important to be rightly understood.[14]

his will: *his determined intention to do good*

sinless perfection: *what the serpent promised Adam and Eve in the Garden of Eden*

> **Romans 7:21–25a** So I find this law at work: When I want to do good, evil is right there with me. For in my inner being I delight in God's law; but I see another **law** at work in the members of my body, waging war against the law of my mind and making me a prisoner of the law of sin at work within my members. What a wretched man I am! Who will rescue me from this body of death? Thanks be to God—through Jesus Christ our Lord!

law: *here, the principle of the sin nature*

"I Can't Do It"

Paul continues to chronicle his experience. He carefully thought out what he was observing and feeling so others could benefit from his grueling experience.

Larry Richards' paraphrase continues, "I know that nothing good exists in the old me. The sin nature is so warped that even when I desire good I somehow can't do it. Sin, dwelling in me, is to blame for this situation. It all seems so hopeless! The fact is that when I want to do right, evil lies close at hand. In my inmost self I delight in God's law. But another principle wars with the desire to obey and brings me to my knees, a captive to the principle of indwelling sin."[15] Paul was not able to achieve righteousness by trying to keep the law. His inability to do so led him to despair and to cry out, *"Who will rescue me from this body of death?"*

He answers his own question with an expression of thanksgiving, for God through Jesus Christ will deliver him.

Something to Ponder

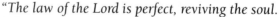

God's laws are meant to keep us from harm, sorrow on this earth, and death in eternity. When we learn this, we *want* to obey God. The psalmists speak of the spiritual man whose *"delight is in the law of the Lord, and on his law he meditates day and night"* (Psalm 1:2). The law is also praised in Psalm 19:

> *"The law of the Lord is perfect, reviving the soul.*
> *"The statutes of the Lord are trustworthy, making wise the*
>   *simple.*
> *"The precepts of the Lord are right, giving joy to the heart.*
> *"The commands of the Lord are radiant, giving light to the*
>   *eyes.*
> *"The fear of the Lord is pure, enduring forever."* (Psalm
>   19:7–9)

This is what Paul means when he says, *"I delight in God's law"* (Romans 7:22). The path we are called to walk is often a troublesome one, but we have God's presence and his Word to fill our hearts and minds. This should be our continuous delight.

Kenneth L. Barker and John R. Kohlenberger III: Romans 7 performs a service by calling into question certain popular notions that lack biblical foundation: that the soul's struggle is essentially against specific sins or habits; that human nature is essentially good [Romans 7:18]; that sanctification is by means of the law; that if one will only determine to do the right, he or she will be able to do it. These are some of the misconceptions that must be removed, and they might have not been removed had the apostle proceeded directly from [Romans 6 to Romans 8]. Without [Romans 7] we would not be able to appreciate to the full the truths presented in the next chapter.[16]

Saint Augustine: These are the words [*"When I want to do good, evil is right there with me"*] of one who is now under grace but still battling against his own lust, not so that he consents and sins but so that he experiences desires which he resists.[17]

> **Romans 7:25b** So then, I myself in my mind am a slave to God's law, but in the sinful nature a slave to the law of sin.

In Summary Of The Struggle

Paul takes a step back to summarize the essence of his struggle. One part of him is a slave to God while another part of him is a slave to sin. He's torn between the two. In the next chapter, we'll look at how Paul puts the resolution of this tension into everyday practice.

Many Christians can relate to what Paul is saying in these verses. We too get frustrated with ourselves. We desperately want to be good, but we can't be. Our hearts hurt. Our minds hurt. Even our bodies hurt because of our own sin. We should find consolation in knowing that the great saint Paul, who wrote more of the New Testament than any other and to whom centuries of Christians are eternally grateful—Paul was in the exact same predicament. He was riddled with his own sin.

Take It to Heart

Study Questions

1. Verse 4 says we died to the law that we might belong to another. What does this mean?
2. What are some of the differences between the old nature and the new nature?
3. How is it that the law is able to show us our sin?
4. How is the law spiritual? What does it mean to be unspiritual?
5. What does Paul mean when he says, *"I myself in my mind am a slave to God's law, but in the sinful nature a slave to the law of sin"* (Romans 7:25)?

CHAPTER WRAP-UP

- As a widow is no longer bound to her deceased husband, neither are we bound to the law because in Christ's crucifixion we died to the law. (Romans 7:1–3)

- The old nature is stimulated by the law to produce fruit to death. The new nature is stimulated by the Holy Spirit to produce fruit unto God. (Romans 7:4–6)

- The law is holy, righteous, and good in that it shows us our sin, but sin within us is aroused by the law and leads to self-destruction. (Romans 7:7–12)

- Sin uses the law to produce death in us. (Romans 7:13)

- Paul wanted to be godly but failed at every turn. He was vexed and bewildered by his behavior. (Romans 7:14–20)

- Tension arises within us because one part of us is slave to God, while the other is slave to sin. Deliverance is found in Jesus Christ. (Romans 7:21–25)

ROMANS 8: THE TRIUMPH OF SPIRIT-GUIDED LIVING

CHAPTER HIGHLIGHTS

- Deliverance from Condemnation
- Our Mind's Focus
- The Holy Spirit
- A Holy Obligation
- Present Testing, Future Triumph
- More Than Conquerors

Let's Get Started

The great triumph of the Christian's faith is total deliverance from **condemnation**. Paul does not say there is nothing in us that deserves condemnation, because there is, but the truth of the Gospel is that Christ Jesus has released us from condemnation. The believer has been imparted perfect righteousness and lives according to the law of the Spirit, which is the law of God.

We are not only forgiven, we have received the Holy Spirit into our very bodies. He is our source of divine power to bring about our necessary sanctification. Paul speaks of our bodies as God's temple: *"Do you not know that your body is a temple of the Holy Spirit, who is in you, whom you have received from God? You are not your own; you were bought at a price. Therefore honor God with your body"* (1 Corinthians 6:19–20).

Romans 8 is where Paul gathers various strands of thought, starting with the Gospel in chapter 1. He links **justification** with **sanctification**.

> **Romans 8:1–2** Therefore, there is now no condemnation for those who are in Christ Jesus, because through Christ Jesus the **law of the Spirit of life** set me free from the **law of sin and death**.

condemnation: being held responsible for and punished for evil acts

justification: the doctrine of being declared righteous in Christ

sanctification: the process by which God brings the Christian to be the person God created him or her to be

law of the Spirit of life: the normal pattern of a life lived in submission to the Holy Spirit

law of sin and death: the normal pattern of a life lived in sin

Jesus Freedom

Here we encounter another of Paul's *therefore*'s. This one takes us all the way back to chapter 3 where Paul said the law's purpose was to silence us before God. Paul has come from pointing out our guilt to *"there is now no condemnation."*

For *"no condemnation"* to have any meaning we must look at the opposite of condemnation—justification. The idea of justification is foundational to this letter and many other of Paul's writings. It happens when we are declared righteous in Christ, but justification goes beyond that. God also accepts us. God not only proclaims us not guilty, he welcomes us to himself with open arms.

> **Romans 8:3–4** For what the law was powerless to do in that it was weakened by the sinful nature, God did by sending his own Son in the likeness of sinful man to be a sin offering. And so he condemned sin in sinful man, in order that the righteous requirements of the law might be fully met in us, who do not live according to the sinful nature but according to the Spirit.

God's Gift

These verses remind us of the anguish in chapter 7. The law makes demands of us, but because of our sinful nature, we are unable to meet those demands. The law is "powerless" to save us.

God could have let us perish in the wrath that our unrighteousness deserves, but because he loves, he sent Christ to do what the law was unable to do. God became one of us, lived a perfect life, and died for our sins. Through Christ God justly condemned sins of the flesh while offering the gift of righteousness to all who believe.

KEY POINT

Grace is knowing that God is for us and with us, even in our sinful condition.

Remember This . . .

The law's purpose is to reveal sin, not to remove it. There is no defect in the law itself. The law was a covenant of works and made no provision for failure if it were to happen. The law leaves us as it finds us, proclaiming with Paul how wretched we are.

What Others are Saying:

Philip Yancey: In *The Art of Forgiving*, Lewis Smedes makes the striking observation that the Bible portrays God as going through progressive stages when he forgives, much as we humans do. First, God rediscovers the humanity of the person who wronged him, by removing the barrier created by sin. Second, God surrenders his right to get even, choosing instead to bear the cost in his own body. Finally, God revises his feelings toward us, finding a way to "justify" us so that when he looks upon us he sees his own adopted children, with his divine image restored.[1]

What Others are Saying:

James R. Edwards: The Christian is like a man who has the right tune in his head but cannot remember all the words. Accordingly, when Paul says that love fulfills the law (Romans 13:8; Galatians 5:14), that is not to assert that Christians are perfect, but that they live . . . according to the Spirit. The present tense of the Greek *peripatein,* "to walk" or live, connotes continued action, forward progress, a pattern of behavior under the Spirit's leading.[2]

Martin Luther: *"For sin He condemned sin."* Blessed Augustine says this about this passage: "For the death of the Lord achieved this, that we no longer fear death and no longer seek material goods or fear temporal evils, in which the carnal wisdom was, in which the precepts of the Law could not be fulfilled."[3]

Matthew Henry: It is the unspeakable privilege of all those that are in Christ Jesus that there is therefore no condemnation to them. He does not say, "There is no accusation against them," for this there is; but the accusation is thrown out. He does not say, "There is nothing in them that deserves condemnation," for this there is, and they see it, and own it; but it shall not be their ruin.[4]

> **Romans 8:5** Those who live according to the sinful nature have their minds set on what that nature desires; but those who live in accordance with the Spirit have their minds set on what the Spirit desires.

Nature And Desire

Paul draws a direct relationship between the essence of one's being and the direction of one's interests. When Paul refers to *"those who live according to the sinful nature,"* he is talking about people who have not accepted the grace of God, non-Christians. The phrase *"have their minds set on"* refers to more than what occupies the mind. It refers to one's *inner desires.* Paul says non-Christians do as their nature dictates. Sadly, they go from one sin to another destroying themselves along the way.

When Paul refers to *"those who live in accordance with the Spirit,"* he is talking about Christians who are controlled by the Holy Spirit. Such Christians want with their innermost beings to do as the Holy Spirit directs them.

Grabbed by Grace

If we determine by the grace of God, *"to live in accordance with the Spirit,"* having our *"minds set on what the Spirit desires,"* God's peace and wisdom will reign in our minds and hearts. Because of God's grace, we are able to catch a glimpse of what life was like before sin entered the world and what it will be like when we go to heaven. With Christ, life as it should have been has been partially restored.

> **Romans 8:6–8** The mind of sinful man is death, but the mind controlled by the Spirit is life and peace; the sinful mind is hostile to God. It does not submit to God's law, nor can it do so. Those controlled by the sinful nature cannot please God.

Let God Mind Your Business

Paul doesn't beat around the bush when it comes to telling his readers what is in store for the sinful man's mind. He uses one word: death. Death is what is in store for people whose minds are focused on sin. In contrast, he says minds controlled by the Holy Spirit will experience life and peace. "Which do you want?" Paul seems to be saying. "Death or life? Pain or peace?"

As the soul is redeemed, the mind must undergo transformation. The Word of God shows high regard for the human mind. Paul told the Corinthians to *"take captive every thought to make it obedient to Christ"* (2 Corinthians 10:5). He puts a premium on a properly focused mind. Throughout his writing, Paul is careful to explain how the sin nature can dominate one's thinking, comprehension, and discernment.

Something to Ponder

You might think as you begin this chapter that Paul is being negative, but sin is not something to be positive about, and Romans is God's definitive word on how God dealt with sin, which has been destroying the human race since the Garden of Eden.

What Paul is sorting out for believers is the difference between flesh and spirit. Here, Paul is not referring to religious do's and don'ts as much as he is pointing to the reality that we are either in the Spirit or in the flesh. We cannot be in both at the same time.

IN OTHER LETTERS   Paul put it this way in his letter to the Philippians, *"Whatever is true, whatever is noble, whatever is right, whatever is pure, whatever is lovely, whatever is admirable—if anything is excellent or praiseworthy—think about such things"* (Philippians 4:8–9). Paul knew that what a person centered his or her mind on would determine the kind of person one would be.

Your Mind's Focus and the Outcome

Focus on What Is . . .	So That You Can Be . . .
True	Discerning, not easily deceived
Noble	Respectable
Right	Morally upright and just
Pure	Chaste and innocent
Lovely	Delightful
Admirable	Praiseworthy and attractive

Kenneth L. Barker and John R. Kohlenberger III: But for the moment Paul wishes to expose the flesh in its stark reality as totally alien to God and his holy purposes. He insists there is a correspondence between one's essential being and what interests that person. The fleshly are occupied with fleshly things, whereas those who possess the Spirit and are controlled by him are concerned with the things of the Spirit.[5]

Adolf Schlatter: Those whom God makes his sons [and daughters] are alive. . . . Paul leaves it to them to determine how to order their physical life in its specifics, in order for the body to remain within its proper bounds. Paul did not formulate ascetic regulations, for he believed in the leadership that the Spirit affords the believers.[6]

What Others
are Saying:

James R. Edwards: Left to itself human nature is red in tooth and claw, locked in combat against God. Whether or not the expressions of human egoism are socially acceptable does not change their fundamental enmity from God and others. "Those controlled by the sinful flesh cannot please God" [Romans 8:8].[7]

> **Romans 8:9–10** You, however, are controlled not by the sinful nature but by the Spirit, if the Spirit of God lives in you. And if anyone does not have the Spirit of Christ, he does not belong to Christ. But if Christ is in you, your body is dead because of sin, yet your spirit is alive because of righteousness.

You Are God's Home

Paul now turns to address his readers. *"You,"* he begins. He reminds them of who they are. They are temples of the Holy Spirit. He tells them it is an unadulterated fact they are not controlled by the sinful nature but by the Spirit. Note that he uses *"Spirit of God"* and *"Spirit of Christ"* interchangeably.

He tells them that if they are looking for God, they need look no further than within themselves because *"the Spirit of God lives in you."* Note that Paul is *not* saying, "You are God," and that is not how his readers would have understood him. He is saying God has taken up residence within them because of their faith in Christ.

Christians often forget that God lives within them; the result of this forgetfulness is frustration and lack of contentment. We need people in our lives who remind us that Christ dwells in us. We also need to be as concerned as Paul was for our fellow Christians so that when the need arises we are quick to remind them of who lives in their hearts.

*Something
to Ponder*

When Paul speaks of having our minds set *"on what the Spirit desires,"* he is pointing the church as a body and as individuals to our control center. The Spirit has labored over the church now for two millennia, seeking to fulfill God's will. Indeed, the church exists today only because of the faithfulness of the Holy Spirit.

*Remember
This . . .*

> **Romans 8:11** And if the Spirit of him who raised Jesus from the dead is living in you, he who raised Christ from the dead will also give life to your mortal bodies through his Spirit, who lives in you.

Just Like New!

This verse reveals a wonderful truth. The Holy Spirit, who raised Jesus from the dead, can infuse our mortal bodies with resurrection power here and now. We're not helpless victims of sin anymore! The life-giving Holy Spirit can overwhelm the power of sin and empower us to lead holy and godly lives.

It is impossible to appreciate fully what God has done for us in sending his Son. We are promised future perfection when the Spirit raises us from the dead at Jesus' return, and even now we are promised access to his transforming power.

Grabbed by Grace

The redemption of our bodies is the crowning act of the redemptive process. The believer's body will be delivered. The effects of sin will no longer be seen on his bride, the church. Jesus will be the only one in heaven with scars. The redemption of our bodies has not yet occurred, so hope is vital to our salvation. We don't hope for what we already possess. Rather, hope points us to that which is yet to be finished.

Remember This . . .

Philip Yancey: Alone, a capella, Jessye Norman (at Wembley Stadium) begins to sing, very slowly:

What Others are Saying:

Amazing grace, how sweet the sound
That saved a wretch like me!
I once was lost but now am found—
Was blind, but now I see.

A remarkable thing happens in Wembley Stadium that night. Seventy thousand raucous fans fall silent before her aria of grace. By the time Norman reached the second verse, "Twas grace that taught my heart to fear, and grace my fears relieved . . . the soprano has the crowd in her hands. . . . Jessye Norman later confessed she had no idea what power descended on Wembley Stadium that night. I think I know. The world thirsts for grace. When grace descends, the world falls silent before it.[8]

What Others are Saying:

Douglas J. Moo: Christian behavior is the necessary mark of those in whom this fulfillment takes place. God not only provides in Christ the full completion of the law's demands for the believer, but he also sends the Spirit into the hearts of believers to empower a new obedience to his demands. Christians now are directed by the Spirit and not by the flesh.[9]

> **Romans 8:12–14** Therefore, brothers, we have an obligation—but it is not to the sinful nature, to live according to it. For if you live according to the sinful nature, **you will die**; but if by the Spirit you **put to death** the misdeeds of the body, **you will live**, because those who are led by the Spirit of God are sons of God.

you will die: *you will be without power*

put to death: *refuse to respond to sinful inclinations*

you will live: *you will have power to live the Christian life*

An Obligation To Live The Good Life

Paul's *therefore* glances back at what he's taught up until now. He has explained the Gospel. He has addressed the differences between Jew and Gentile. He has clearly outlined the need for righteousness and explained how righteousness has been provided for us. He has clarified the principle of justification by faith using Abraham and David as examples, and he has explained that reconciliation has been secured through the blood of Jesus Christ.

exhortation: *strong encouragement; admonition*

Paul moves from instruction to **exhortation**, from what God has accomplished to the importance of our response. He outlines the needed response in one word: obligation. In the original text it means, "one who owes a moral debt." We cannot earn or buy our salvation, but we are called by God to follow him. In Christ, we have adequate resources to serve our God, the king of heaven and earth. This is our moral debt, our obligation, and the end result of filling this obligation is life! The good life!

☞ **GO TO:**

James 4:7 (Satan)

Hebrews 3:7–15 (Holy Spirit)

Remember This . . .

Satan is diametrically opposed to anything that compels us to be submissive to the will of God, but we are called to resist <u>Satan</u> and listen to the voice of the <u>Holy Spirit</u>.

☞ **GO TO:**

Mark 14:36; Galatians 4:6 (Father)

> **Romans 8:15–16** For you did not receive a spirit that makes you a slave again to fear, but you received the Spirit of sonship. And by him we cry, "*Abba*, <u>Father</u>." The Spirit himself testifies with our spirit that we are God's children.

"No Fear" Isn't Just A Brand Name

Paul continues to shower his readers with the benefits of being believers. Here he says we are no longer chained to fear—fear of God's wrath, of death, or of where we will end up finally. We are not slaves to fear. We are children of God and as such, Paul encourages us to cry to God as if he were our "Daddy," which is a good translation of *Abba*. Like children with their father, we ought to run to him when we're hurt, ask lots of questions, and trust him when he says everything is going to be okay.

How do we know we are God's children? We feel it deep down. We sense the Holy Spirit's promptings, we feel a new closeness to God, we are more free in our interaction with him. If you don't feel it, believe it. If you believe it and follow through with action, just be patient, you are bound to feel it eventually.

Philip Yancey: God may be the Sovereign Lord of the Universe, but through his Son, God has made himself approachable as any doting human father. In Romans 8, Paul brings the image of intimacy even closer. God's spirit lives inside us, he says, and when we do not know what we ought to pray "the Spirit himself intercedes for us with groans that words cannot express."[10]

What Others are Saying:

> **Romans 8:17** Now if we are children, then we are heirs—heirs of God and co-heirs with Christ, if indeed we share in his sufferings in order that we may also share in his glory.

Our Inheritance

In Paul's letters, the idea of inheritance is strongly influenced by Roman law. According to Roman law, a person received his or her inheritance rights and was considered co-owner of all his or her parents' tangible and intangible assets from birth, though he or she did not take full possession of the inheritance until the parents' death. Paul's point, therefore, is that as soon as we are "reborn," as soon as we put our faith in Christ, we are <u>coheirs with Christ</u> in all that God owns. It is God's pleasure to share with his children what is his.

We will not receive the full extent of our <u>inheritance</u> until we enter the full presence of God, but even now God blesses us with the enjoyment of his possessions.

Our precious relationship with "*Abba*, Father" carries a cost, as

☞ **GO TO:**

Philippians 3:10–11; 2 Timothy 2:12 (coheirs with Christ)

1 Peter 1:4 (inheritance)

all close relationships do. Paul solemnly reminds Christians that they are called as sons and daughters to *"share in his sufferings in order that we may also share in his glory."*

Esther K. Rusthoi writes in one of her hymns, "It will be worth it all when we see Jesus, life's trials will seem so small when we see Christ; one glimpse of His dear face all sorrow will erase, so bravely run the race 'til we see Christ.'"[11] Being coheirs with Christ implies a participation in the fellowship of his sufferings.

Grabbed by Grace

The floodgates of God's grace open wide when it comes to our inheritance. We are heirs:

- of the promises God makes to his children
- of righteousness
- of the kingdom of God
- of God
- along with Jesus Christ
- of eternal life

glory: wonder, splendor

> **Romans 8:18** I consider that our present sufferings are not worth comparing with the **glory** that will be revealed in us.

Looking Ahead: A Lesson In Driving

I have a friend, Danny, who owns a driving school. About a year ago, my wife and I took a refresher driving seminar from him to review our driving habits, good and bad. Danny told us the most important thing about driving is using your eyes well. The best way to use your eyes is to look as far ahead as possible.

This is somewhat like Paul's spiritual vision. To stay faithful to the task at hand, to bear the present sufferings and testing, he reminds us to look far ahead into the future. All of the pain, hard work, self-denial, and ridicule we now face is *"not worth comparing with the glory that will be revealed in us."* Once we get to heaven all that we've dealt with here will be insignificant. Also, if our eyes are <u>fixed on Jesus</u> we are more likely to stay out of life's ditches.

☞ **GO TO:**

Hebrews 12:2
(fixed on Jesus)

> **Romans 8:19–21** The **creation** waits in eager expectation for the sons of God to be revealed. For the creation was subjected to frustration, not by its own choice, but by the will of the one who subjected it, in hope that the creation itself will be liberated from its bondage to decay and brought into the glorious freedom of the children of God.

creation: all created things

Are We There Yet?

Not only do humans look forward to *"the glory that will be revealed in us,"* all of creation does. As the Fall brought all kinds of affliction to humankind, it injured creation too. Paul says the healing of creation will not take place until the hour of Christ's return.

Have you ever listened to a pastor or teacher whose lesson was so relevant to you that you found yourself leaning forward, hanging onto every word? This is the picture Paul is painting when he uses the words *"eager expectation."* Creation is leaning forward in anticipation of the day of our glorification.

Something to Ponder

It often seems like society is more interested in saving whales than unborn babies. While there are strict laws regarding whaling procedures, in many places it is legal to kill unborn babies. Respect and love for the earth are a part of God's plan, but worship of nature is not. We can rest assured that one day the earth will be healed.

What Others are Saying:

John Chrysostom: Whatever these sufferings may be, they belong to this present life, but the blessing to come stretches out forever. Since Paul had no way of giving a detailed description of these or of putting them before us in human language, he gives them a name which is used of things we especially desire: glory.[12]

Saint Jerome: When the children of God attain glory, creation itself will be delivered from its slavery.[13]

> **Romans 8:22–23** We know that **the whole creation** has been groaning as in the pains of childbirth right up to the present time. Not only so, but we ourselves, who have the firstfruits of the Spirit, groan inwardly as we wait eagerly for our **adoption** as sons, the redemption of our bodies.

the whole creation: the entire material universe

adoption: here, God's public acknowledgment of our relationship with him

☞ GO TO:

Genesis 6; 2 Peter 3:3–7 (Noahic flood)

Galatians 5:22–26 (fruit)

Noahic: of Noah

fruit: character traits Christians ought to exhibit—love, joy, peace, patience, kindness, goodness, faithfulness, gentleness, and self-control

Remember This . . .

What Others are Saying:

mitigated: made less severe

KEY POINT

Hope is essential in the battle of waiting. Hope keeps our hearts tender and believing.

Creation's Contractions

Paul continues his discussion of the yearning of creation. The upheaval in creation—the earthquakes, the famines, the **Noahic flood**, the violent storms—all of these are a result of the Fall. It's obvious that Paul has great compassion for creation, which would not be in its present state of frustration if we had not fallen. He likens creation's groaning to the pains of childbirth. The pains of childbirth are intense, but they are also what tells us new life is on the way. Creation's pain, therefore, is both a consequence of the Fall and a prophecy of redemption.

The creation is groaning, as are we. We have the **fruit** of the Holy Spirit, the grace of God has come our way, yet we are in a waiting cycle. Each generation is in that same cycle, waiting to be adopted.

Paul uses the concept of adoption to describe redemption. The word *adoption* comes from two Greek words, *huios*, meaning "son," and *thesis*, meaning "to place." Thus, adoption literally means "the placing as a son." It means a son or daughter is given to a family to which he or she does not naturally belong.

John Calvin: When we console ourselves with the hope of a better condition, the feeling of our present miseries is softened and **mitigated**.[14]

Kenneth L. Barker and John R. Kohlenberger III: Because an element of our salvation—the redemption of the body—is held in reserve, we have hope. If all were ours now, there would be no place for this expression. Since the object of our hope is not yet realized, "we wait for it patiently."[15]

> **Romans 8:24–25** For in this hope we were saved. But hope that is seen is no hope at all. Who hopes for what he already has? But if we hope for what we do not yet have, we wait for it patiently.

Pilgrim's Hope

Part of our salvation is yet to be given us, namely the redemption of our bodies, so we wait in patient hope. If all the benefits of salvation were ours now, we would have no reason to hope. As it is, we walk the road of life in worship to the God whose full presence we will one day enjoy. We see the dark tunnel of death before us, but we know what awaits on the other side, so we hope.

IN OTHER LETTERS What form should our hope take? Should we sit around and twiddle our thumbs until we go to heaven? Paul answered these questions in one of his letters to the Corinthians. He said, *"Always give yourselves fully to the work of the Lord, because you know that your labor in the Lord is not in vain"* (1 Corinthians 15:58b). The work we do for God is of eternal value. It doesn't go into some cosmic trash can as soon as we go to heaven. It lasts forever, so we should "give ourselves fully" to the work of God.

> **Romans 8:26–27** In the same way, the Spirit helps us in our weakness. We do not know what we ought to pray for, but the Spirit himself **intercedes** for us with groans that words cannot express. And he who searches our hearts knows the mind of the Spirit, because the Spirit intercedes for the saints in accordance with God's will.

intercedes:
communicates with God
on our behalf

Our Devoted Prayer Partner

God uses both hope and the ministry of the Holy Spirit to support believers in the midst of life's burdens, tests, and disappointments. The Holy Spirit helps us precisely in those places where we are weakest. Paul points out that we do not know what our real needs are, but he assures us that God does and that he will see to those needs. God always does what is best for us no matter what it costs him or us.

The Holy Spirit prays on our behalf with groans. We get the sense from these verses that the groans to which Paul refers are a better form of spiritual communication than words. Perhaps this is because words are limited. Some things cannot be expressed with words. If we take this as true, we may also take it as true that the Holy Spirit's groans are not subject to the same limitation. They may be able to express things that otherwise are inexpressible. In any case, Paul assures us that the Holy Spirit prays for us, and this is for our benefit.

Prayer is a difficult discipline that we all need to develop. Jesus spent a lot of time in prayer and his disciples asked him, *"Lord, teach us to pray, just as John taught his disciples"* (Luke 11:1). The Holy Spirit and the Word of God teach us how to have a faithful prayer life. We find many helpful prayers in the Book of Psalms, God's prayer book for the church of the ages.

What Others are Saying:

Dietrich Bonhoeffer: A Christian fellowship lives and exists by the intercession of its members for one another, or it collapses. . . . How does this happen? Intercession means no more than to bring our brother into the presence of God, to see him under the Cross of Jesus as a poor human being and sinner in need of grace. Then everything in him that repels us falls away; we see him in all his destitution and need. . . . Intercession is a daily service we owe to God and our brother.[16]

> **Romans 8:28** And we know that in all things God works for the good of those who love him, who have been called according to his purpose.

God's A Hard Worker

After reading this verse one might wonder, "Wait a minute. Does this mean that if I fail to love God, he won't work for my good?" Paul seldom talks about believers' love for God. When he does, he does not talk about it as a requirement for God to fulfill his promises. Because love for God is a natural response to God's grace and mercy, when Paul says *"those who love [God],"* he is referring to all believers. Paul knew very well that as a Christian, he failed to love God in the sense that he struggled to obey God. We saw this back in chapter 7. The fact that he struggled, however, is evidence that he was God's own. God always does what is best for his own.

What Others are Saying:

Philip Yancey: The New Testament epistles repeatedly tell us that love for God, which means acting in loving ways toward God, nurtures the relationship and leads toward growth. I do not get to know God, then do his will; I get to know him more deeply *by* doing his will. I enter into an active relationship, which means spending time with God, caring about the people he cares about, and following his commands—whether I spontaneously feel like it or not.[17]

Meet Paul—To Paul, love for God meant obedience to God. Many people today think love for God is a feeling. We think if we say, "I love God," God should bend over backwards to make our lives luxurious. When our lives turn out less than luxurious, we begin to doubt God's love, maybe even his existence. Paul's concept of loving God was rooted in the truth that we are sinners, deserving only condemnation, and God is our holy Creator and Judge who in his mercy rescued us from death.

There is an attitude prevalent within our culture that says, "I deserve this. I have a right to that." We see this attitude reflected in billboards and other advertisements that gleam with attractive slogans like, "You deserve a break today" and "Buy this car. You're *worth* it." These slogans are appealing because we want to believe that we're good people, deserving anything we want, even though we know deep down that we're not good people. Paul knew the only thing we had a right to was condemnation. Our attitude, therefore, should be one of gratefulness and contentment, not entitlement and greediness.

Something to Ponder

> **Romans 8:29–30** For those God **foreknew** he also **predestined** to be conformed to the likeness of his Son, that he might be the firstborn among many brothers. And those he predestined, he also called; those he called, he also justified; those he justified, he also **glorified**.

foreknew: *to have intimate, accurate knowledge of future events*

predestined: *preordained, determined beforehand*

glorified: *perfected, freed of sin and made to be like God*

This Is Your Destiny

Paul started a discussion about sharing in the sufferings of Christ back in verse 16. He said our sufferings will seem like nothing when we get to heaven. He said all of creation groans under the weight of the Fall and longs for our glorification. He said the Holy Spirit helps us in our weaknesses. He then said God works all things for the good of those who love him.

Continuing in this spirit of encouragement, now Paul says God chose us for himself. He chose us to be saved from sin and death and he chose us to be conformed to the likeness of his son. He's saying, "Look, God chose you for this. God. The almighty Creator of the universe. And if God chose it, it's as good as done no matter how hard life is. You can count on it." We learn, therefore, that at the end of being with Christ in his sufferings we will be glorified with Christ in heaven.

Grabbed by Grace

God in his sovereignty promised Christ's followers that they will take on the character and characteristics of their Master. God's people are predestined by his grace and mercy to be restored into the very image we were originally created to be.

> **Romans 8:31–32** What, then, shall we say in response to this? If God is for us, who can be against us? He who did not spare his own Son, but gave him up for us all—how will he not also, along with him, graciously give us all things?

A Done Deal

From here to the end of the chapter Paul explains how secure the position of the Christian is. Nothing is more certain than our glorification. Glorification is when we will enter heaven, experience the full presence of God, and be given new bodies. God has willingly given up his son for our sins so our place in his kingdom is a done deal.

Wouldn't it be strange if a father gave his son a brand-new Porsche but sold the tires off it and replaced them with cheap tires? If the father went to the trouble of giving his son a new Porsche, wouldn't he give him the tires too?

That's how it is with God, Jesus, and us. God has sacrificed his beloved and only son. Whatever it costs him to give us anything more is negligible because he has already given us his most precious possession. God gave us his son. We ought not doubt his willingness to give us every other good thing.

Remember
This . . .

Paul does not deny that we go through hard times, but he wants us to see those hard times in light of the truth that when we enter into heaven, we'll look back and wonder what all the fuss was about. We'll wonder this not because our sufferings are without pain right now but because heaven is going to be that fulfilling!

> **Romans 8:33–34** Who will bring any charge against those whom God has chosen? It is God who justifies. Who is he that condemns? Christ Jesus, who died—more than that, who was raised to life—is at the right hand of God and is also interceding for us.

Q&A

Here Paul starts a series of questions and then answers them. His first questions are, *"Who will bring any charge against those whom God has chosen?"* and, *"Who is he that condemns?"* Paul may have been alluding to the fact that Satan is always accusing us. Satan constantly points out the difference between what we profess and how we live (as if Satan were interested in righteousness), but God dismisses Satan's accusations because God has made up his mind to be for us. Because all sin is committed against God, only God has the right to condemn. If God does not condemn us, and he doesn't because our sin has been paid for, no one does.

> **Romans 8:35–37** Who shall separate us from the love of Christ? Shall trouble or hardship or persecution or famine or nakedness or danger or sword? As it is written: "For your sake we face death all day long; we are considered as sheep to be slaughtered." No, in all these things we are more than conquerors through him who loved us.

We Shall Overcome

His second question is, *"Who shall separate us from the love of Christ?"* Again, Paul is trying to convince his readers that come what may, the really important questions have been answered. Nothing will separate us from the love of Christ. Paul quotes from Psalm 44:22 to remind us that suffering is nothing new to godly people. Suffering has been the burden of followers of God since the Old Testament, Paul says.

Jesus said, *"In this world you will have trouble. But take heart! I have overcome the world"* (John 16:33). Jesus told us in no uncertain terms that we would have trouble so we should not be surprised when we do. He also said, however, that he has overcome the world. In other words, the world has tried to beat him, but it failed. Jesus prevailed over the world and because we are linked to Christ, we too will overcome the world.

> **Romans 8:38–39** For I am convinced that neither death nor life, neither angels nor demons, neither the present nor the future, nor any powers, neither height nor depth, nor anything else in all creation, will be able to separate us from the love of God that is in Christ Jesus our Lord.

Love Keeps Hangin' On

The apostle seems to pull out all the stops in these last verses of Romans 8. God's love and provision for his own are presented in exalted and passionate language. The apostle speaks of God's purpose in calling out a people who would love him.

Paul emphasizes the certainty of our sanctification. If we are in Christ Jesus, we will be in heaven one day with Christ. He puts the emphasis on the fact that *"we know"* this. This is a hope that is certain, even though we are in a posture of waiting.

We need to ask ourselves, do we love him? A yes to this question will solve most of the schisms and factions that Satan has created in the church.

You might be eloquent in discussing predestination, you might have solved the so-called free will issue, but if you *"have not love, [you are] only a resounding gong or a clanging cymbal"* (1 Corinthians 13:1). The church Jesus came to build needs to rededicate her efforts to living in Christ's love and proclaiming the Gospel.

Oswald Chambers: Huge waves that would frighten an ordinary swimmer produce a tremendous thrill for the surfer who has ridden them. Let's apply that to our own circumstances. The things we try to avoid and fight against—tribulation, suffering, and persecution—are the very things that produce abundant joy in us. "We are more than conquerors through Him" "*in* all these things"; not in spite of them, but in the midst of them.[18]

Study Questions

1. Why is the law powerless to save a person who sincerely seeks to keep it?
2. How does our mindset influence our spiritual journey?
3. What does it mean to be controlled by the Holy Spirit? Isn't this another form of bondage?
4. We are coheirs with Christ. What does this mean?
5. What does the Holy Spirit do?

CHAPTER WRAP-UP

- Christ set us free from the law of sin and death. Therefore, there is no condemnation in our future. (Romans 8:1–4)

- Our mind's focus is essential to becoming the people God created us to be. (Romans 8:5–8)

- The Holy Spirit is within us and is giving us life. He helps us pray and is with us in our weaknesses. (Romans 8:9–11)

- We have an obligation to live according to the Holy Spirit, which will bring us blessings. (Romans 8:12–17)

- Suffering is a very real part of living in a sin-sick world. God wants us to get a biblical view of suffering. Hope sustains us while we wait for God's transforming grace to mold our character. (Romans 8:18–25)

- We have been predestined to be conformed to the image of the risen Christ. God has promised that there is nothing *"in all creation"* that will be able to separate us from the love of God. (Romans 8:29–39)

Part Four

JEWS AND GENTILES

REVEREND FUN

"I'm sorry, Mr. Stein, 'Because I'm a descendant of Abraham' is not the answer to the big question . . . on to Mr. Cohen, What did you have for, 'Why should you get into heaven?'"

ROMANS 9: GOD'S IN CHARGE

Let's Get Started

In chapters 1 to 8 Paul explained the details of the New Covenant. The New Covenant was different from the Old Covenant. The Old Covenant, which came through Moses, said God would reward Israel if the nation obeyed God, and punish Israel if it disobeyed God. Israel failed on their part of the deal. The New Covenant, Paul explained, imparted righteousness to all those who believed in Christ, Jew and Gentile alike. The Jews, therefore, might have made the accusation that God was being unfair to the Jews by changing his mind and being inconsistent. It is this accusation that Paul addresses in chapters 9 to 11.

Paul points out that God has not been inconsistent. He has always imparted righteousness on the basis of faith. Moreoever, God is sovereign, which means he has always been free to deal with any people as he chooses. He is not bound by what humans think of him. In other words, God's in charge.

In chapter 9 Paul demonstrates that even though the Jews had failed to accept God's promises, the Word of God had not failed. A great many Jews fell away because they did not seek righteousness by faith as Abraham had.

> **Romans 9:1–4a** I speak the truth in Christ—I am not lying, my conscience confirms it in the Holy Spirit—I have great sorrow and unceasing anguish in my heart. For I could wish that I myself were cursed and cut off from Christ for the sake of my brothers, those of my own race, the people of Israel.

No Lie

Paul was about to say something that he knew his readers would find outlandish so he starts with a preface. He says he is speaking the truth, but not only that, he says he is speaking the truth *"in Christ."* He says he is not lying. He says his conscience confirms it, but not only that, he says his conscience confirms it *"in the Holy Spirit."* By this time his readers may have been thinking, "Okay, okay, we believe you. *Out* with it already."

He does come out with it, and what he says is quite sobering. Paul is tormented over the failure of his people to receive Jesus Christ. He says he would take condemnation on himself if it would save his fellow Jews. By this time in his life Paul knew enough about Jesus to believe he was the fulfillment of **the prophetic message**, and he desperately wanted his fellow Jews to believe the same.

Paul was a Jew. He loved his Jewishness and never strayed from his Jewish heritage. What he is attempting to do in Romans 9 is explain how and why the Jews—<u>God's chosen people</u>—had rejected their Messiah. A number of questions needed to be answered:

1. Had God abandoned the Jewish people?
2. What further role did Israel as a nation play in God's plan?
3. In the face of human rejection, does God abandon his promises?
4. Can man foil the sovereign workings of God?

In time Paul answers all of these questions for the Jewish believers.

☞ **GO TO:**

Amos 9:13–15;
  Zechariah 14:1–9
  (the prophetic
  message)

Genesis 12:1–3;
  15:1–21
  (God's chosen people)

the prophetic message:
*the Old Testament
promises concerning
Israel*

☞ **GO TO:**

Luke 19:41–44
  (he wept)

*Something
to Ponder*

Meet Paul—Paul said if it was possible for his own condemnation to bring salvation to the Jews, he would wish condemnation upon himself. When we remember that hell is a place completely absent of God, full of torture and pain forever, it is obvious Paul had extraordinary compassion for his unbelieving brothers and sisters. It is similar to the kind of love Jesus demonstrated when <u>he wept</u> over Jerusalem.

Not many of us would wish condemnation on ourselves in exchange for the salvation of others. Not many of us cry over people who do not know God. How is it that Paul and Jesus had this much compassion for lost people? Perhaps it was a combination of knowing how much unbelievers were missing and what they were doomed for. They were missing the everlasting joy of God. They were doomed for eternal separation from God. There was one thing, and only one thing, that would grant them one and save them from the other: faith in Christ. Paul and Jesus were in agony because they could not force the Jews to believe. That was something the Jews had to do on their own.

> **Romans 9:4b–5** Theirs is the adoption as sons; theirs the divine glory, the covenants, the receiving of the law, the temple worship and the promises. Theirs are the patriarchs, and from them is traced the human ancestry of Christ, who is God over all, forever praised! Amen.

A Listing Of Blessing

In the midst of his grief and reflection, Paul reviews Israel's God-given blessings. These blessings were designed by God to support and affirm his people in their spiritual journey. Paul lists seven spiritual privileges that belonged to the Jewish people:

1. *They were adopted as sons.* Moses was to tell Pharaoh *"This is what the Lord says: Israel is my firstborn son"* (Exodus 4:22). Who else could claim adoption as <u>sons</u>?

2. *They saw the divine glory.* The Israelites experienced the very presence of God in **theophanies**.

3. *They had the covenants.* God entered into <u>covenants</u> with Abraham, Moses, and David.

4. *They received the law.* God gave Moses the <u>law</u> on Mount Sinai.

5. *They had <u>temple</u> worship* (latreia, *"the sacred place"*). The Temple was ordained and pleasing to God as a place of worship, praise, and spiritual fellowship.

6. *They had the promises (especially the promise of Messiah).* Hundreds of promises fill their sacred writings.

7. *They had the Patriarchs.* Abraham, Isaac, Jacob, David, and all the prophets that God lists in Scripture belong to the nation of Israel.

☞ **GO TO:**

Jeremiah 31:9; Hosea 11:1 (sons)

Exodus 3:2; 24:10 (theophanies)

Genesis 5:18; Exodus 19:5; Deuteronomy 29:1; 2 Samuel 7:21 (covenants)

Deuteronomy 5:1–22 (law)

2 Chronicles 7:11; Psalm 11:1 (temple)

theophanies: *visible manifestations of God*

What a heritage! The Jews had been given an array of spiritual treasures, yet in the end they rejected God their king and the blessings of his kingdom. Paul was bearing the burden of their foolishness, but the same God whom the Jews rejected was the God who sustained Paul in his grief.

> **Romans 9:6–7a** It is not as though God's word had failed. For not all who are descended from Israel are **Israel**. Nor because they are his descendants are they all Abraham's children.

Israel: God's chosen people

The Real Israel

Pastor Mark Driscoll writes, "On the surface it appears that God had attempted to redeem Israel and had failed."[1] But Paul goes beneath that surface mentality and says, *"It is not as though God's word had failed."* Paul's primary emphasis is on God's purposes, not Israel's failures. To build a strong argument for the truth, Paul first dispels all false presumptions.

KEY POINT

God does not fail.

Though it seemed safe to assume that if you were from Israel, you were then a child of promise, that simply was not the case: *"For not all who are descended from Israel are Israel. Nor because they are his descendants are they all Abraham's children."* Here Paul establishes that there is a distinction between ethnic Israel and the *"Israel of God"* (Galatians 6:16).

Paul has been preparing to say this since chapter 2 where he confronted those who called themselves Jews. He made it very clear: *"A man is not a Jew if he is only one outwardly. . . . No, a man is a Jew if he is one inwardly"* (Romans 2:28–29). Here the apostle reaches the core of the matter: It's not the natural born who are the children of God, but the spiritually born who are the children of God through promise.

What Others are Saying:

James D. G. Dunn: The depth of the feeling expressed here would be almost melodramatic were it not for the strength of the oath introducing it. . . . Paul would insist, he is being *true* to his heritage in taking the gospel to the Gentiles. And it is precisely the misunderstanding of that claim which causes him such continuous and painful anguish, for it means that most of his fellow Jews are failing to enter into their own heritage.[2]

Where?
When?

> **Romans 9:7b–9** On the contrary, "It is through Isaac that your offspring will be reckoned." In other words, it is not the natural children who are God's children, but it is the children of the promise who are regarded as Abraham's offspring. For this was how the promise was stated: "At the appointed time I will return, and Sarah will have a son."

A Promise Kept

His primary evidence is God's word to Sarah: *"At the appointed time I will return, and Sarah will have a son."* God had promised Abraham and Sarah that even though they were well beyond child-bearing age, they would have a son, born of promise, to bless all people (see GWWB, pages 38–39). Then Sarah got pregnant and Isaac, the son of promise, was born.

☞ **GO TO:**

Ephesians 2:1–3;
 Romans 5:12–21
 (dead)

> We are not naturally spiritual. We are <u>dead</u> in trespasses and sins. To be children of Abraham, called *"children of God,"* we must be *"born of the Spirit of God."* Salvation is of God, totally apart from what we do. Augustine put it succinctly, "God does not choose us because we believe, but that we may believe."[3] Works may follow, which goes back to Paul's discussion in chapter 8 where he addresses moral obligation, but they don't earn us any favor either before salvation or after. If we serve in God's kingdom, we are simply doing what we should be doing as members of the family of God.

Something to Ponder

D. Martyn Lloyd-Jones: Paul refers to the fact that Jews, in contrast with Gentiles, had not obtained the righteousness of God. This was because of their unbelief. So if a man is saved, it is because God has saved him. But if a man is lost, that is to be attributed to his own rejection of the gospel and his rebellion against God's way of salvation.[4]

What Others are Saying:

> **Romans 9:10–13** Not only that, but Rebekah's children had one and the same father, our father Isaac. Yet, before the twins were born or had done anything good or bad—in order that God's purpose in election might stand: not by works but by him who calls—she was told, "The older will serve the younger." Just as it is written: "Jacob I loved, but Esau I hated."

☞ **GO TO:**

Genesis 25:19–26
(family)

Jacob: God's Choice

Paul goes beyond God's word to Abraham and Sarah to the <u>family</u> of the son of promise. Isaac and his wife Rebekah gave birth to twin boys named Jacob and Esau (see GWWB, page 57). Paul was responding to the possible objection that Ishmael was not Abraham's child and therefore Paul's argument that God elects certain people and not others didn't hold any water. Paul is careful to explain that Jacob and Esau had the same father; God chose Jacob, not Esau.

God was creating a line that would one day bring forth the promised Messiah. The arrival of twins proposed a potential problem. According to customary human experience, the boys should stand on equal terms before God and man.

Due to God's sovereign will, that could not be. God made a distinction between Jacob and Esau before the twins arrived. This was a sovereign decision. The boys' characters had not been shaped, and they had performed no deeds that could form a basis for evaluation. Moreover, God decreed that the older of the two brothers would serve the younger, something contrary to the custom of the day.

As the boys grew into their manhood, they were both in need of the typical kinds of correction that take place in childhood. One was not necessarily any more spiritual than the other.

Something to Ponder

The passage is not talking about hatred in the sense of antagonism or fierce anger toward another person. God bestowed many blessings on Esau and his descendants, a manifestation of grace and love. In the biblical world this was legal language. A person would say, "I hated so-and-so" in his or her will to indicate which people had been written out of the estate. The passage is saying God decisively rejected any claim that Esau might have had to the covenant. History proved that God had chosen one of the twins and rejected the claim of the other twin.

What Others are Saying:

Larry Richards: The verse does not mean God condemned Esau before his birth. In its O.T. context ["Esau I hated"] means that God decisively rejected Esau's claim to the covenant promises which would be his as older son.[5]

God's grace is unfettered. His love, his covenants, his promises, and his Son are demonstrations of his unconditional commitment to his people. A God who could be manipulated by the will of his creatures would be a dangerous God. We can see this negative attribute in Satan, who is the god of this world, causing evil wherever he can manipulate willing subjects.

Grabbed by Grace

Peter Stuhlmacher: But Sarah's pregnancy is only the first example of God's free elective grace in Israel's history. It is no different with Isaac's wife Rebecca. When she became pregnant (by Isaac) and the twins Esau and Jacob were still not yet born, God documented the freedom of his providence, which acts according to the principle of **predestination**, in that his creative word of promise determined that the older must serve the younger.[6]

What Others are Saying:

predestination: in Greek, proorizo, to mark out ahead of time, to predetermine

Romans 9:14–15 What then shall we say? Is God unjust? Not at all! For he says to Moses, "I will have mercy on whom I have mercy, and I will have compassion on whom I have compassion."

Passionate Compassion

Here Paul anticipates an objection from the Romans which is not unlike an objection we commonly hear today. Many feel the principle of **election** makes God unjust or unfair. No matter how much grace and blessing people have experienced, this attack on God's character surfaces generation after generation.

But God has a right to be God. It's not wrong to try and understand these deep truths, but we need to be humble and respectful in that learning process. We should also remember that God did not have to save anybody. We all deserve death. In his great mercy he decided to save some.

Paul takes his readers back to Exodus 33 where Moses and **Yahweh** had a **tent meeting**. It was during one of these conversations that God said to Moses, *"I will cause all my goodness to pass in front of you, and I will proclaim my name, the Lord, in your presence. I will have mercy on whom I will have mercy, and I will have compassion on whom I will have compassion"* (Exodus 33:19). God does not need our permission to do what he wants to do. He is God, we are not.

election: an exercise of God's free choice of some for his own special purposes

Yahweh: name for God, meaning "I am"

tent meeting: Moses met with God at the entrance of a special tent

☞ **GO TO:**

Exodus 33:7–9 (tent meeting)

How does mercy differ from grace? How are they partners? Mercy is God's compassionate response to man's need. Grace is God's determination to have mercy on all because of Christ, despite the fact that mercy is not merited.

> **Romans 9:16–18** It does not, therefore, depend on man's desire or effort, but on God's mercy. For the Scripture says to Pharaoh: "I raised you up for this very purpose, that I might display my power in you and that my name might be proclaimed in all the earth." Therefore, God has mercy on whom he wants to have mercy, and he hardens whom he wants to harden.

A Heart Like Granite

For an example of God's sovereign will, Paul takes readers back to the days of Pharaoh in Egypt. God was merciful to Pharaoh, but Pharaoh's pride kept him from seeing the glory of God in God's servant Moses.

judgments: punishments from God

God did not change Pharaoh's nature or manipulate Pharaoh's will. God revealed more and more of himself through the **judgments**, and Pharaoh reacted to God's self-revelation by rejecting God and his will. This is called "revelatory hardening," when God reveals himself to a human and the human's reaction is to harden his or her heart toward God. An analogy for this is what the sun does to wax or clay. When wax is heated by the sun it softens because of the nature of wax. When clay is heated by the sun it hardens because of the nature of clay. In the same way, when God revealed more and more of himself to Pharaoh, Pharaoh's heart hardened because of Pharaoh's essential nature.

☞ **GO TO:**

Exodus 14:17 (Red Sea)

After the final judgment when Pharaoh began to pursue the Jews and entered the <u>Red Sea</u>, God hardened Pharaoh's heart again. This was "judicial hardening." Judicial hardening is when a person is already hard-hearted and God hardens his or her heart even more. Judicial hardening is a punishment for being totally committed to rebellion against God.

In neither case did God cause Pharaoh to act against his essential nature. God permitted Pharaoh to become Pharaoh ("raised him up") because he knew full well who he was and how he would behave. Pharaoh chose to rebel against God. God used his rebellion to accomplish his own purposes.

James R. Edwards: *Desire and effort* were in fact very much part of Paul's commitment to Christ (Philippians 3:12–16), but they had nothing to do with his (or Israel's) choosing by God. Human effort is a necessary response of gratitude and commitment to God for his grace in Christ Jesus, but it neither merits nor maintains grace. With regard to election God remains totally free, not to employ arbitrary (or worse, malevolent) designs, but to express mercy.[7]

Martin Luther: ["God will have mercy on whom he wants to have mercy"] is a harsh answer for the proud and those who think they know everything, but for the meek and the humble it is sweet and pleasing, because they despair of themselves; and thus God takes them up.[8]

> **Romans 9:19–21** One of you will say to me: "Then why does God still blame us? For who resists his will?" But who are you, O man, to talk back to God? "Shall what is formed say to him who formed it, 'Why did you make me like this?'" Does not the potter have the right to make out of the same lump of clay some pottery for noble purposes and some for common use?

Yackety-Yack, Don't Talk Back

We want the final word. It's human nature. We feel we have the right to challenge God and even think it's smart or cute. The old nature, as we learned earlier in this letter, will always resist the truth. It is only the new nature that begins to trust in the wisdom and grace of God.

The accusation behind the questions, *"Then why does God still blame us? For who resists his will?"* is this: God is unfair because he blames us for his own decisions. This accusation assumes that we are innocent to begin with, and we are not. God never condemns innocent people; he condemns sinners. He is under no obligation to save anyone, yet he does save those whom it pleases him to save.

We know that God, who is both righteous and **omniscient**, always makes wise choices. The problem is that we disagree with his will and fail to discover his wisdom and love, while living in the old-nature rebellion.

Paul uses a metaphor to explain further. He presents God as a

omniscient: *all-knowing*

potter. Just as the potter makes decisions about his creation, doesn't the God who made all things have the same prerogative? And just as it would be ridiculous for a lump of clay to talk back to the potter, it is ridiculous for us to talk back to our Creator.

James R. Edwards: Right is not right because God does it; rather, God does it *because* it is right. God's righteous will, as revealed in the Ten Commandments and in the rules of fairness and justice associated with them, is ultimate, and not even God can transcend it. . . . There is a moral code in creation only because there is a corresponding moral order in the Creator. This passage does not depict or defend a cosmic bully. God is perfect love and perfect justice.[9]

> **Romans 9:22–24** What if God, choosing to show his wrath and make his power known, bore with great patience the objects of his wrath—prepared for destruction? What if he did this to make the riches of his glory known to the objects of his mercy, whom he prepared in advance for glory—even us, whom he also called, not only from the Jews but also from the Gentiles?

Gracious Patience

An important thing to remember is that every human on the planet will glorify God, willingly or not, in heaven or in hell. Either people will glorify God as objects of his mercy and glory, or they will glorify God as objects of his wrath and power.

The phrase *"prepared for destruction"* might imply that God makes up his mind to send people to hell even before he creates them, but this is not likely. The preparation refers to what unbelievers do despite what their consciences tell them. Such people are "preparing" themselves for destruction.

Paul points out the patience of God in that God tolerates the sins of the wicked for a time. He says he tolerates wickedness *"to make the riches of his glory known to the objects of his mercy."* He does this in two ways. One was already mentioned in reference to Pharaoh. Pharaoh was raised up, his heart was hardened, and his sins accumulated so God could more fully display his wrath in judging him in the end. The second way he shows his glory is in delaying his wrath to give sinners a chance to repent.

> **Romans 9:25–26** As he says in Hosea: "I will call them 'my people' who are not my people; and I will call her 'my loved one' who is not my loved one," and, "It will happen that in the very place where it was said to them, 'You are not my people,' they will be called 'sons of the living God.'"

Come On In

Aren't those wonderful words? When someone says "come on in," we feel included. We feel like our company is desired. None of us wants to be alone or left on the outside. With Christ's death and resurrection, God stood at the threshold of his kingdom, looked at the Gentiles, and said, "Come on in."

Paul was fond of quoting Scripture to prove his points. Here he uses Scripture to prove that Gentiles will be part of God's kingdom. He quotes Hosea 2:23 and Hosea 1:10, both of which refer to when Israel fell from God's favor and was later restored. Here Paul is using the first quote (Hosea 2:23) to refer not to Israel, but rather to the Gentiles. Paul wasn't the only one to do this. Peter did it too in 1 Peter 2:10.

Paul may have been using the second quote from Hosea 1:10 to refer to the Gentiles also, but it's possible he was referring to the Jews. In any case, Paul's point is that God's kingdom would be made up of both Jews and Gentiles and that God's choice to include people he previously excluded is not an innovation. In fact, it is in the Jews' best interest not to scorn God for this. If it were not for God's willingness to welcome those who were previously on the outside of his kingdom, yes the Gentiles would be on the outside, but so would the Jews!

KEY POINT

Both Jesus and Gentiles will be in heaven.

> **Romans 9:27–29** Isaiah cries out concerning Israel: "Though the number of the Israelites be like the sand by the sea, only the remnant will be saved. For the Lord will carry out his sentence on earth with speed and finality." It is just as Isaiah said previously: "Unless the Lord Almighty had left us descendants, we would have become like Sodom, we would have been like Gomorrah."

Faithful Remnant

Remember that beginning with chapter 9 Paul is answering the accusation that God was being unfair to the Jews in establishing the New Covenant. Another question Paul wanted to answer was whether God's purpose for the Jews had failed because not all Jews were believing in Christ. Throughout chapter 9 Paul has been explaining that God's purpose did not fail because God never intended to save every Jew. In the verses quoted previously, however, Paul quotes from Isaiah to point out that God has always had a faithful **remnant** of Jews. This was true in Paul's time as well.

The remnant idea goes back to Romans 2 when Paul explained the difference between those who had been circumcised outwardly and those who had been circumcised inwardly. "The remnant" to which Paul refers is the number of Jews who had come to Christ. Paul understood this at a very personal level because he himself was one of the remnant.

Someone steeped in the Old Testament might raise the charge that God had abandoned the people whom he foreknew, the Jews, but Paul says otherwise. God provided a way for all people, including Jews, to be saved.

remnant: a portion of a larger group

Take It to Heart

In many ways Paul can be compared to Christians who come from non-Christian families. Such Christians may be tempted to turn their backs on their families, thinking only of how their parents or siblings wronged them. When he became a Christian, Paul did not ignore his fellow, unbelieving Jews. He was in anguish because many of the Jewish race, the race from which Jesus came, did not put their faith in Christ. Paul knew that if they did not repent and believe, they faced eternal destruction—just like the people in Sodom and Gomorrah. Christians who come from non-Christian families should follow Paul's example.

Something to Ponder

People who may look like God's favorites, because of how joyful they are, are not his favorites. They are simply more humble and more honest about sin and are always ready to seek forgiveness. Moreover, joyful Christians are joyful because they have found out that in the long run, righteousness is more fun than sin!

> **Romans 9:30–33** What then shall we say? That the Gentiles, who did not pursue righteousness, have obtained it, a righteousness that is by faith; but Israel, who pursued a law of righteousness, has not attained it. Why not? Because they pursued it not by faith but as if it were by works. They stumbled over the "stumbling stone." As it is written: "See, I lay in Zion a stone that causes men to stumble and a rock that makes them fall, and the one who trusts in him will never be put to shame."

Stumbling Stone

Paul concludes this section like a true orator: *"What then shall we say?"* It's as if he's looking for a way to put a period at the end of this sentence before he enters the next phase of the dialogue.

He finds an apt way. He points out the difference between the two peoples, the reason God receives the Gentiles and rejects the Jews. The Gentiles found that by embracing Jesus Christ by faith they could attain righteousness. But the Jews chased after righteousness by trying to keep the law, not by faith, but by religious works. They continued to embrace the **shadows** and reject the **substance**. They rejected the merits of their Messiah for their own supposed good works.

To articulate his point, Paul quotes Isaiah 28, a passage which depicts Christ as the Rock. Instead of a stepping stone to raise them up, he becomes a stumbling stone. But those who "[trust] *in him will never be put to shame."*

One of the greatest promises in all of Scripture is located in Romans 9:30–33. If our trust is in the Rock of Ages we will never be put to shame. We might have to walk through the fire, but he will be with us, bearing our pain and shame.

We ought to pursue righteousness by having faith in Christ, not by running after the law. We will never catch up with the law because the law is beyond our reach. But Christ is a different story. He raced with the law side-by-side and came out the winner. The law fell over dead, and Christ was given the gold medal. He is our righteousness now, and he does not challenge us to race him. He <u>walks</u> toward us. Will we embrace him, or run hopelessly after the law?

shadows: *the promises of God which point to Christ*

substance: *the Christ who came as Jesus of Galilee*

Remember This . . .

Take It to Heart

☞ **GO TO:**

Revelation 3:20 (walks)

Kenneth L. Barker and John R. Kohlenberger III: If God's judgment had been unsparing, the nation would have become as truly wiped out as Sodom and Gomorrah [Romans 9:29]. But the divine judgment is tempered by unfailing mercy, of which the remnant is the eloquent proof.[10]

Study Questions

1. Why does Paul begin this chapter with a preface?
2. The Jews had been given a rich heritage. Paul names seven characteristics that made the people of Israel different. What are they?
3. Why are people offended by the election concept?
4. What two historical events does Paul use to discuss the sovereignty of God in election?
5. What does Scripture mean by "remnant"?

CHAPTER WRAP-UP

- Paul's heart was in anguish over Israel's rejection of their Messiah. His pain was for them, for the shame it brought upon God, and for the despair it brought to his heart. (Romans 9:1–5)

- God chose a line through which the messianic hope would be carried. God used this to demonstrate the principle of election. For God's plan to remain infallible, it has to remain God's plan. Man can add nothing to the purposes of God. (Romans 9:6–21)

- How we pursue righteousness has serious consequences. God will not accept man's works as a substitute for faith in Jesus Christ. Only those who choose to put their faith in Christ will be saved. They are called *"the remnant."* (Romans 9:22–33)

ROMANS 10: FAITH AVENUE

CHAPTER HIGHLIGHTS

- Real Zeal
- Two Kinds of Righteous-ness
- The Source of Faith

Let's Get Started

There are times when our hearts feel like they are going to break. A divorce, the death of a loved one, an accident that leaves a friend crippled for life—events like these make our hearts heavy and our spirits downcast. The apostle Paul was going through such a time. When loved ones do not embrace the truth, it hurts. Often anxiety and feelings of estrangement set in.

Another way of being downcast comes from compromising on that which you know in your heart and mind to be true. When we compromise the truth of God's Word—exactly what Satan wants us to do—we become hypocrites.

Paul felt deeply the rejection of his Jewish brothers, yet he remained faithful to the Jewish Messiah that brought him the message of God's mercy and grace. Though Paul was in pain because many Jews were lost, his spirit was free.

> **Romans 10:1–2** Brothers, my heart's desire and prayer to God for the Israelites is that they may be saved. For I can testify about them that they are zealous for God, but their zeal is not based on knowledge.

The Zeal Deal

Paul addresses his readers as "brothers." Here he is addressing the Jews, his natural brothers, not his Christian brothers. It is obvious that Paul identified with his fellow Jews. He cared for them inexpressibly.

It was not long before Paul wrote his letter to the Romans that he was zealously seeking a righteousness by the law. He had been where the Jews were. At one time Paul thought Jesus and his followers were traitors of his beloved Judaism because they did not seek righteousness the same way he and other Pharisees did.

What Paul sought, however, he sought in ignorance, thus he says the Israelites' zeal for God is not based on knowledge. This is because in many cases the Israelites *refused* to know anything about the righteousness God offered through Christ.

Take It to Heart

Note that Paul acknowledges the Israelites' zeal for God. He is not accusing the Jews of laziness. He's saying their zeal is in the wrong direction. This should remind us that being passionate for God is not enough. First we must be willing to admit that our own agenda may not be God's agenda. Then we must be knowledgeable about how God wants us to be passionate for him.

False Zeal vs. Real Zeal

☞ **GO TO:**

John 2:17; Psalm 69:9 (zeal)

Usually <u>zeal</u> is necessary for communicating what you feel deeply. In Romans 12:11 Paul exhorts, *"Never be lacking in zeal, but keep your spiritual fervor, serving the Lord."* Obviously there's a valid place for zeal. But paradoxically, it is Israel's zeal that created their greatest historical blunder. Their zeal created a mob mentality. Theirs was a zeal built on emotions, not God's will.

In his commentary on the Book of Romans, D. Martyn Lloyd-Jones offers a number of indicators for false or inappropriate kinds of zeal.

First, "zeal must always be tested and examined." The Jews' zeal was not according to knowledge. They needed to carefully examine what they were doing and encouraging others to do.

Second, a zeal that "has been whipped up or organized" may well be a false zeal.

Third, a zeal that "puts greater emphasis upon doing than upon being" always alerts caution.

Fourth, in a "false zeal it is the activity, rather than the truth" which is at the center.

Fifth, "when methods, organization and the machinery are very prominent" you have evidence of a false zeal.

carnal: fleshly

Sixth, when the zeal has a **carnal** sense about it, it is a false zeal.

Seventh, "false zeal dislikes being questioned. It resents inquiry." It has no patience with any examination.[1]

The above addresses some of the characteristics of false zeal, but what about true zeal? True zeal is a natural expression of one's emotions and convictions. It's a demonstration of who we are. Godly zeal reflects grace and maturity, not manipulation, for true righteousness does not seek to **beguile**. Finally, knowledge is the decisive factor in the **litmus test** between true and false zeal. The presence of knowledge indicates true zeal; the absence of it signals false zeal.

beguile: to trick or deceive

litmus test: a test in which a single factor is decisive

What Others are Saying:

D. Martyn Lloyd-Jones: You cannot make your own spirit fervent. If you try to do so it will be a false zeal. The Holy Spirit alone can make people truly fervent. It is the fire from the altar of heaven that alone can burn in the heart and give us a concern for the lost, and make us do something about them. That is what you need. You need a baptism of the Spirit of God, you need the fire of the Spirit! And you should give yourself no rest or peace until you have it.[2]

> **Romans 10:3–4** Since they did not know the righteousness that comes from God and sought to establish their own, they did not submit to God's righteousness. Christ is the end of the law so that there may be righteousness for everyone who believes.

The Law's End

The Jews had no idea that righteousness could be a gift. They knew it was an attribute of God. In fact, they prided themselves on knowing their God was righteous whereas pagan gods were not, but if you had said to a Jew, "Righteousness is a gift," he or she would have looked at you like you belonged in a straitjacket.

As for human righteousness, the Israelites thought the way to be righteous was by keeping the Mosaic law and Rabbinic traditions. As long as a Jew observed the holy feasts and the Sabbath, he or she assumed all was fine. Because of (1) how ignorant they were, and (2) how preoccupied they were with their own self-made ideas of human righteousness, the Jews did not even look for the gift of "God's righteousness." They did not know such a thing existed.

Of course, the Jews were *not* righteous. Their righteousness and God's righteousness were as different as monopoly money is from real greenbacks issued by the U.S. Treasury.[3] So, what was the solution? Christ. Christ, Paul explained, was "the end" of the law in at least three ways.

1. The law leads us to Christ.
2. Christ lived the perfect life that the law required.
3. Christ caused the law to disappear from the scene (*"We are not under law but under grace."*)

Christ fulfilled the requirements of the law, and Christ's righteousness is credited to the believer's account.

Take It to Heart

Remember This . . .

☞ **GO TO:**

Acts 9:1–19 (Damascus)

As a result of the Jews' **recalcitrant** wills, *"their foolish hearts were darkened"* (Romans 1:21). This is a serious warning for all who confess faith in God, as did the Jews, but refuse to submit to the righteousness of God as revealed in Christ. Such an attribute is evidence of a false, nonbiblical zeal.

Paul speaks plainly about Israel's failure, but not in a reproachful manner. He speaks out of a sense of duty to declare the truth. As we observed in Romans 9 and here again in this chapter, the apostle feels a deep love for his native heritage. He has a Jewish heart and appreciates his Jewish roots. Yet Paul knew their spiritual condition, because their condition was his own prior to his <u>Damascus</u> road experience.

 Meet Paul—Paul is up front about his desire for Israel. He wanted them to be saved. His pre-Calvin doctrines (this was nearly 1700 years before Calvin and the other Reformation fathers) did not prevent him from believing, praying, and going to the lost. The doctrines of election and predestination were never barriers to Paul; they were open windows from heaven. He knew God loved the world and that he was called by God to go and preach God's love to the world. He felt this intimately when preaching to his Jewish countrymen.

> **Romans 10:5–8** Moses describes in this way the righteousness that is by the law: "The man who does these things will live by them." But the righteousness that is by faith says: "Do not say in your heart, 'Who will ascend into heaven?'" (that is, to bring Christ down) "or

> 'Who will descend into the deep?'" (that is, to bring Christ up from the dead). But what does it say? "The word is near you; it is in your mouth and in your heart," that is, the word of faith we are proclaiming.

The Nearness Of God

Once again Paul goes back to the Old Testament to show his fellow Jews where they've gone wrong. He refers to Moses, the man through whom the Jews received the law. First Paul shows the Jews what is Moses' definition for a *"righteousness that is by the law."* In short, Moses said that righteousness by the law is attained by keeping the law. The person who keeps the law will live. The only snag is that anyone who does not keep the law—and none of us does—is condemned.

Paul then moves on to another passage from Moses, but this one is used to describe a *"righteousness that is by faith."* Here is the passage from which he quotes:

> *The Lord your God will circumcise your hearts and the hearts of your descendants, so that you may love him with all your heart and with all your soul, and live. . . . Now what I am commanding you today is not too difficult for you or beyond your reach. It is not up in heaven, so that you have to ask, "Who will ascend into heaven to get it and proclaim it to us so we may obey it?" Nor is it beyond the sea, so that you have to ask, "Who will cross the sea to get it and proclaim it to us so we may obey it?" No, the word is very near you; it is in your mouth and in your heart so you may obey it.* (Deuteronomy 30:6, 11–14)

This passage starts with a heart devoted to God and proceeds to point out that following God is not something out of our reach. We do not need to reach for heaven because in Christ, heaven has come to us. If we submit our lives to God, his will is near to us—as close as our mouths that praise him and as close as our hearts that lodge a desire to please him.

 Meet Paul—Lest someone suppose God used Paul because he did such a great job at keeping the law, here is what Paul wrote to his missionary-friend, Timothy, *"Christ Jesus came into the world to save sinners—of whom I am the worst. But for that very reason I was shown mercy so that in me, the worst of sinners, Christ might display his unlimited*

patience as an example for those who would believe on him and receive eternal life" (1 Timothy 1:15–16). Paul had no illusions about his own sin. He knew that it was God's mercy, not his own merit, that had snatched him out of the self-destruction of his depravity.

Something to Ponder

Many throughout the generations were humbled and had a wonderful walk of faith with God. Among the outstanding ones were the **patriarchs** and the **prophets**. But there were many others also. In short, the concept of a*"righteousness that is by faith"* was not a new one, but it hit a major snag among the nation's leaders when Jesus came on the scene.

Remember This . . .

The law gave Israel God's moral requirements, which they couldn't fulfill, and which God used to show them their need for repentance. The continuation of his love was in bringing Jesus the Messiah. The promise of his coming is throughout the whole Old Covenant. One who believes a promise has faith in the promise giver.

patriarchs: *Abraham, the founder of the Jewish people, his son Isaac, and grandson Jacob*

prophets: *spokespersons commissioned by God to communicate his words*

confess: *publicly express*

> **Romans 10:9** That if you **confess** with your mouth, "Jesus is Lord," and believe in your heart that God raised him from the dead, you will be saved.

Mouth And Heart

Once a Muslim approached a missionary in an Arab country. The Muslim wanted to prove the ridiculousness of this verse so he said to the missionary, "Jesus is Lord," and proceeded to explain that he didn't really believe it, but because the Bible said all he had to do was confess it, God was therefore obligated to let him enter heaven. The missionary looked at the Muslim and in a tone loud enough for other Muslims to hear he said, "I'm glad you have confessed that Jesus is your Lord." The Muslim slunk away in a hurry.

It's one thing to say the words, it's another thing to confess them and to show what's in your heart by acting accordingly.

☞ **GO TO:**

Ephesians 2:9–10 (boast)

carnal: *worldly, non-Christian*

The path to faith always seems like a bad choice to the **carnal** mind. Works make us feel significant, like we have a right to something. They make us feel like we have something to <u>boast</u> about. But the path of faith leads us to the truth, which is that we are sinners, have nothing to boast about, and are infinitely blessed by God.

Grabbed by Grace

Paul said something very interesting to the Philippians about confessing Jesus as Lord. He said, *"Therefore God exalted [Christ] to the highest place and gave him the name that is above every name, that at the name of Jesus every knee should bow, in heaven and on earth and under the* earth, *and every tongue confess that Jesus Christ is Lord, to the glory of God the Father"* (Philippians 2:9–11). In other words, each and every person who ever lived will eventually confess that Jesus is Lord. Paul is not saying everyone will be saved. He's saying both saved people who go to heaven and lost people who go to hell will acknowledge the lordship of Christ. Christians will acknowledge it in joy, non-Christians will acknowledge it in despair.

KEY POINT

The only way to be saved is through Jesus Christ.

What Others are Saying:

D. Martyn Lloyd-Jones: [regarding the battle with intellectualism and the Gospel] I say once more that the most ignorant, the most illiterate, and the most benighted can believe this message and be saved by it in a second . . . you are not saved by a knowledge of doctrine! You are saved by the Lord Jesus Christ and what He has done on your behalf . . . thank God! We do not have to drag Him down or lift Him up. He has done it all! He has come; He has done the work; He has risen again . . . 'Only believe'![4]

James R. Edwards: What is humanly impossible—to scale the heights or descend the depths—has been revealed by God in the law, but ultimately in Christ. All noble, pious, and heroic attempts to demonstrate human righteousness are only active unbelief. It is not we who bring Christ to people, but Christ who sends us to them with his saving word.[5]

Charles Hodge: They were not to regard the resurrection and the ascension of Christ as impossible. But the whole context shows that the purpose of the apostle is to contrast the legal and the gospel methods of salvation—to show that the one is impracticable, the other easy. By works of the law no flesh living can be justified; whereas, whosoever simply calls on the name of the Lord shall be saved.[6]

Something to Ponder

A person who is saying the same kinds of things today that Paul said nearly two thousand years ago is Billy Graham. For a number of years, I've served as chair of the Billy Graham Phone Center in Seattle, Washington. I've participated in over forty of the telecasts. I've watched God use Billy Graham to present the Gospel in each of these crusades. He always presents this apostolic message with grace and clarity. The Spirit of God comes upon the hearts of thousands of people, and they come forward to *"confess with* [their] *mouth, 'Jesus is Lord.'"* It is the power of the Gospel through the faithful preaching of a man who was himself saved by that Gospel. It always blesses my heart to listen to the Gospel being preached.

> **Romans 10:10–13** For it is with your heart that you believe and are justified, and it is with your mouth that you confess and are saved. As the Scripture says, "Anyone who trusts in him will never be put to shame." For there is no difference between Jew and Gentile—the same Lord is Lord of all and richly blesses all who call on him, for, "Everyone who calls on the name of the Lord will be saved."

You Are Invited

Here Paul explains how the Gospel manifests its power: *"It is with your heart that you believe and are justified."* God changes your heart to be ready to receive the Gospel. The Holy Spirit causes you to be born again. He comes to live with you and in you. It is by God's grace and mercy that this occurs.

Further, *"it is with your mouth that you confess and are saved."* Believe and confess are two inseparable aspects of coming to faith in Jesus Christ. Conversion is not an intellectual show-and-tell, but an intentional and public witness of your faith in the risen Christ.

The way the apostle presents this explanation of the Gospel's power shows the Christian two very essential things: First, to say you believe without confession hints at betrayal; and second, to confess without really believing is self-deception, resulting in hypocrisy. These are two of Satan's best shots. Avoid them at all cost.

Paul writes, *"For there is no difference between Jew and Gentile."* What does he mean? There is no difference when it comes to the necessity of salvation. We are all sinners. Earlier in his letter, Paul reminded the church that *"this righteousness from God comes through faith in Jesus Christ to all who believe. There is no difference, for all have sinned"* (Romans 3:22–23).

There is no difference because God said there isn't: *"The same Lord is Lord of all and richly blesses all who call on him, for, 'Everyone who calls on the name of the Lord will be saved'"* (Romans 10:12–13). God has spoken and we need to listen for his voice. Obedience to the truth is evidence that you love God and respect his Word.

Something to Ponder

What Others are Saying:

Douglas J. Moo: Central to the Reformers' teaching about salvation was their distinction between "law" and "gospel." "Law" is whatever God commands us to do; "gospel" is what God in his grace gives us to do. The Reformers uniformly insisted that human depravity made it impossible for a person to be saved by doing what God commands; only by humbly accepting, in faith, the "good news" of God's work on our behalf could a person be saved.[7]

Adolf Schlatter: Believing is the effort of the heart and confessing that of the mouth. If faith is accomplished by the heart, righteousness is the result, and if confession is made with the mouth, salvation is its fruit . . . righteousness liberates from guilt, and salvation from death. The former orders the inner life, hence Paul attributes it to the heart. The latter renders the believer part of the community that is destined to life.[8]

D. Martyn Lloyd-Jones: What I am trying to say was put in a pithy phrase by one of the great Puritans who went out from this country to New England in the 1630's, a man called Thomas Hooker, who lived and preached in Cambridge, Massachusetts. He put it like this: "If a man hath faith within, it will break forth at the mouth." And that, I believe, is exactly what the Apostle is saying here: that this true, heartfelt, sincere belief in the context of saving faith will inevitably give expression to itself.[9]

> **Romans 10:14–15** How, then, can they call on the one they have not believed in? And how can they believe in the one of whom they have not heard? And how can they hear without someone preaching to them? And how can they preach unless they are sent? As it is written, "How beautiful are the feet of those who bring good news!"

Dirty Feet Are Beautiful To God

In this passage, Paul transitions from proclaiming that all who call on the Lord will be saved to exploring the nuts and bolts of how this is done. He introduces five *how's* into his discourse.

1 His first *how* is this: *"How, then, can they call on the one they have not believed in?"* Paul moves from what is required of the seeker to the role of the believer. He addresses this again in his letter to the Corinthians: *"'No eye has seen, no ear has heard, no mind has conceived what God has prepared for those who love him'— but God has revealed it to us by his Spirit. The Spirit searches all things, even the deep things of God. For who among men knows the thoughts of a man except the man's spirit within him? In the same way no one knows the thoughts of God except the Spirit of God"* (1 Corinthians 2:9–11). Thus, the Holy Spirit participates in the communication of the Gospel and in the conversion of the soul. Paul is serving God by giving God the glory and declaring his truth.

He goes on to reveal God's method: *"the Lord has assigned to each his task. I planted the seed,* **Apollos** *watered it, but God made it grow. So neither he who plants nor he who waters is anything, but only God, who makes things grow"* (1 Corinthians 3:5–7).

We see from these two passages that God sent out servants to plow and cultivate the soil and to plant the seeds of the Gospel. It is the mission of the church to do the work of **evangelism**—to prepare the way and to spread the good news. It takes the grace of God to make the seeds take root. The Spirit of God touches people's hearts, making them open to hearing the Gospel message. We need to trust the Holy Spirit for his grace to move hearts.

2 The second *how* is closely linked to the first: *"How can they believe in the one of whom they have not heard?"* Here Paul reminds believers that faith depends on knowledge. The Gospel has to be communicated, and preaching is God's primary method. One must hear the Gospel before receiving or rejecting the Lord. This is an important truth to bring with us as we go about our lives.

Apollos: *an early Christian leader, mentioned in Acts 18:24–28*

evangelism: *sharing the Gospel with others*

There are many wonderful ways to sow the seed of God's love. One way is simply by showing love toward others—this will lead people to inquiry in a world filled with pain and loneliness.

wind: here, an image used to represent the Holy Spirit

3 Paul's third *how* is this: *"How can they hear without someone preaching to them?"* This is God's call to the church to be a servant people. We are called to serve, to do the work of the kingdom for the glory of God and for the fulfillment of the great commission. Our service is to bear witness to the saving power of Jesus Christ.

4 Paul's fourth *how* is this: *"How can they preach unless they are sent?"* Here Paul addresses the need for order, discipline, and organization. Being sent suggests one should operate under an appointed mentor or authority or society that has a vision from God. Being sent addresses accountability on the part of the one going and the one staying. Our message does not originate with us, but with God. He and his Word are the final authority. God has appointed leaders to do his bidding.

5 The apostle turns his final *how* into a statement: *"How beautiful are the feet of those who bring good news!"* This was the message that was **heralded** when Israel began to return from her captivity in Babylon. It announces the favor of the Lord to the Holy City of Jerusalem. It was a proclamation of peace—good tidings after years of servitude. Paul's emphasis on *"the feet of those who bring good news,"* points to the need for servants who will go forth in the name of God to make the message of love personal, therefore **incarnational**.

herald: to proclaim or announce important news

If the proclamation of peace was considered good news—and indeed it was—how much more is the promise of eternal life through Jesus Christ our Lord. The Gospel is not merely a philosophy or an idea, though it does significantly influence one's worldview. The Gospel is a life-transforming message that tells people how to be who they were created to be.

incarnational: represented in human flesh

William S. Plumer: All the ecclesiastical authorities in the world cannot impart to men the gift of preaching aright. They must have an unction to teach them all things. They must be called and sent by the Lord himself. There is much cause to fear that some refuse to preach who are duly called; and that others obtrude themselves into the sacred office without any divine mission.[10]

What Others are Saying:

Martin Luther: But this is a new acquisition opposed to, or above, Aristotle, who taught that righteousness is produced by actions, especially external and frequent actions. But this civil righteousness is reprobate before God. But true righteousness comes into being by believing the words of God with the whole heart, as had been said [before], Romans 4:3: *"Abraham believed God, and it was reckoned to him as righteousness."*[11]

> **Romans 10:16–21** But not all the Israelites accepted the good news. For Isaiah says, "Lord, who has believed our message?" Consequently, faith comes from hearing the message, and the message is heard through the word of Christ. But I ask: Did they not hear? Of course they did: "Their voice has gone out into all the earth, their words to the ends of the world." Again I ask: Did Israel not understand? First, Moses says, "I will make you envious by those who are not a nation; I will make you angry by a nation that has no understanding." And Isaiah boldly says, "I was found by those who did not seek me; I revealed myself to those who did not ask for me." But concerning Israel he says, "All day long I have held out my hands to a disobedient and obstinate people."

A Lesson In Contrasts

Paul makes it very clear that the Father's offer of righteousness by faith was extended to all, Jews and Gentiles alike. But unfortunately not everyone accepted the offer. And it was the official rejection by the Jewish leaders that caused Paul so much anguish. He knew what this would ultimately mean to the nation.

The Jews had ample opportunity to hear the Word of God, both by **general revelation** and by **special revelation**. They heard, but they did not accept God's invitation. Paul uses Old Testament Scripture to point out the sad reality that the Gentiles, who for a long time were ignorant of God, were in the end more accepting of God's invitation than the Jews, whom God actively pursued over and over again throughout history. The idea is that while God sought after the Jews, they rejected him. The Gentiles, who were not even looking for God, found and believed in him.

☞ **GO TO:**

Psalm 19:1–4, 7–11;
Romans 1:19–20
(general revelation)

1 Corinthians 2:10–13
(special revelation)

general revelation: what can be deduced about God from the natural universe

special revelation: information given to human beings by God, especially in the Scriptures

The phrase *"all day long"* is an expression of how long-suffering God is in his love for people. His invitation is still open. He is still holding out the gift of his eternal presence.

Something to Ponder

What Others are Saying:

Saint Augustine: The preaching of predestination should not hinder the preaching of perseverance and progress in faith, so that those to whom it has been given to obey should hear what they ought to hear. For how will they hear without a preacher?[12]

Charles Hodge: The universal revelation of God in nature, was a providential prediction of the universal proclamation of the Gospel . . . the manifestation of God in nature, is, for all his creatures to whom it is made, a pledge of their participation in the clearer and higher revelations.[13]

Study Questions

1. What was wrong with the Jews' zeal for God?
2. How does "righteousness by law" differ from "righteousness by faith"?
3. How does one receive the Lord Jesus as his or her Lord and Savior?
4. When Paul says in verse 12, *"there is no difference between Jew and Gentile,"* what does he mean?
5. What's Paul's point in saying *"how beautiful are the feet of those who bring good news"*?

CHAPTER WRAP-UP

- Israel had a zeal for God, but their zeal wasn't based on knowledge. They had rejected the Gospel. (Romans 10:1–5)

- The law has no saving potential. It helps us see ourselves more clearly, more honestly. Righteousness by the avenue of faith is the only sure way of securing a relationship with God. (Romans 10:6–13)

- Faith comes from hearing the message. And the message is heard through the Word of Christ. This makes the Christian faith a personal faith, grounded in daily experience, and a faith that will last eternally. (Romans 10:14–21)

ROMANS 11: ISRAEL'S DESTINY

CHAPTER HIGHLIGHTS

- Paul the Jew
- The Remnant
- Mercy for the Gentiles
- Grafted In
- God's Promise
- God Be Praised

Let's Get Started

In chapter 9 Paul emphasized God's sovereignty in choosing Israel to be his people. In chapter 10 Paul pointed out that Israel had consistently been reluctant to accept God's gift of *"righteousness that is by faith."* Chapter 10 ended with the sobering charge that Israel is a *"disobedient and obstinate people."*

So, we have God's sovereign choice of Israel on the one hand and Israel's obstinance on the other. Will God give up on Israel? Will he find a way, despite Israel's disobedience, to preserve and enact his purpose? These are the questions Paul addresses in chapter 11.

> **Romans 11:1–2a** I ask then: Did God reject his people? By no means! I am an Israelite myself, a descendant of Abraham, from the tribe of Benjamin. God did not reject his people, whom he foreknew.

No Rejection For The Remnant

Paul is determined to help the Romans rightly understand Israel's fall. He was determined to do so not because of a selfish desire for his own peace, though surely this was a motivating factor. Rather, Paul sought God's will and wanted to state it accurately.

When Paul says *"his people,"* he has in mind the remnant he referred to in Romans 9:27–29. Though most Jews were disobedient throughout the Old Testament and when Paul was teaching,

God had not given up on *"his people."* We remember that *"not all who are descended from Israel are Israel"* (Romans 9:6).

Paul includes himself in the discussion for at least two reasons. One was to present himself as evidence that God had not rejected the Jews. If God had rejected the Jews, he would not have given Paul such a prominent role in spreading the Gospel. A second reason was to remind the Jews that he was one of them. He was therefore qualified to speak with fairness about their situation.

What Others are Saying:

D. Martyn Lloyd-Jones: But in chapter 11 he (Paul) goes further. He looks into the future and shows how this great and grand purpose of God is going to be carried out in its glorious fulness, both as regards Gentiles and Jews. So there is a new theme here. The present has been explained but the question now is, What of the future? The Jews are outside, are they always to be there?[1]

> **Romans 11:2b–6** Don't you know what the Scripture says in the passage about Elijah—how he appealed to God against Israel: "Lord, they have killed your prophets and torn down your altars; I am the only one left, and they are trying to kill me"? And what was God's answer to him? "I have reserved for myself seven thousand who have not bowed the knee to Baal." So too, at the present time there is a remnant chosen by grace. And if by grace, then it is no longer by works; if it were, grace would no longer be grace.

Sidonian: from Sidon, a Phoenician kingdom near Israel

King Ahab: king of Israel's Northern Kingdom

Baal: a Canaanite term for "god"

☞ **GO TO:**

1 Kings 16:29–33 (King Ahab)

Judges 2:13; 1 Kings 19:18 (Baal)

God's Track Record

In this passage, Paul takes his readers back to 1 Kings 19 where we find the account of Elijah fleeing from Jezebel, who was the **Sidonian** wife of **King Ahab**. This pagan woman had been promoting **Baal** worship throughout the land (see GWMB, pages 136–138).

Elijah had just had a whale of a victory on Mt. Carmel (see illustration, page 157) against 450 prophets of Baal. When Ahab informed Jezebel of Elijah's astounding victory, she sent a threatening note to Elijah telling him she would have his head in the next twenty-four hours.

Elijah buckled. He fled out into the desert south of Beersheba to hide and pray. While there, *"the word of the Lord came to him: 'What are you doing here, Elijah?'"* (1 Kings 19:9). Elijah was feeling like the battle was over and he was the only faithful servant

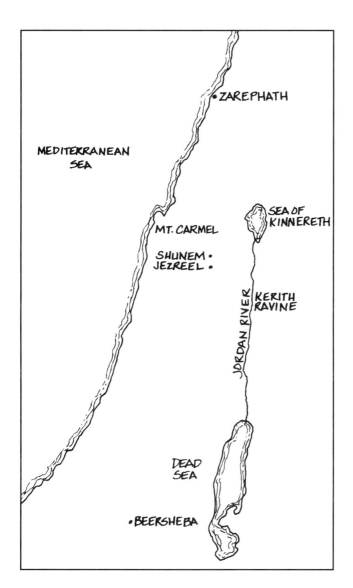

This map shows Mt. Carmel where Elijah fought the prophets of Baal. After learning that the queen wanted to have him killed, Elijah fled south of Beersheba.

left in the land. He was ready to give up because he thought he was alone. But God informed him, *"I [have reserved] seven thousand in Israel—all whose knees have not bowed down to Baal and all whose mouths have not kissed him"* (1 Kings 19:18). In this case, seven thousand does not mean an exact head count; rather, it suggests that which is complete, maybe even more than one can count. The *"seven thousand"* of Israel were the remnant.

Paul brings up this Old Testament story as a way of saying God has always had a faithful remnant of Jews. It was true in the dark days of Elijah, and it's true now. God has not and will not reject Israel.

☞ **GO TO:**

2 Chronicles 20:15 (battle)

Grabbed by Grace

works: *merit earned by what an individual does*

What Others are Saying:

In the battle against the forces of evil, it's easy to get overwhelmed. We feel like we're the lone sentinel on a hill. In those moments, we forget that the <u>battle</u> is God's to fight, not ours. Paul was reminding the Jews who were faithful to Jesus Christ that *"at the present time there is a remnant chosen by grace,"* just as God had reserved a godly number in Elijah's day.

We can only rightly understand God's elective purposes when we understand that God is sovereign. We do not become part of God's remnant through our efforts; it is a gift of God. The larger lesson in this context is this: *Since the remnant has been secured by the grace of God, the remnant stands as a pledge that God will continue to show favor toward Israel as a whole.*

Paul is reminding Israel, as well as the Gentiles, that salvation has always been a matter of God's grace. Israel was called into existence by the grace of God. The Church was called into existence by God's grace. And the future heavenly reward of both groups rests on God's grace.

Verse 6 says, *"And if by grace, then it is no longer by **works**; if it were, grace would no longer be grace."* He's clarifying his reference to *"a remnant chosen by grace,"* Grace and works are opposites. Like oil and water, grace and works due to their diverse characteristics cannot mix, and when we do mix them, we spoil both.

John Calvin: The grace of God and the merit of works are so opposed to one another that if we establish one we destroy the other. If, then, we cannot allow any consideration of works in election without obscuring the unmerited goodness of God . . . those fanatics, who make the worthiness which God foresees in us the cause of our election, must consider what answer they are to give to Paul.[2]

> **Romans 11:7–10** What then? What Israel sought so earnestly it did not obtain, but the elect did. The others were hardened, as it is written: "God gave them a spirit of stupor, eyes so that they could not see and ears so that they could not hear, to this very day." And David says: "May their table become a snare and a trap, a stumbling block and a retribution for them. May their eyes be darkened so they cannot see, and their backs be bent forever."

Israel Goes Bad

"Don't pity the Israelites," Paul says. They sought God in the wrong way. Recall in Romans 9:31 when the apostle reminded us that Israel *"pursued a law of righteousness."* They did not seek God by faith. Now we find out more about the consequences of those actions.

In their vain attempt to establish their own adequacy—their own standing before God—they refused, knowingly and unknowingly, to receive the <u>righteousness</u> that comes from God. Rejection of God starts with one act, and it snowballs from there. Each rejection of God afterward gets easier and easier. The result was that God hardened the unbelieving Jews' hearts. He gave them a *"spirit of stupor."*

Grace is the sign of **the elect**, for the elect obtain righteousness by trusting in divine grace, not in the works of the flesh—no matter how sincere they are. Though there is a *"remnant chosen by grace"* (Romans 11:5), most people in Israel failed to attain divine righteousness.

Earlier Paul told the Roman believers that *"God has mercy on whom he wants to have mercy, and he hardens whom he wants to harden"* (Romans 9:18). We can only resist his will so long, and then the hardening takes place. When hearts are hardened, they resist the grace of God, and people without grace are people under judgment.

Judgment is such a serious matter that the apostle throws the weight of Scripture behind his argument for God's truth. The Jews had **the Law**, **the Prophets**, and **the Writings**. Paul quotes from all three—Deuteronomy 29:4, Isaiah 29:10, and Psalm 69:22—to make sure his hearers understand. Paul knows if you mess with the truth, you undermine all of what's best in life.

The Route Of Resistance

Two things happen to those who continue to resist when God holds out his hands of grace, mercy, and love.

First, they become hardened, making it difficult to receive truth in the future. This hardening produces a **flinty** heart and permanent bluntness. It's like a spiritual tattoo—nearly impossible to reverse.

Second, God removes blessings from their lives. In the biblical world the table was a symbol of prosperity that represented the

☞ **GO TO:**

Romans 1:17 (righteousness)

the elect: *one of Paul's terms for Christians*

Remember This . . .

the Law: *first five OT books*

the Prophets: *writings of the prophets*

the Writings: *Psalms and the wisdom literature*

flinty: *rocklike, inflexible, or inert*

pleasures of life. So when the psalmist prayed, *"may the table set before them become a snare,"* he was asking God to take pleasure out of the lives of those who rejected God.

KEY POINT

We cannot mock the grace of God and hope to be at peace in our heart, spirit, soul, or body.

IN OTHER LETTERS

In his second letter to the Corinthians Paul answered the question of how he and his ministry partner, Apollos, should be viewed. He wrote, *"Not that we are competent in ourselves to claim anything for ourselves, but our competence comes from God"* (2 Corinthians 3:5). Paul's statement reflects how indebted he felt toward God. He knew that his salvation, even his competence as a minister of Christ, came not from himself but from God.

What Others are Saying:

Billy Graham: Pope John Paul II has stated, "Our future on this planet, exposed as it is to nuclear annihilation, depends on one single factor: humanity must make a moral about-face." But the question that confronts us is, how can this happen. . . . Man himself must be changed. The Bible teaches that this is possible through spiritual renewal. Jesus Christ taught that man can and must have a spiritual rebirth.[3]

Martin Luther: Every arrogant heretic is first caught by his ignorance of the truth; for when he despises this, he is already in the snare. Then he accepts what seems to him to be true; and he is trapped again, because he smugly walks through life as if he were free beyond the snare and the trap. Finally, he stumbles against everything which goes contrary to him and thus turns off his hearing.[4]

> **Romans 11:11–12** Again I ask: Did they stumble so as to fall beyond recovery? Not at all! Rather, because of their transgression, salvation has come to the Gentiles to make Israel envious. But if their transgression means riches for the world, and their loss means riches for the Gentiles, how much greater riches will their fullness bring!

Israel Is Green With Envy

Paul now turns his attention from the remnant to Israel as a whole. He asks if there is any hope. Will Israel ever get back up? Are they doomed forever? *"Not at all!"* Paul answers. He explains that while the Jews are rejecting God, God will sow the gospel seed among the Gentiles to make the Jews envious. Paul is saying the Jews will see God's blessing upon the Gentiles and they'll get jealous. He goes on to say if the *"transgression"* of the Jews brings riches to the Gentiles, their return to God will bring even greater riches to the Gentiles!

Because Israel did not welcome Christ, God opened his gift of salvation to the Gentiles. Prior to Christ the only way for a Gentile to identify himself or herself as a follower of Yahweh was to identify with God's covenant people and submit to God's law as a Jew. With Christ Gentiles no longer had to convert to Judaism. If they put their faith in Jesus, they were not Jews, they were Christians!

Something to Ponder

Here we see a real hint of the future salvation of Israel. God in his grace and power is bringing great good out of the foolishness of Israel. They were offered the righteousness of God, but rejected it for the old way of the law. The consequence has been enormous—centuries of testing and grief. But all is not lost.

Remember This . . .

The glory of God is clearly revealed in this unusual process of making good out of failure. Gathering people from among the nations, Jesus created the very <u>church</u> that he said he would build. Christianity became reality, but not without hope for Israel. Today's remnant from Israel is secured in that they come into God's kingdom through their Messiah, the Lord Jesus Christ.

Grabbed by Grace

Kenneth L. Barker and John R. Kohlenberger III: A word should be said about "loss" [Romans 11:12]; this is a military figure. An army loses a battle because of heavy casualties. In other words, as surely as Israel's defeat (identified with her stumbling) has brought the riches of God's grace to the Gentiles on a large scale so the conversion of Israel to her Messiah [Romans 11:26] will bring even greater blessing to the world.[5]

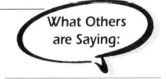
What Others are Saying:

☞ **GO TO:**

Matthew 16:17–20 (church)

*paratoma: transgression,
sin*

Adolf Schlatter: Israel's fall is God's work, as the Scripture declared it; yet God's action is always goal-oriented. Did Israel stumble in order to fall? If so, only wrath would be at work in its destiny and God's grace would not be seen. Israel's fall denotes guilt; it is a ***paratoma*** and therefore what Israel suffers has been prepared for them by wrath. But grace will be made manifest even in what it suffers, because its fall brings about the salvation of those who are of the nations.[6]

> **Romans 11:13–15** I am talking to you Gentiles. Inasmuch as I am the apostle to the Gentiles, I make much of my ministry in the hope that I may somehow arouse my own people to envy and save some of them. For if their rejection is the reconciliation of the world, what will their acceptance be but life from the dead?

Holy Branches, Batman!

Paul links this paragraph with the preceding one. He wants to make certain that the Gentiles are paying attention. It's important for the unity and the growth of the church that the Gentiles catch the full importance of what Paul is saying and doing. He emphasizes that he's the apostle to the Gentiles.

It is good that they understand him to be the *"apostle to the Gentiles,"* but he doesn't want them to forget that he's a witness to the Jews as well. Christ doesn't have two bodies of people. The Church he is building is *"one body and one Spirit—just as you were called to one hope . . . one Lord, one faith, one baptism; one God and Father of all"* (Ephesians 4:4–6). It is made up of Jews and Gentiles. Paul pays close attention to his ministry because he knows that the more the Gentile world responds to the Gospel, the more the Jews will be aroused to action.

**Something
to Ponder**

God's work is being carried out even if the Jews continue to reject their Messiah. Paul has been given spiritual eyes to see exactly what the Father is doing.

> **Romans 11:16** If the part of the dough offered as firstfruits is holy, then the whole batch is holy; if the root is holy, so are the branches.

A Down Payment With More To Come

Paul uses two analogies—the dough and the root—to teach a significant concept without making a prophetic announcement. *"Part of the dough"* is the present number of Jews that have bowed to Jesus as their Lord; they are the *"firstfruits,"* the elect.

The second analogy—*"the root"*—addresses their beginning or the source of their life. Covenantally, their root goes back to Abraham whose place in their history and theology is beyond dispute.

Paul is pointing to the future restoration of the nation of Israel to God. He did not expect this to happen in his own lifetime, though he hoped his work would help to convert *"some"* (Romans 11:14). He expected the nation's restoration to happen sometime in the indefinite future.

D. Martyn Lloyd-Jones: The general warning to us is this, that we must be very careful that we never "write people off" as being beyond redemption. We must denounce unbelief, we must denounce error more, but we must never write people off. We must never say that someone "cannot be saved." We do not know. . . . We have a serious view of sin, but that does not mean we condemn the sinner.[7]

> **What Others are Saying:**

> **Romans 11:17–18** If some of the branches have been broken off, and you, though a wild olive shoot, have been grafted in among the others and now share in the nourishing sap from the olive root, do not boast over those branches. If you do, consider this: You do not support the root, but the root supports you.

Prepare To Be Pruned

The olive tree (see illustration, page 164) is a familiar and beautiful part of the landscape in Israel. It's a symbol of both strength and blessing. David penned in Psalm 52:8, *"But I am like an olive tree flourishing in the house of God; I trust in God's unfailing love for ever and ever."*

Paul uses the branch of an olive tree to picture what God has done in connecting the Gentiles, those *"wild olive shoots,"* into the cultivated olive tree, Israel. In Paul's metaphor, some of the olive tree's branches were broken off and wild shoots were grafted into the tree.

A slow-growing olive tree such as this one was a common sight in Israel during New Testament times. Its fruit was crushed and the oil was extracted and used for cooking, lighting, and mixing ointments and perfumes. One tree could produce twenty gallons of oil. The wood was hard and had many uses as well.

God was turning the Gentiles into a fruit-bearing people. This left no room for boasting. Paul told the Gentiles, *"If you do [boast], consider this: You do not support the root, but the root supports you."* Paul is pointing them to the very source of their lives: God. God is the Keeper of the vineyard, the ultimate Gardener.

> **Romans 11:19–21** You will say then, "Branches were broken off so that I could be grafted in." Granted. But they were broken off because of unbelief, and you stand by faith. Do not be arrogant, but be afraid. For if God did not spare the natural branches, he will not spare you either.

You See The Hole, Now Step Around It

The Gentiles were now recipients of all the blessings of belonging to God. Many Jews had rejected God and therefore did not receive these blessings. The Gentile temptation to boast must have been enormous.

Paul warns the Gentile Christians not to repeat the sins of the Jews. The Jews did not depend on God for their salvation, but their own works. Paul tells the Gentiles to remember that the only reason they were grafted into the tree of God's kingdom was because they depended on God. If they now let go of their dependence on God, God could just as easily break them off of the tree as he broke off the self-reliant Jews.

Saint Jerome: Whenever I see a synagogue, the thought of the apostle always comes to me—that we should not boast against the olive tree whose branches have been broken off but rather fear. For if the natural branches have been cut off, how much more we who have been grafted on the wild olive should fear, lest we become like them.[8]

> **Romans 11:22–24** Consider therefore the kindness and sternness of God: sternness to those who fell, but kindness to you, provided that you continue in his kindness. Otherwise, you also will be cut off. And if they do not persist in unbelief, they will be grafted in, for God is able to graft them in again. After all, if you were cut out of an olive tree that is wild by nature, and contrary to nature were grafted into a cultivated olive tree, how much more readily will these, the natural branches, be grafted into their own olive tree!

Stern Kindness

In this passage, we see Paul holding out hope for the Jews: if they *"do not persist in unbelief, they will be grafted in, for God is able to graft them in again."* Unbelief is what kills. Belief is what gives life. If the Jews simply give up persisting in their unbelief, Paul says, then the kindness and power of God will reestablish them in the kingdom of God.

Paul had the heart to perceive what was on the horizon for his fellow Jews. The phrase *"how much more readily will these, the natural branches, be grafted into their own olive tree"* (Romans 11:24b) shows that Paul had hope for the Jews. The apostle sees that God's original plan for the Jewish nation will unfold naturally when unbelief is out of the way.

In this passage we see the vastness of the character and personhood of God. He is able to be kind in his sternness and stern in his kindness, all while remaining righteous. This is a feat that is difficult for humans. We are usually mean in our sternness and permissive in our kindness.

God Commands Kindness

parable: *a story that teaches a lesson*

In the **parable** of the unmerciful servant, a servant is unable to repay his master **ten thousand talents** he owed him and begged for mercy. The master *"took pity on him, canceled the debt and let him go"* (Matthew 18:27).

ten thousand talents: *approximately twelve million dollars*

one hundred denarii: *about eighteen dollars*

Then the forgiven servant met one of his fellow servants who owed him **one hundred denarii** (see illustration, page 167). The forgiven servant refused to forgive the fellow servant and had him thrown in prison.

When the master of the servants heard what happened he said, *"You wicked servant . . . I canceled all that debt of yours because you begged me to. Shouldn't you have had mercy on your fellow servant just as I had on you?"* (Matthew 18:32–33). The servant was sent off to prison until he had paid the ten thousand talents. Jesus concluded his parable, *"This is how my heavenly Father will treat each of you unless you forgive your brother from your heart"* (Matthew 18:35).

accountable: *obligated*

Once we have learned the grace of kindness, we are **accountable** to distribute that same kindness to others. This is an unconditional condition in God's kingdom.

mystery: *an aspect of God's plan not revealed in the Old Testament*

> **Romans 11:25–27** I do not want you to be ignorant of this **mystery**, brothers, so that you may not be conceited: Israel has experienced a hardening in part until the full number of the Gentiles has come in. And so all Israel will be saved, as it is written: "The deliverer will come from Zion; he will turn godlessness away from Jacob. And this is my covenant with them when I take away their sins."

The Defeat Of Conceit

KEY POINT

With God nothing is impossible!

Paul wants the Gentiles to be knowledgeable of the *"mystery."* By *"mystery"* Paul is referring to the future salvation of the bulk of Israel. He wants the Gentile Christians to know this so they won't be conceited about their own part in God's plan. They did not

Denarius

One denarius, pictured here, was one day's wage for the average worker at the time Paul wrote Romans.

permanently replace the Jews as God's chosen people. They were not the be all and end all of God's activity throughout history. Paul says part of the reason Israel experienced a hardening was so the full number of Gentiles could enter God's kingdom. In other words, the Gentiles are on very shaky ground when they look down on hardened Israel because if it were not for Israel's hardening, many Gentiles would not have been saved!

Furthermore, Paul says when the full number of Gentiles are saved, Israel as a nation will be saved. This will happen at the return of Christ (*"when the deliverer will come from Zion"*). We do not need to interpret the passage to mean every living Jew will be saved at the return of Christ, only that Israel as a nation will turn to him.

Something to Ponder

Paul may have mentally compared Israel's future conversion to his own conversion. Paul was not converted until Christ appeared to him and confronted him with the question, *"Saul, Saul, why do you persecute me?"* To this very day the nation of Israel has not turned to Christ, and Paul knew two millenia ago that their conversion would not take place until Jesus came back. When at last Jesus does come back, Israel will likely have an experience that is comparable to that of Paul's encounter with Christ on the Damascus Road.

Romans 11:28–29 As far as the gospel is concerned, they are enemies on your account; but as far as election is concerned, they are loved on account of the patriarchs, for God's gifts and his call are irrevocable.

Beloved Enemies

Paul explains a two-sided truth to the Gentiles. He says the unbelieving Jews are God's enemies in the sense that they have rejected God's gift of righteousness by faith. God will use the Jews' unbelief to bring the *"full number of Gentiles"* into his kingdom.

On the other hand, Paul says God loves the unbelieving Israelites because ever since the faith of Abraham, Israel has been God's specially chosen people.

Paul insists that God's gifts and God's call are irrevocable. Nothing can defeat or even frustrate the promises of God. God promised that the sins of the nation of Israel would be taken away in Isaiah 59:20–21, and God always makes good on his promises.

Take It to Heart

God has not given up on the Jewish race *"on account of the patriarchs,"* which is to say that somehow there is a connection between the faith of the founders of Judaism and the Jews of today. This truth should remind us that the things we say and do, good or bad, have an effect on the generations that follow us. Children whose mothers and fathers make prayer a priority are more likely to pray themselves, children whose parents are abusive are more likely to be abusive later in life. This is simply the God-created order of things.

> **Romans 11:30–32** Just as you who were at one time disobedient to God have now received mercy as a result of their disobedience, so they too have now become disobedient in order that they too may now receive mercy as a result of God's mercy to you. For God has bound all men over to disobedience so that he may have mercy on them all.

The Pendulum Swings Both Ways

Paul reminds the Gentiles that they too were once disobedient. God used the disobedience of the Israelites to show mercy to the Gentiles. Many Gentiles left their disobedience to embrace God's mercy. Now it was the Jews who were in disobedience, and God would eventually use the mercy he showed to the Gentiles to bless Israel.

The emphasis here is on mercy, a word which appears four times in these three verses. Only God's mercy can save people. In chapter 9 Paul quoted God as saying, *"I will have mercy on whom I have mercy,"* implying that God will not have mercy on everyone. Here, Paul points out how *inclusive* God's mercy is by saying, *"For God has bound all men over to disobedience so that he may have mercy on them all."* It does not follow that God is obligated to save each and every person on the planet. It does follow, however, that God will show mercy to all groups of people. He will not show mercy to one race at the expense of another.

We also learn from this passage that to appreciate mercy, we must see it against the dark background of our disobedience, another word which appears four times in these three verses. We are tarnished with our sin, but God's mercy burns away our impurities and leaves us brilliant with his glory.

What Others are Saying:

James Montgomery Boice: Sin abounds! But it is precisely in that context and against that dark and tempestuous background that the mercy of God flashes forth like lightening.[9]

James R. Edwards: The Greek word for "bound over" means to "shut up" or "imprison" and is a close parallel of Galatians 3:22. Gaugler [another commentator] likens verse 32 to a master key which opens all the doors to Paul's gospel. . . . That may be an overstatement, but it certainly is the master key to Romans 9–11. What a breathtaking conclusion: God goes so far as to hand over *all* peoples to disobedience.[10]

Remember This . . .

God took the common thread that runs through all humanity—sin—and did something beautiful with it: *"For God has <u>bound all</u> men over to disobedience so that he may have mercy on them all."* In showing mercy to sinful people, God proves how superhuman he is.

☞ **GO TO:**

Romans 3:9–20 (bound all)

> **Romans 11:33–36** Oh, the depth of the riches of the wisdom and knowledge of God! How unsearchable his judgments, and his paths beyond tracing out! "Who has known the mind of the Lord? Or who has been his counselor? Who has ever given to God, that God should repay him?" For from him and through him and to him are all things. To him be the glory forever! Amen.

To God Be The Glory

Paul's understanding and explanation of God's righteous dealings with all humankind bring him to a new height of spiritual joy. He bursts forth in song, quoting from Isaiah 40:13 and Job 41:11! Paul's doxology expresses his bewilderment at the superiority of God. Specifically, Paul mentions the wisdom, knowledge, judgments, paths (or ways), and mind of God.

Paul also points out that God does not owe us anything because whatever we give God came from him. We can't even praise God without his assistance.

Take It to Heart

In our sinfulness and finiteness, it is often difficult to see and understand the wisdom of God: *"Oh, the depth of the riches of the wisdom and knowledge of God! How unsearchable his judgments, and his paths beyond tracing out!"* We cannot fully understand God's plan, but worship is a godly response when the glory of God reaches our hearts. Simple praise is a way to honor and adore our Savior. Blaise Pascal, a great servant of God in the seventeenth century, taught that what the mind cannot know the heart may know by other reasons.

God decides what to do without the assistance of counselors. It is impossible for us to lay hold of him. He is God, the only God, Father, Son, and Holy Spirit.

What Others are Saying:

James Montgomery Boice: The reason we do not see great periods of revival today is that the glory of God in all things has been largely forgotten by the contemporary church. It follows that we are not likely to see revival again until the truths that exalt and glorify God in salvation are recovered. Surely we cannot expect God to move among us greatly again until we can again truthfully say, "To him [alone] be the glory forever! Amen."[11]

Study Questions

1. Why was Paul so concerned about Israel's rejection of God?
2. In Romans 11:7–10, what does Paul mean by *"a spirit of stupor"*?
3. Was Israel's fall permanent?
4. In Romans 11:25–32, what mystery is Paul seeking to explain?
5. How were the unbelieving Jews God's enemies and yet at the same time loved by God?
6. Against what should we see God's mercy and why?

- Paul explains that he was from the tribe of Benjamin and also a descendant of Abraham. He presents himself as Exhibit A, showing that God has not rejected his people. (Romans 11:1–2)

- A second matter that needs clarification is the remnant *"chosen by grace"*—those who believe in Jesus as the Messiah of God. (Romans 11:3–6)

- Israel's fall has opened the door for the Gentiles to enter into the kingdom of God. Paul calls this *"riches for the world"* and *"riches for the Gentiles."* As the apostle to the Gentiles, he is seeking to arouse his own people to envy, hoping to make some breakthrough in their hearts. (Romans 11:7–16)

- Paul presents an olive tree metaphor. The branches that were broken off made room for the Gentiles to be grafted in. But the fact that they were broken off portrays the unbelief of the Jews. This bothered Paul greatly. (Romans 11:17–24)

- Paul knows that we cannot have complete insight, but ignorance is not acceptable in the Christian community. When God gives, he doesn't turn back. His gifts and call are irrevocable. This speaks of God's faithfulness and mercy. (Romans 11:25–31)

- For Paul, worship is a result of careful study and a love for God. Paul's doxology is an expression of worship and praise. (Romans 11:33–36)

Part Five

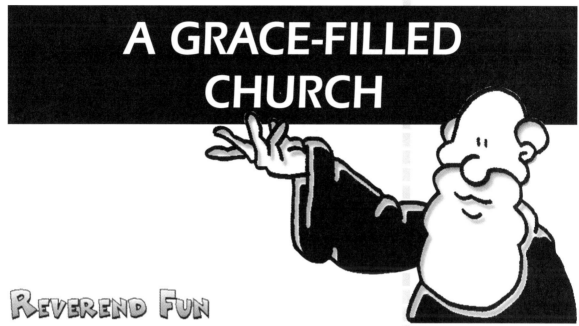

A GRACE-FILLED CHURCH

REVEREND FUN

"Pastor said all good gifts come from above, and I wanted to be sure that I catch mine."

ROMANS 12: HOW TO DO CHURCH

CHAPTER HIGHLIGHTS

- Living Sacrifice
- Mind Renewal
- Humility
- God-given Gifts
- Sincere Love

Let's Get Started

Now Paul changes the topic of discussion. He has spent the better part of the preceding chapters discussing how sinful humans can come into a right relationship with God. Having addressed this matter thoroughly, in chapter 12 he moves on to discuss how having a right relationship with God should affect our everyday lives, especially within our church community.

> **Romans 12:1** Therefore, I urge you, brothers, in view of God's mercy, to offer your bodies as living sacrifices, holy and pleasing to God—this is your spiritual act of worship.

Sacrifice Your Body

The use of *therefore* is the apostle's way of signaling a transition and an important summary of all that's gone before. You can find this same method used in Romans 3:20, 5:1, and 8:1.

The Temple in the Old Covenant was a building. In the church, the body of the believer is the Holy Spirit's temple. In the Old Covenant the blood of bulls, goats, and calves was the <u>sacrifice</u>, but under the blessing of the New Covenant, the <u>sacrificial blood</u> is Christ's. In the Old Covenant the priests handled the sacrifices and were permitted to enter the Holy of Holies only once a year (see illustration, page 176). In the New Covenant believers be-

☞ **GO TO:**

Leviticus 4:1–12; Hebrews 8; 1 Peter 2:4–10 (sacrifice)

Hebrews 9:14 (sacrificial blood)

Floor Plan of the Temple

This illustration shows the layout of the Temple. The High Priest could enter the Holy of Holies only once a year. Because of Christ, believers now have unrestricted access to God.

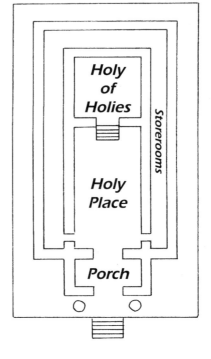

☞ **GO TO:**

Hebrews 4:14–16
(High Priest)

High Priest: *one who offered a sacrifice atoning for all sins*

priests: *represent God to others, communicate with God on behalf of themselves and others*

came priests with direct access to the Holy of Holies—God's presence—at all times.

Christians are believer-priests and are identified with Christ, our great **High Priest**. The church is a kingdom of **priests**—called, gifted, and sent into the world to serve the Savior. The priesthood is not an office that you attain by doing good works, going to seminary, or being ordained. Christ solemnly bestowed the title of priest on us when we accepted his blood as atonement for our sins. Our gifts will help determine how we exercise our priestly duties.

Old and New Covenants Compared and Contrasted

Old: *Old Covenant Priests:* human, imperfect, sinners, mortal
New: *New Covenant Priests:* human, redeemed, representing Christ our High Priest

Old: *Temple:* actual, physical building, God's presence in the Holy of Holies
New: *Temple:* believers' bodies, in which the Holy Spirit resides

Old: *Animal Sacrifices:* repeated, outward, reminder of sin; could not perfect sinner
New: *Jesus the Sacrifice:* brought once-for-all cleansing from sin for all who believe in God's Son

Old: *Who benefits?* A select group of people; called to be God's people of promise
New: *Who benefits?* Every tribe, tongue, people, nation . . . all people

Presenting our bodies as living sacrifices is an essential part of godly worship. There is nothing inherently evil about the human body. Our bodies are capable of sin or righteousness, evil or good. Because God created our bodies, we need to bring them under God's control. If our attitudes and actions are right, we become an offering *"pleasing to God."*

Remember This . . .

A. W. Tozer: We're here to be worshippers first and workers only second. God meant that a convert should learn to be a worshipper, and after that he can learn to be a worker. The work done by a worshipper will have eternity in it.[1]

What Others are Saying:

> **Romans 12:2** Do not conform any longer to the pattern of this world, but be transformed by the renewing of your <u>mind</u>. Then you will be able to test and approve what God's will is—his good, pleasing and perfect will.

☞ **GO TO:**

1 Peter 3:1–2;
   Philippians 4:7 (mind)

Mind Bath

We are either being **conformed** or transformed. God calls us to a life of transformation. A **transformed** life requires renewal of the mind. We ought to think differently as Christians than we thought as non-Christians. Often Paul writes about having the mind of Christ. We must begin to think about our circumstances and goals the way Christ would think about them. We must use a new perspective, a perspective that takes practice and self-discipline to develop.

conformed: *squeezed into the world's mold*

transformed: *changed from the inside out*

Robert Haldane: It is not the conduct merely, but the heart itself, of the Christian that is changed; and it is from the renewal of the mind that the conduct is also renewed.[2]

What Others are Saying:

Adolf Schlatter: The believer does not fall prey to the servitude of the body and does not draw his thinking and action from the wisdom of this world, but differs from the world because of a new character, and for this he is indebted to God's mercy that does not reckon his sins to his account.[3]

IN OTHER LETTERS

Paul said this to the Philippians about having a Christlike perspective: *"Your attitude should be the same as that of Christ Jesus: Who, being in very nature God, did not consider equality with God something to be grasped, but made himself nothing, taking the very nature of a servant, being made in human likeness. And being found in appearance as a man, he humbled himself and became obedient to death—even death on a cross!"* (See Philippians 2:5–8.) Renewing our minds so that we have the perspective of Christ is a matter of humbling ourselves to the extent that we become servants to those around us.

> **Romans 12:3–5** For by the grace given me I say to every one of you: Do not think of yourself more highly than you ought, but rather think of yourself with sober judgment, in accordance with the measure of faith God has given you. Just as each of us has one body with many members, and these members do not all have the same function, so in Christ we who are many form one body, and each member belongs to all the others.

The Body Shop

Paul was able to address issues that hindered the growth of the church. What he said was relevant to all believers.

Paul thought too highly of himself before he converted, which is one of the reasons he persecuted the church, but later he became aware of how destructive pride is. He exhorts believers to be sober in their judgments as an act of faithfulness to God. We are not to promote ourselves because to do so is to act out of our <u>sin nature</u>. When our sin nature drives our attitudes and actions we *"cannot please God"* (Romans 8:8).

☞ **GO TO:**

Romans 7:14–20
(sin nature)

Grabbed by Grace

The grace that Paul received was the gift of apostleship. This gift, in serving the kingdom and overseeing the church, gave him a godly authority that was unique to his calling. As members of the Body of Christ, we all serve different functions. We are not all called by God to be apostles. We all have different jobs to do.

The Christian body is a bit like an orchestra. Different

instruments play different notes, but all the sounds blend harmoniously into beautiful music. Imagine if the violins refused to play. The symphony would be missing an important melody. Similarly, if one group of believers within the Body of Christ refused to perform its function, the church would not work right. This is why Paul reminds his readers to think soberly and *"in accordance with the measure of faith God has given you."*

KEY POINT

Humility is not thinking little of yourself, but thinking nothing of yourself.

Philip Yancey: I see the confusion of politics and religion as one of the greatest barriers to grace. C. S. Lewis observed that almost all crimes of Christian history have come about when religion is confused with politics. Politics, which always runs by the rules of ungrace, allures us to trade away grace for power, a temptation the church has been unable to resist.[4]

What Others are Saying:

John Chrysostom: Paul addresses these words not to one group of people only but to everyone. The governor and the governed, the slave and the free, the ignorant and the wise, the woman and the man, the young and the old—all are included.[5]

> **Romans 12:6–8** We have different **gifts**, according to the grace given us. If a man's gift is prophesying, let him use it in proportion to his faith. If it is serving, let him serve; if it is teaching, let him teach; if it is encouraging, let him encourage; if it is contributing to the needs of others, let him give generously; if it is leadership, let him govern diligently; if it is showing mercy, let him do it cheerfully.

gifts: Holy Spirit–given abilities to minister to others

Spread The Wealth

Paul knows that gifts come from God to help Christians do ministry. He wants believers in Rome to be useful to each other, and he knows that right actions grow out of right attitudes.

Eugene Peterson's *The Message* renders the passage this way, "So since we find ourselves fashioned into all these excellently formed and marvelously functioning parts in Christ's body, let's just go ahead and be what we were made to be, without enviously or pridefully comparing ourselves with each other, or trying to be something we aren't.

"If you preach, just preach God's Message, nothing else; if you help, just help, don't take over; if you teach, stick to your teach-

☞ **GO TO:**

Ephesians 4:7–8, 11–16; 1 Corinthians 12:1–11 (gifts)

ing; if you give encouraging guidance, be careful that you don't get bossy; if you're put in charge, don't manipulate; if you're called to give aid to people in distress, keep your eyes open and be quick to respond; if you work with the disadvantaged, don't let yourself get irritated with them or depressed by them. Keep a smile on your face."

We will help each other most if we focus on whatever task God has set before us. We will become ineffective members of the body if we compare ourselves to other members or if we grumble about our role. God created us with certain gifts for certain jobs. Each job is absolutely crucial to our overall task of being Christ to the world.

Spiritual Gifts in Romans 12

Gifts	Paul's Admonition	The Gift's Effect
Prophesying (verse 6)	Do it in proportion to your faith.	People are built up.
Serving (verse 7)	Serve.	God's work is accomplished.
Teaching (verse 7)	Teach.	Spiritual growth occurs.
Encouraging (verse 8)	Encourage.	Emotional needs are met.
Contributing (verse 8)	Give generously.	Physical needs are met.
Leading (verse 8)	Govern diligently.	Things run in an orderly way.
Showing mercy (verse 8)	Do it cheerfully.	Burdens are borne thoughtfully.

What Others are Saying:

Larry Richards and Gib Martin: Paul urges believers to see themselves within the context of the body rather than as isolated individuals. "Don't think of yourselves more highly than you ought," he says. Instead believers are to see themselves as part of a body, to which they each contribute. . . . The focus is on relationships within the body, rather than on the relationships of individual believers or of the body to the larger community.[6]

Mark Driscoll: In the church community we discover that we belong to others, and that God has given each of His children gifts and abilities to be a means of grace to others. As we discover this gift and God's will for its use we then know how to glorify God.[7]

James R. Edwards: Some gifts appear to be natural talents strengthened by the Spirit, whereas others are unique abilities following conversion. They are and remain gifts, however. True to their name, they are spiritual endowments for ministry within Christ's body; they are not *our* possessions or status-builders.[8]

> **Romans 12:9–10a** Love must be sincere. Hate what is evil; cling to what is good. Be devoted to one another in brotherly love.

Love Will Keep Us Together

The apostle uses two forms of the word *love* to communicate his message, *agape* and *philadelphia*. Agape is used in 1 John 4:8: *"God is love [agape]."* It is also used in John 3:16, *"For God so loved the world that he gave his one and only Son."* This love is a description of God's attitude toward the human race.

Paul says *"Love [agape] must be sincere"* (Romans 12:9). In other words, if love is not sincere, it is not love.

The second word for love used in this text is *philadelphia*. It literally means, "love for man." It suggests tender affection. In Jesus' dialogue with Peter in John 21:15–17, we see these two words used in a context that helps us to understand the difference in their meaning. When Jesus asked Peter, "Do you love [*agape*] me?" Peter responded, "Yes, Lord, you know that I love [*phileo*] you." Peter used the more general word for love, expressing his affections; whereas, the Lord used *agape*, a love that is centered in the will, not in the emotions. God's love [*agape*] will produce emotional responses, but it is a love that goes beyond feelings. It is a love based on commitment. God is capable of loving the unlovely.

Christ within us makes our love real and complete. Due to the Fall, we are not inclined to be sincere. When our love is tested and life gets hard, we are likely to give up on a person and look for someone nicer to love. Paul says, "No way! Don't do that. Love like Christ loved—with complete commitment and brotherly feeling."

> **Romans 12:10b–13** Honor one another above yourselves. Never be lacking in zeal, but keep your spiritual fervor, serving the Lord. Be joyful in hope, patient in affliction, faithful in prayer. Share with God's people who are in need. Practice hospitality.

Be A Determined Disciple

Our love for one another is to be lived out as we see Christ expressed individually through Christians around us. It is not meant to be locked up between our ears as a mere concept or good idea. Love for fellow Christians is not based on how attractive or useful they are to us. It is based on the truth that because other Christians are now in a very real sense our family, we are obligated to look after them. We are to shoulder one another's burdens.

Paul says never to be lacking in zeal and to keep our spiritual fervor. What he means is don't let yourself get bored with Christ. Think of when Jesus called to Peter and Andrew in their fishing boat. There they were, going about their workaday business, when Jesus showed up and said, "Follow me." Peter and Andrew could have said, "Naw, we've got work to do, but thanks anyway," but they didn't. *"At once they left their nets and followed him"* (Matthew 4:20). Now Jesus is asking us to follow him. Will we stay in our boats or will we follow? Paul is saying, "Keep making the decision to follow Christ. Don't get lazy."

Take It to Heart

☞ **GO TO:**

Matthew 10:11
(sent them)

Hospitality means, literally, having a love for strangers, and practice means to pursue. So, Paul is telling his readers to pursue a love for strangers. Without hospitality, the spread of the Gospel during the days of the infant church would have been significantly hindered.

Jesus encouraged his disciples to depend on the kindness and hospitality of their countrymen when he <u>sent them</u> out on missions. Godly hospitality is a powerful way to build your spiritual walk.

What Others are Saying:

Dietrich Bonhoeffer: The first service that one owes to others in the fellowship consists in listening to them. Just as love to God begins with listening to His Word, so the beginning of love for the brethren is learning to listen to them. It is God's love for us that He not only gives us His Word but lends us His ear. So it is His work that we do for our brother when we learn to listen to him.[9]

Billy Graham: We fail to overcome temptation when we forget to trust the Lord or when we are too lazy or too proud to call on His strength. . . . The natural, easy, pleasing way is self-indulgence and moral softness. The hard way is self-denial and self-discipline, which incidentally, is commanded in the Word of God. We have too many soft Christians today! One of the best ways to overcome temptation is to keep busy for the Lord. Find something to do for Him. Seek to serve Him. Once you are willing, He will open innumerable doors of service for you.[10]

Charles R. Swindoll: Fortunately, grim, frowning, joyless saints in Scripture are conspicuous by their absence. Instead, the examples I find are of adventurous, risk-taking, enthusiastic, and authentic believers whose joy was contagious even in times of painful trial. Their vision was broad even when death drew near. Rules were few and changes were welcome. The contrast between then and now is staggering. The difference, I am convinced, is grace.[11]

What Others are Saying:

> **Romans 12:14** Bless those who persecute you; bless and do not curse.

Put Down Your Big Stick

Jesus said, *"Love your enemies and pray for those who persecute you"* (Matthew 5:44) and, *"If someone strikes you on one cheek, turn to him the other also"* (Luke 6:29a). Here, Paul is saying something very similar.

Persecution can come in many different forms. Someone may mock your values, laugh when you mention the name Jesus, or call you unintelligent for believing in God. The way to be a follower of Jesus when someone persecutes you is to respond with blessing. Our tendency is to get angry and to act out of that anger. We might yell at our persecutor or call him or her names. We might feel so wounded that all we can do is cry. We may even want to take up arms against our persecutors. Paul says to bless your persecutors. In other words, when someone shows hatred for you or God, respond by showing that person love. This is perhaps the most difficult part of Christian living.

Keep in mind Paul and his readers were living in a time of great <u>persecution</u>. James the son of Zebedee was beheaded by command of King **Herod**. At that same time, Peter was put into prison, all before the year A.D. 44 Andrew, Philip, and Jude all died through persecution in the years following the death of James. In A.D. 44 persecution under **Nero** was swift and massive. The blood of the martyrs stained the soil of the entire Roman Empire. We have no record of the final

☞ GO TO:

Acts 12:1–4
  (persecution)

Herod: *king of Judea,* A.D. *37–44*

Nero: *Nero Claudius Caesar, Roman emperor,* A.D. *37–68; notoriously cruel*

Something to Ponder

---

stages of Paul's trial in Rome, but we do know it ended in martyrdom in A.D. 67 or 68. Records indicate he died of decapitation.

 Meet Paul—Paul lived by the word that God wrote on his heart, and he died because of that word. He was free to live for God, and he was free to die for God. He had one motive: to glorify God.

> **Romans 12:15–16** Rejoice with those who rejoice; mourn with those who mourn. Live in harmony with one another. Do not be proud, but be willing to associate with people of low position. Do not be conceited.

Be An All-Around Companion

To rejoice with those who are being blessed is easy if we too are being blessed. When someone is rejoicing while we are going through a tough time, it is much more difficult to rejoice. Yet, the mature Christian can and will respond to Paul's admonition.

The other side of this spiritual theorem is also a challenge: *"mourn with those who mourn."* This is how Jesus loved. He did not run from people in grief. He wept with them. Think of Mary and Martha who were grieving over the loss of their dear brother, Lazarus. Jesus wept with them.

Jesus also associated with people of low position, as Paul encourages us to do. He called Matthew, for example, to be his disciple. Matthew was a tax collector, which in that culture meant that he was the lowest of the low, lower even than a prostitute. The reason for this was because as a tax collector, Matthew had turned on his own people (the Jews) to collect taxes for the Roman Empire and pocket some for himself. The Jews would have thought very little of Matthew, yet he became one of Jesus' biographers when he wrote the Book of Matthew.

All Together Now

This set of admonitions has that everyday kind of feeling about it. Living harmoniously with one another can be hard work; in fact, it *usually* is. It seems that our likes and dislikes are forever bumping into one another.

But the truth is, we need to seek to live in a way that our personality quirks and our personal oddities don't create tension and division in the fellowship. We should never seek to cause emotional trauma.

The word translated "harmony" is *phroneo,* and it means "to think, to be mindful of." It does away with unreasoned opinions. Leaders must treat opinions with grace, and at the same time test them against the facts and against the Word of God.

For the sake of godly harmony, if an opinion is not in accord with the truth, we need to disregard it, while seeking to walk with the one who espouses it.

> **Romans 12:17** Do not repay anyone evil for evil. Be careful to do what is right in the eyes of everybody.

Positive Charges For A Negative World

In this group of charges, Paul gives explicit counsel on how to face hostility and indifference. His instruction stems from a lifetime of studying God's Word and experience on the mission field. Paul never talked nonsense.

When we meet Jesus and his grace brings us under the shelter of his love, that is only the beginning point. **Sanctification** takes a lifetime. We bring our bad habits, our lack of understanding, and our lack of control with us when we join the community called church.

sanctification: becoming like Christ

Paul exhorts, *"Do not repay anyone evil for evil."* This admonition is obviously on the mark, but most of us are not ready to obey it in those early years of our spiritual journey. The Holy Spirit has to burn it on our souls so that a right response will happen when we are touched by evil and want to get revenge.

The apostle takes us a step further when he says, *"Be careful to do what is right in the eyes of everybody."* Someone once asked me, "Does everybody mean *everybody*? My wife? My neighbor? The guys I work with?"

I asked him what he thought. After a moment of silence, he responded, "It's not possible!"

I know only one person who has fulfilled this charge, and that is Jesus. But his fulfillment of this charge is sufficient, for Jesus gives us the wisdom, grace, and desire to seek this kind of righteousness.

> **Romans 12:18–21** If it is possible, as far as it depends on you, live at peace with everyone. Do not take revenge, my friends, but leave room for God's wrath, for it is written: "It is mine to avenge; I will repay," says the Lord. On the contrary: "If your enemy is hungry, feed him; if he is thirsty, give him something to drink. In doing this, you will heap burning coals on his head." Do not be overcome by evil, but overcome evil with good.

Your Right To Revenge Has Been Revoked

Paul knows what living in the world is like when he says, *"If it is possible, as far as it depends on you, live at peace with everyone"* (Romans 12:18). For peace to be a reality, all parties must want peace and seek it. We have watched the peace negotiations between Israel and Palestine over the past thirty years, and we have yet to see a real, lasting, secure peace. We don't have the power nor do we have divine permission to manipulate other people's motives or hearts. It took a divine work in our soul to bring us to the place where we have <u>peace</u> with God. We have to be patient while we wait for God to work in the hearts of others.

☞ **GO TO:**

Romans 5:1–2 (peace)

One of the great destroyers of the peace process at the human level is the spirit of revenge. Knowing this, the apostle concludes his instruction with a negative and a positive: (1) Don't take revenge, and (2) Be kind to your enemy.

Paul says that by showing kindness to our enemies, we will heap burning coals on their heads. What does he mean? Larry Richards writes, "Most suggest kindness induces a stinging sense of remorse in those whose actions merit punishment. It may be that remorse will only be felt on judgment day and unrequited kindness shown to the wicked and rejected will be the cause of even more severe judgment."[12]

Only God is qualified to avenge our enemies, though our feelings say otherwise. The cross is how God handled revenge. He took on man's sin as the only way to destroy the need for revenge. In so doing, he demonstrated how to overcome evil with good. The cost was tremendous, but the results are stupendous.

Revenge is a doctrine in several world religions. They have a perverted view of God, according to this text. But Jesus is our Savior and our model of righteousness. In the resurrection he literally overcame evil with good. Revenge is a doctrine of Satan, and that is exactly why we feel so strongly tempted to make things right in whatever fashion we might choose.

Something to Ponder

What Others are Saying:

James R. Edwards: God is not complacent in the face of evil, but his just wrath is of a wholly different character from human vengeance, which often and easily is fueled by self-interest, excess, and vindictiveness. The early church broke ground at this point, for in Judaism revenge was permissible against non-Israelites or in cases of personal injury. Paul categorically excludes revenge: Do not take revenge, my friends, but leave room for God's wrath (v. 29). "The anger of man does not work the righteousness of God" (James 1:20, RSV).[13]

Martin Luther: Do not be overcome by evil. That is, see to it that he who hurts you does not cause you to become evil like him and that his iniquity does not overcome your goodness. For he is the victor who changes another man to become like himself while he himself remains unchanged. But rather by your well-doing make him to become like you. Let your goodness overcome his wickedness and change him into you.[14]

Saint Augustine: The evil man who is overcome by good is set free, not from an exterior, foreign evil but from an interior, personal one, by which he is more grievously and ruinously laid waste than he would be by the inhumanity of an enemy from without.[15]

Study Questions

1. How is offering our bodies as living sacrifices an act of worship?
2. We are to be transformed by the renewal of our minds. How do the mind and the Spirit interact?
3. What is the meaning of Paul's statement in verse 3: "Do not think of yourself more highly than you ought"?
4. Paul lists seven key gifts that have been graciously given. What is the purpose of these gifts?
5. A key principle in this chapter is, "Love must be sincere" (Romans 12:9). How might you check the sincerity of your love for God and for your fellow man?

- God does not want animal sacrifices under the New Covenant. He wants us to be living sacrifices by following him daily. (Romans 12:1)

- Sin has marred our thoughts so we need to renew our minds in order to live transformed lives. (Romans 12:2)

- Humility is a character trait that both Jesus and Paul stress as essential if our service is to be useful to God. (Romans 12:3)

- Gifts are an important part of God's plan to reach the world in Jesus' name. Paul lists seven essential gifts in the building of the church as a community. (Romans 12:4–8)

- Love must be sincere. God's love enables believers to walk in a world full of sinful people. We must not be overcome with evil. We must contend for the faith in such a manner that our opponents will have to respect our way of living and being. (Roman 12:9–21)

ROMANS 13: GOD AND COUNTRY

Let's Get Started

The situation between the church and the government was tense in Paul's day. How could the Roman Christians entrust themselves and their families to a government that persecuted them and denied them civil rights, and later had them executed simply for their allegiance to Jesus Christ? How could this government be **ordained** by God?

ordained: established

Nevertheless, the church leaders consistently upheld the New Covenant teaching that civil authorities were ordained by God and had every right to exercise restraint on a person's body but not the soul.

Christians were to obey the law of the land, respect the civil authorities, and pay their taxes whether they agreed with the authorities or not. If secular rulers violated their own authority, it was the duty of Christians to testify to the truth, but only by using peaceful means.

Undergirding the New Covenant teaching is the knowledge that God is in control and that we should respect the government whether we like it or not. In Proverbs 8:15–16 God says, *"By me kings reign and rulers make laws that are just; by me princes govern, and all nobles who rule on earth."* God is the final authority regardless of who sits in the authority seat on earth.

> **Romans 13:1** Everyone must submit himself to the governing authorities, for there is no authority except that which God has established. The authorities that exist have been established by God.

President Of The Universe

Paul talked a lot about how to be righteous before God in Romans 1–12 and about how to live out that righteousness in different areas of one's life on earth. The believer's relationship to the government, or state, is one of those areas. In chapter 13 Paul talks about how Christians should conduct themselves in relation to a government that often contradicts God's nature and values. God doesn't want the rotten barrel to spoil the good apples, but his preservation plan is not what we might expect.

We must remember the historical context of the Roman people. Jews had been kicked out of Rome by Claudius and had only recently been allowed to reenter when Paul wrote his letter. The Jewish Christians who returned might very well have felt hostility for the Roman government because of the way they had been treated previously.

Paul's words are unswerving. Those in authority are under God's sovereign control, whether they realize it or not. God gives the authorities that exist, Christian or non-Christian, permission to rule. There is no authority, regardless of how it seems, except that which God has established.

In God We Trust

In the United States and Canada we've enjoyed decades of unparalleled freedom and prosperity. Generally speaking, government has been our friend, not our foe. We've had our civil rights protected and our conservative values upheld in the halls of government and in our justice system. We can worship God according to our conscience and in full submission to his Word.

The apostle lived in a very different culture than we do today. Being disciples of the God whom they addressed as Creator and Lord placed believers in harm's way even if they were Roman citizens, as was the apostle Paul. Paul had nothing to benefit from promoting submission to governmental authority, but it was the will of God. Therefore he took his stand.

Times for us are changing, and the foes of God's Word are beginning to gain ground in our schools, universities, and government. Evil men and women have weaseled their way into places of power. Fortunately the press has not been blind to the consequences of America's shift in values and the social decay of recent times.

Today, lead stories in newspapers and news magazines are asking what has gone wrong in America. They regularly point out the destructive permissiveness of society, people's failure to demonstrate common decency, and the large-scale invasion of greed, just to mention a few. You don't have to be Christian to admit that the moral health of our society is declining.

Take It to Heart

One thing that contributes to our society's moral decline is that Christians are not communicating the Gospel as much or as clearly as they should be. This is at least partly because Christians are confused by the counter-scriptural declarations dominant within our culture that "there is no right or wrong" and "humans are basically good."

Our response should not be to run and hide or to wait quietly until it all goes away. Rather, we need to know the truth and communicate it in love. The Scriptures tell us there is right and wrong. Every one of us has done wrong. We are therefore separated from God, and our only recourse is to confess our sin before God and ask him to forgive us on the basis of Christ's sacrifice.

Remember This . . .

The writer of Psalms struggled with submitting to the government because it was doing wrong. Examining what the psalmist said helps us to gain a biblical perspective about civil submission. The psalmist prayed, *"The kings of the earth take their stand and the rulers gather together against the Lord and against his Anointed One"* [Christ]. Then the psalmist heard God's answer: *"The One enthroned in heaven laughs; the Lord scoffs at them"* (Psalm 2:2, 4). The psalmist understood that God had nothing to fear from earthly government. He laughed at their puny attempts to fight against him. We need to realize the same thing. No matter how bad our governments are, no matter how much they go against God, God is not afraid of them. He will have the final word.

What Others are Saying:

Martin Luther: Thus the spirit of the believers cannot be or become subject to anyone, but is exalted with Christ in God, holding all things under its foot . . . the "soul" which is the same as man's spirit, insofar as it lives and works and is occupied with visible and temporal matters, ought to be "subject for the Lord's sake to every human institution" (1 Peter 2:13). For by this submission it is obedient to God and wills the same things that He wills; and thus through this subjection it is victorious over all these things.[1]

Everyone Means EVERYone

To understand Paul's sternness when he says, *"Everyone must submit himself to the governing authorities,"* we need to examine the word *everyone*. The Greek *pasa psucha* is best translated "every soul." "Everyone" is sometimes used in a broad way, which makes its meaning much less demanding. Paul was referring to each and every individual on earth.

Paul is explaining a spiritual law that we are all subject to in principle just as we are to the Ten Commandments. There is no authority except those that God ordains so to oppose a government when its laws are not in contradiction with God's law is equivalent to opposing God himself.

What Others are Saying:

James Montgomery Boice: The problem for us is not so much that God has established whatever rulers there may be. . . . The problem is that we are told that it is the duty of Christians to obey those who exercise such authority, and that includes *all* authorities, not just kings and presidents but also policemen, judges, schoolteachers, bosses, and other such "governing authorities."[2]

> **Romans 13:2–3** Consequently, he who rebels against the authority is rebelling against what God has instituted, and those who do so will bring judgment on themselves. For rulers hold no terror for those who do right, but for those who do wrong. Do you want to be free from fear of the one in authority? Then do what is right and he will commend you.

Rebel With A Cause

☞ **GO TO:**

Matthew 5:14 (lights)

What about Christians who rebel against the authority? We are in the world to shine as <u>lights</u>. When we disobey the rules of our society, we are punished. That too is God's sovereign will! Our freedom in Christ does not free us from society's laws and if we break them, from traffic tickets to prison, we will feel the consequences.

In a democracy or a republic we have certain power through the ballot box, but once the ballot is cast and the tally is in, we still must live under the appointed authorities.

The apostle follows up his teaching on rejecting authority with a forthright statement: *"Do you want to be free from fear of the one in authority? Then do what is right and he will commend you."* He means, for example, "Do you wish not to worry when you see a policeman in an unmarked car? Well, drive the speed limit, stop at all the stop signs, and you won't have to be afraid of getting a ticket. You might even receive a compliment for good driving."

To Obey Or Not To Obey

There are two ways that a person upholds the law. One way is by obeying it. The other way is to disobey the law when it is unjust, but to accept the consequences. In both ways a person upholds the law.

Martin Luther King was willing to go to jail for his civil disobedience and in going to jail he upheld the law. Some people dodged the draft in the Vietnam era and fled to Canada. In fleeing to Canada they did not uphold the law. They were willing to disobey the law, but they were not willing to accept the consequences for doing so.

> Whenever we have to decide whether or not to obey a law of man that contradicts a law of God, we must have faith. It is our duty to speak out against injustices done by our government and our bosses, but we will likely face consequences.

Take It to Heart

What Others are Saying:

Pelagius: The ruler is set up by God to judge with righteousness, so that sinners might have reason to be afraid should they sin.[3]

James R. Edwards: Paul thus approached the relation of church and state not as a **Sadducee** who lived from the advantages of the state, nor as a **Zealot** who lived to overthrow the state, nor as a **Pharisee** who divorced religion from the state, nor as a Roman citizen for whom the state was an end in itself. Paul wrote as a free man in Christ, and he appeals to the church to be equally free in obedience to the state, but not conformed to it.[4]

John Calvin: "Render then to all what is due" . . . Now this passage confirms what I have already said—that we ought to obey kings and governors, whoever they may be, not because we are constrained, but because it is a service acceptable to God; for he will have them not only to be feared, but also honoured by a voluntary respect.[5]

Sadducee: *first-century liberal, religious, political party*

Zealot: *first-century religious, political party that called for armed rebellion against Rome*

Pharisee: *first-century religious, political party that called for strict observance of OT law*

Good Government

Paul says the function of government is to be God's agent for good in that government provides a rule of law that guards against **anarchy** and the excesses associated with it. Even bad governments protect its citizens to some extent from injustices like murder and robbery. Even bad governments provide roads and streetlights.

By implication Paul is saying that if a government is truly evil, it is bound to fall. If a government fails to maintain order and respect its citizens to the extent that uncontainable masses of people turn against that government, the only possible outcome is that the government will fall.

Two examples of governments that fell are that of German leader Adolf Hitler and Chilean President Augusto Pinochet. Hitler's government fell because of external pressure, while Pinochet's government caved in on itself because of internal pressure. Both governments were too evil to sustain themselves.

Count On Consequences

When Paul says the government *"bear[s] the sword,"* what he means is that the government has the power to coerce people to do things. Governments coerce behavior in many different ways, from creating laws to imposing taxes to using police force.

Paul is addressing the moral consequences that are linked with the issue of authority. He gives two reasons why we should obey authority: to avoid punishment and because our conscience demands it.

The responsibilities associated with authority move in both directions, from subjects to their authorities and from authorities to their subjects. In a family children are under the authority of their parents from day one, but parents are ultimately subject to the Lord's authority. Paul told parents in his letter to the Ephesians, *"Fathers, do not exasperate your children; instead, bring them up in the training and instruction of the Lord"* (Ephesians 6:4).

In the business world owners have the responsibility of overseeing the work of employees, to treat them with respect, to create safe work conditions, and to pay them fairly for their service. On the other hand the employees are responsible to God to give a day's work for a day's pay.

In the political realm those who are appointed or elected into office are to be genuinely concerned with the lives of the people they are called to serve, showing compassion and acting in good faith. Those of us who live under their authority are to show respect and honor, even when we disagree with a particular political philosophy. Paul points out that we should pay our taxes.

Did Jesus Pay His Taxes?

Jesus showed respect for the government of his day when he answered the question, *"Is it right to pay taxes to Caesar or not?"* (Matthew 22:17). Jesus knew his questioners were trying to trick him and charge him with **insurrection** so he asked to see one of the coins used to pay taxes. There was an inscription of Caesar on the coin (see illustration below). Jesus said to his questioners, *"Give to Caesar what is Caesar's, and to God what is God's"* (Matthew 22:21). Jesus' submission to civil authorities, concerning money or death on a cross, was perfect.

insurrection: *rebellion against established authority*

Coins, Then and Now

Coins inscribed with important figures have remained much the same for centuries. The silver coin used in Jesus' time featured the portrait of Augustus Caesar, the first emperor of Rome. An American quarter shows the head of George Washington, the nation's first president.

What Others are Saying:

unequivocally: *without doubt*

doctrinaire: *person who tries to put abstract theory into effect without regard for practical problems*

impediment: *hindrance, roadblock*

debt: *obligation*

Ravi Zacharias: How do you come to terms with what the human nature essentially is? Jesus taught **unequivocally** that the self-will within each life, which seeks absolute autonomy and bends to no higher law than one of its own, is in rebellion of the highest order, inevitably descending to the lowest level of indignity and indecency. No good can come if the will is wrong. This teaching of Jesus is often dismissed as **doctrinaire** and as an **impediment** to human creativity. Yet in the proverbial wisdom of every culture it is sustained and proven again and again.[6]

Billy Graham: Every Christian in every nation—totalitarian, democratic, or somewhere in between—decides daily to be loyal to Christ and the kingdom He is building or to give in to this age and its values.[7]

> **Romans 13:7–10** Give everyone what you owe him: If you owe taxes, pay taxes; if revenue, then revenue; if respect, then respect; if honor, then honor. Let no **debt** remain outstanding, except the continuing debt to love one another, for he who loves his fellowman has fulfilled the law. The commandments, "Do not commit adultery," "Do not murder," "Do not steal," "Do not covet," and whatever other commandment there may be, are summed up in this one rule: "Love your neighbor as yourself." Love does no harm to its neighbor. Therefore love is the fulfillment of the law.

Won't You Be My Neighbor?

Thus far, Paul's main admonition is, *"Give everyone what you owe him."* Owe nothing to anyone. Make sure you meet all your obligations. The only exception is our debt of love that we owe one another. We are never paid up on our debt of love. Every day we go deeper and deeper in debt on that account.

Paul says, *"he who loves his fellowman has fulfilled the law."* In other words, by loving we fulfill *"the righteous requirements of the law"* (Romans 8:4). We do this not by striving after the law but by doing what the Holy Spirit prompts us to do.

Paul sums up all of the commandments that are about relating to others with one principle: *"Love your neighbor as yourself."* The Greek for *"neighbor"* here is derived from "one who is near." In other words, we should not decide who our neighbor is on the basis of race, socioeconomic status, or political affiliation. Our neighbors are those who are near to us—our families, our friends, people at church, our coworkers, the person who rings up our groceries, and the people who live with us in our city or town.

Take It to Heart

"Give everyone what you owe him" is a universal spiritual law. As Christians, it's our duty to do this. Paul isn't just talking about books or money you borrowed and forgot to return or repay, although these are important. We owe more than just money and things. It is our debt to bring Christ to the world. It is our debt to be loving to our neighbors.

Sometimes we may be unaware of our debts to others. Ask God to reveal to you what you owe and to whom. When he does, waste no time in reconciling those debts. No matter what kind of debt is in question, the best thing a debtor can do is repay the debt as soon as possible.

When we are told to love our neighbor as ourselves, we discover the burden of God's heart. He is asking us to do as he is doing. The debt of love is unqualified, and it grants no exceptions. The Greek word for *love* in this context is *agape*. This isn't an abstract concept. *Agape* love seeks out people who are ready to receive love. Just as God searches for and finds us so that he may show love to us, we are to do the same with people around us.

Something to Ponder

Real love rarely happens without conscious effort. Ask yourself how you might show love to those around you. An unexpected card or gift can work wonders. Maybe you need to sit down and have a long talk with someone you've been in conflict with. Think carefully how those around you would best feel loved by you, and then take action. Those who actively love often receive far more than what they give.

Take It to Heart

Origen: In many cases debt is equivalent to sin. Paul therefore wants us to owe nothing on account of sin and to steer clear of debts of this kind, retaining only the debt which springs from love, which we ought to be repaying every day.[8]

What Others are Saying:

Saint Augustine: This law [love your neighbor as yourself] is not written on tables of stone but is shed abroad in our hearts through the Holy Spirit who is given to us.[9]

Philip Yancey: Jesus said God is like a shepherd who leaves ninety-nine sheep inside the fence to hunt frantically for one stray. . . . God loves people not as a race or species, but rather just as you and I love them: one at a time. We *matter* to God. In a rare moment when he pulled back the curtain between the seen and the unseen worlds, Jesus said that angels rejoice when a single sinner repents. A solitary act on this speck of a planet reverberates throughout the cosmos.[10]

salvation: total deliverance when Jesus returns

> **Romans 13:11** And do this, understanding the present time. The hour has come for you to wake up from your slumber, because our **salvation** is nearer now than when we first believed.

Wake Up And Smell The Coffee

Paul tells the Roman Christians to love while on earth but to do so with the knowledge that the fulfillment of their salvation is always drawing closer. Christ was not afraid to touch lepers and dead people. His love within us compels us closer to people who do not know him. But as Christ's focus on following his Father put him at a distance from the degenerate world, so should our hope in God's promises keep us far from the temporary and self-destructive pleasures of the world.

Paul says the reason we need to be awake is, *"because our salvation is nearer now than when we first believed."* Salvation is pictured a number of ways in Scripture: (1) Salvation is that moment we are saved, when Jesus becomes our Savior and Lord, (2) salvation is progressively unfolding in our lives as we become more like Christ, and (3) salvation sometimes refers to the **final judgment** when there will be complete deliverance from all that pollutes and condemns (see GWPB, pages 181, 208).

Paul is saying be aware of who you are and what your mission is. Are you living a fruitful life while you're waiting for that heavenly moment? The apostle wants to make certain God's people are not lulled to sleep by the sweet talk of the world. None of us knows when our call home will come, but we do know the call will come. Paul is saying, "Be ready!" (see GWPB, pages 229–230).

☞ **GO TO:**

1 Corinthians 7:29–31;
1 Peter 4:7–10;
1 John 2:18 (nearer)

Revelation 20:11–15 (final judgment)

final judgment: last reward, or punishment, at history's end

While Paul is speaking to a particular people—the church in Rome—he's presenting a universal subject, a message for the whole church. When he says, *"the present time,"* he isn't referring to clock time, but to the interval between Christ's first and second comings (see GWPB, pages 180–182). When Paul calls the church to *"wake up from* [its] *slumber,"* he's asserting what must be our constant attitude if we are concerned about a faithful walk with God. We must <u>stay alert</u> and not be lured away from God by the petty indulgences of this world.

Remember This . . .

☞ **GO TO:**

Ephesians 5:14
(stay alert)

> **Romans 13:12–14** The night is nearly over; the day is almost here. So let us put aside the deeds of darkness and put on the armor of light. Let us behave decently, as in the daytime, not in orgies and drunkenness, not in sexual immorality and debauchery, not in dissension and jealousy. Rather, clothe yourselves with the Lord Jesus Christ, and do not think about how to gratify the desires of the sinful nature.

Move Over, Armani

Paul continues to expand his closing exhortation by using images of slumber and night. Both night and slumber are times when the mind becomes less active and we feel our weaknesses—tiredness, fatigue, fearfulness, weariness, dullness, indifference. We want to be left alone.

This imagery suggests vulnerability or evil, as in the time just before the Flood (see GWBI, pages 9–11). Jesus comments on this event saying, *"As it was in the days of Noah, so it will be at the coming of the Son of Man. For in the days before the flood, people were eating and drinking, marrying and giving in marriage, up to the day Noah entered the ark"* (Matthew 24:37–38; see GWPB, pages 11–12). The picture is one of people who are focused not on eternal matters but on matters of this world. Paul wants us to have eyes to see what is important for eternity.

God calls us to put away our nighttime clothing, to wear clothing fit for the day. Our behavior is to be appropriate to our calling. Listen carefully to God's call: *"So let us put aside the deeds of darkness and put on the armor of light. Let us behave decently, as in the daytime, not in orgies and drunkenness, not in sexual immorality and debauchery, not in dissension and jealousy."* This sounds like downtown San Francisco, Chicago, L.A., or any other metropolis around the world. Orgies, drugs, drunkenness, and debauchery were the scene in Paul's day, and they're the scene in our day too. Humanity hasn't improved, culture hasn't made things better, and the twenty-first century will surely repeat the errors and sins of the twenty centuries preceding it.

Paul's solution is for people to *"put on the armor of light."* This armor is an interior armor. He tells the church in Ephesus (see illustration, page 4) to *"put on the full armor of God, so that when the day of evil comes, you may be able to stand your ground"* (Ephesians 6:13). Light is a powerful metaphor throughout Scripture. Light scatters darkness. Light makes God's path visible. To put on the *"armor of light"* is to put on Jesus Christ.

Grabbed by Grace

debauchery: *extreme indulgence of one's appetites, leading one morally astray*

Instead of participating in the **debauchery** of this sick world, Paul says to *"clothe yourselves with the Lord Jesus Christ, and do not think about how to gratify the desires of the sinful nature."* By the grace of God we can do this. Christ works in the hearts of believers, scattering our darkness, healing our woundedness, putting up barricades against the evil one, inspiring the use of our gifts, strengthening our weak limbs, and preparing us for the battle on today's front, as well as for our journey home.

If our relationship with Jesus is truly honest, it will have the edge of adventure that keeps the mind directed toward righteousness and away from the lust of the flesh.

What Others are Saying:

John Calvin: Now to put on Christ, means here to be on every side fortified by the power of his Spirit, and be thereby prepared to discharge all the duties of holiness; for this is the image of God renewed in us, which is the only true ornament of the soul.[11]

Teacher: Jesus

Robert Benson: The culture we live in teaches us to get what we can, outsmart the other guy, vote for the folks who will protect our interests, buy everything that is not nailed down, and rent a storage facility if you cannot hold it all in the house you can barely afford. The **Teacher** calls us to give ourselves away, to stop worrying about tomorrow, to do good to the ones that hate us, to seek only the kingdom.[12]

Saint Augustine: Provision for the flesh is not to be condemned if it has to do with the needs of bodily health. But if it is a question of unnecessary delights or luxuries, a person who enjoys the delights of the flesh is rightly chastised. For in that case he makes provision for the desires of the flesh, and *he who sows in the flesh will reap corruption in the flesh.*[13]

Study Questions

1. Is submission to governing authorities necessary for everyone or just for some?
2. Identify five areas of your life in which you live under authority.
3. How can we free ourselves from the fear of those in authority?
4. How does conscience work against or with authority?
5. According to Paul's analysis, why do we pay taxes?
6. We are to leave no debt outstanding except the debt of love. What is the debt of love?
7. How does one put aside the deeds of darkness?

CHAPTER WRAP-UP

- It is sin if a believer fails to submit to the governing authorities. God has established the need and the rule of authority. (Romans 13:1)

- Fear of authority is unnecessary. If we do what is right, the authority will do right by us. God is the author of all authority and will be with us when we are tested. (Romans 13:2–7)

- God wants us to extend love to one another, giving witness to the love and grace of God, which makes salvation possible. (Romans 13:8–14)

ROMANS 14: KEEPING PEACE

Let's Get Started

Have you ever argued with fellow Christians about the right way to baptize people or about whether or not it's okay for Christians to smoke or drink alcohol? These and other issues have traditionally been referred to as "disputable matters," matters about which Christians disagree because Scripture does not speak decisively about them. Issues like adultery and theft are not disputable matters, of course, because Scripture is clear about such matters.

The disputable matters to which people pay attention may change throughout history, but the existence of disputable matters is nothing new. In chapter 14 Paul begins a discussion about the disputable matters of his own day. We do not know how much Paul knew about the inner workings of the Roman church so it is difficult to tell whether he is responding to information he had somehow gathered from the Roman church or if he is merely addressing issues that were what he considered generally important at the time. Regardless, Paul obviously thought the issues found in Romans 14 were worth discussion.

> **Romans 14:1** Accept him whose faith is weak, without passing judgment on disputable matters.

KEY POINT

The existence of disputable matters is nothing new.

Catch The Little Foxes

The person of weak faith in Paul's day was the person who thought that some foods were **unclean**. The weak believed, for example, it was wrong to eat meat that had been offered to idols. Paul says, "Accept that person." To "accept" in Greek literally means, "keep on taking to yourselves." We are responsible for maintaining fellowship with those who are weak of faith. Ungracious handling of disputable matters creates stress and disintegration in Christian communities.

Wise Solomon wrote, *"Catch for us the foxes, the little foxes that ruin the vineyards, our vineyards that are in bloom"* (Song of Songs 2:15). It was the little things, such as what one ate and how one observed special religious days, that created tension in the Body of Christ. Little things are the little foxes that keep the vineyard from bearing fruit for God's glory. These matters create much negative, useless discussion that causes division and grief.

> **Romans 14:2–3** One man's faith allows him to eat everything, but another man, whose faith is weak, eats only vegetables. The man who eats everything must not look down on him who does not, and the man who does not eat everything must not condemn the man who does, for God has accepted him.

In God's Kingdom, We're All The Same Height

We don't know all the details of the dispute, but Paul does give us enough of them to speculate. The believers in Rome may have been arguing about whether or not it was okay to eat meat that had been offered to idols (see illustration, page 205). If believers thought eating such meat was wrong and could not be certain that the meat sold at market had not been offered to idols, they may have become vegetarians. Jewish believers may have been concerned about whether or not they should continue to **eat kosher** foods. The Gentile believers may have believed Christians should live an ascetic lifestyle, becoming vegetarians and drinking only water. Paul commands each individual to follow his or her own conscience.

---

unclean: animals, which, according to Mosaic law, were unfit to eat

☞ **GO TO:**

Romans 15:7 (accept)

---

eat kosher: follow strict dietary rules, including not mixing meat and dairy items

☞ **GO TO:**

Exodus 23:19; 34:26;
  Leviticus 17
  (eat kosher)

Romans 14:4 Who are you to judge someone else's servant? To his own master he stands or falls. And he will stand, for the Lord is able to make him stand.

Mind Your Master

It's easy to judge others and look down on them as having weak faith. But Paul says, "Give it up! Let God be the judge. It's not your job to judge others. God has already accepted those people." When it comes to disputable matters, each individual is to be responsible to God, not to pastors, not to the pope, not to elders, not to boards, not to the general feeling of a congregation, not to anyone but God.

By careful control of our <u>thoughts</u>, we can help build a fellowship where judgment on *"disputable matters"* is under the control of the Holy Spirit. He gives us the grace necessary to nuture each other despite our differences.

Believers are at different levels of spiritual maturity. We come from diverse backgrounds that affect our attitudes and behaviors. One of the first lessons we need to learn in order to live harmoniously is to stop judging each other.

 GO TO:

2 Corinthians 10.5, 1 Corinthians 10:23–24 (thoughts)

Remember This . . .

Something to Ponder

Take It to Heart

judge: condemn

The Jews were used to following certain dietary laws of the Old Covenant that were no longer necessary when Christ came because Christ was the fulfillment of the law. The Jewish Christians had a difficult time making this transition, and the Gentiles needed to be sensitive.

Neither the one *"whose faith is weak"* nor the one *"who eats everything"* is free to condemn the other. Here is where Paul pulls the rug out from under both parties. God accepts both as long as neither pass judgment on the other (see GWHN, pages 151–157).

Paul asks the Roman believers, *"Who are you to **judge** someone else's servant?"* We all agree that it's silly for someone to give orders to another person's servant or household worker. And that's the point Paul is making. We are all servants of God and only God. He's our boss. When we try to tell others how to act in disputable matters, we are wrong. To act as a judge when it comes to disputable matters is to perform duties that belong to God alone. To do so is arrogant and sinful.

What Others are Saying:

Larry Richards: Actually, all of us differ from others in significant ways. We Christians have different opinions about what a believer should and shouldn't do. Some think women should be ordained; others violently disagree. . . . These differences tended then and now to divide believers into subgroups of "them" and "us." And all such antagonistic divisions are harmful to community! All distort the unity and ministry of Jesus' church.[1]

John Calvin: As you would act uncourteously, yea, and presumptuously among men, were you to bring another man's servant under your own rules, and try all his acts by the rule of your own will; so you assume too much, if you condemn anything in God's servant, because it does not please you; for it belongs not to you to prescribe to him what to do, and what not to do, nor is it necessary for him to live according to your law.[2]

> **Romans 14:5–8** One man considers one day more sacred than another; another man considers every day alike. Each one should be fully convinced in his own mind. He who regards one day as special, does so to the Lord. He who eats meat, eats to the Lord, for he

> gives thanks to God; and he who abstains, does so to the Lord and gives thanks to God. For none of us lives to himself alone and none of us dies to himself alone. If we live, we live to the Lord; and if we die, we die to the Lord. So, whether we live or die, we belong to the Lord.

Follow The Leader

Paul continues to explain how people of differing opinions or preferences can still live in harmony with one another. Paul knows how important it is to have harmonious relationships within the family of God. He knows that disunity is the surest way to destroy the work of God. Paul addresses sacred days and eating meat, the subjects that were important to his readers. He urges each person to seek God's will earnestly for himself or herself.

He tells them to learn to live with whatever they are fully convinced is true, but not to be the judge of those who disagree. God's grace freed Paul to accept the differences of fellow believers without doing violence to the Word of God. This was a lesson that both Jew and Gentile had to learn if harmony was to exist between them.

IN OTHER LETTERS To the Colossian church Paul wrote, *"Therefore*

do not let anyone judge you by what you eat or drink, or with regard to a religious festival, a New Moon celebration or a Sabbath day. These are a shadow of the things that were to come; the reality, however, is found in Christ" (Colossians 2:16–17). Here again we find Paul pointing to Christ, whose coming caused a shift from Old Covenant thinking to New Covenant thinking. If the Roman Christians were successful at making that shift, the result would be the apprehension of true righteousness and the defeat of worthless legalism.

When you are convinced that your own position on any given disputable matter is not in contradiction to the will of God, you are free to live out your faith, but this freedom is not without obligation.

As we grow in grace and in the knowledge of Christ, we will discover from time to time that we need to reevaluate our position. We need to be humble when such times come because we serve one who is infinite in love, knowledge, wisdom, and holiness. He demands growth.

Something to Ponder

William S. Plumer: We belong to God, our life and our death are ordered by him; we are accountable to him for the use we make of our liberty, in things uncommanded; and if we make a right use of that liberty, we do glorify God living or dying, and are the property of the Lord, not of one another.[3]

Peter Stuhlmacher: The mutual acceptance which Paul here commends thus has its model in Jesus' own conduct toward sinners . . . but the strong, who eat everything, as well as the weak, who renounce the consumption of meat, should both abstain from reacting toward one another with disdain or condemnation.[4]

> **Romans 14:9–12** For this very reason, Christ died and returned to life so that he might be the Lord of both the dead and the living. You, then, why do you judge your brother? Or why do you look down on your brother? For we will all stand before God's judgment seat. It is written: "'As surely as I live,' says the Lord, 'every knee will bow before me; every tongue will confess to God.'" So then, each of us will give an account of himself to God.

Who Are You To Judge?

Paul is still concerned with the spirit of judgment that exists in the assembly and continues to discuss it with them. He has let them know that both groups will answer to God in the coming day.

There is a huge difference between discerning what is right and wrong for oneself and imposing those standards on others. It is Christ's responsibility to be our <u>judge</u>. The Lord's death and resurrection makes him both the Lord of the dead and of the living. His qualifications are impeccable and eternal. Christ is God's measuring rod. Paul says to all Christians: How do you measure up? Are you really qualified to be a judge?

☞ **GO TO:**

James 4:11, 12 (judge)

IN OTHER LETTERS

Christ is the only person qualified to determine who is right and who is wrong in disputable matters. This is why Paul told the folks in Corinth, "*Therefore judge nothing before the appointed time; wait till the Lord comes. He will bring to light what is hidden in darkness and will expose the*

motives of men's hearts. At that time each will receive his praise from God" (1 Corinthians 4:5). Instead of using our ability to discern right from wrong on others, we should use it on ourselves, remembering that there will come a day when God will judge us.

Take It to Heart

We all need daily cleansing from the bad habit of judgmentalism, which surfaces in gossip, in harsh language, in disrespect, and in convenient hearsay. Paul concludes this passage, *"So then, each of us will give an account of himself to God."* Let us become accountable now, so on the judgment day we can give glory to God.

In becoming more accountable to him, God makes gracious provision for the changing of our hearts and minds. Here are some tips to keep you accountable:

1. Place yourself under the leadership of godly leaders who will disciple you.

2. Develop a relationship with two or three people who will hold you accountable. These are friends that walk with the Lord and keep **close accounts**.

close accounts: deal with sinful attitudes and actions quickly

3. Get into the habit of Bible reading; listen to the voice of the Holy Spirit.

4. Pray for ways to share your faith in Christ; stay humble and real.

5. Develop a regular habit of worship and praise where the Word is taught.

6. As you get your footing, reach out to others and build relationships.

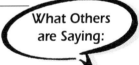

What Others are Saying:

John Chrysostom: It is not the law which will demand an account from us but Christ. You see how Paul has released us from the fear of the law.[5]

Charles R. Swindoll: What a wonderful future [and present] God has for people who accept grace. It is almost too good to be true. When George MacDonald, the great Scottish preacher, was talking with his son about the glories of the future, his little boy interrupted and said, "It seems too good to be true, Daddy.". . . "Nay, laddy, it is just so good it must be true!"[6]

> **Romans 14:13–14** Therefore let us stop passing judgment on one another. Instead, make up your mind not to put any stumbling block or obstacle in your brother's way. As one who is in the Lord Jesus, I am fully convinced that no food is unclean in itself. But if anyone regards something as unclean, then for him it is unclean.

You Are What You Eat

Paul uses the better part of what remains in this chapter to address the "strong" Christians—the Christians of Paul's time who believed no food was unclean. Paul is candid about his own position concerning the food issue. As a Jew, he confesses that he sees no food as unclean (see GWHN, pages 151–164). This places Paul among the "strong" believers, but the possible division that could result over food is far more important to Paul than bringing everyone around to his own way of thinking.

The question Christians need to ask is not, "Do I have freedom to do this?" but "If I do this, will I offend another brother or sister?"

Paul Roots For Reconciliation

Paul is determined to bring this clash between believers to a godly conclusion. There were two issues to confront:

1. They disagreed about what to eat.
2. They were passing judgment on one another.

Paul reasons with his readers. He exhorts them to think of each other.

The best solution was for both parties to lay down their swords and continue toward an enlightened dialogue. Sword wielding, if it continued, could lead to deeply felt divisions that lasted for years, if not forever.

Too often believers are driven by emotions rather than logic. In this case the emotions of Paul's readers were likely blocking the way to a real solution. Paul had to address their situation like a referee breaking up a hockey fight.

 Meet Paul—Paul was able to see the Romans' situation from at least three different angles.

1. He saw the difficulty the Jews were going through because he was a Jew himself and had for most of his life lived by the laws of the Old Covenant.

2. He saw the Gentile's temptation to look down on the Jews because he shared their belief that no food was unclean.

3. He saw the situation from a Christlike perspective because Paul's first loyalty was to God and God's kingdom.

What Others are Saying:

Stanley K. Stowers: The weak hold to false beliefs about things like food and special days that they would use as criteria for not accepting others in the community who act more in line with the boldness and freedom of Jesus' faithfulness. The strong are inclined to accept the weak only in order to attack their superstitious beliefs with rational arguments, acting like philosophers subjecting the foolish to therapy of the passions of reason.[7]

> **Romans 14:15** If your brother is distressed because of what you eat, you are no longer acting in love. Do not by your eating destroy your brother for whom Christ died.

Food Isn't Worth It

Paul tells the strong believers to forego their freedom in front of weak believers. Selfish insistence on freedom can destroy the spiritual development of others, and obviously the spiritual development of fellow Christians is more important than our own exercise of certain freedoms. Paul points out that the principle to follow is the principle of love. Let love make your decision about whether or not to eat meat or observe holy days. Let love guide your relationships with other Christians.

IN OTHER LETTERS In his second letter to the Corinthian church, Paul clearly speaks to this matter. He says God *"has made us competent as ministers of a new covenant—not of the letter but of the Spirit; for the letter kills, but the Spirit gives life"* (2 Corinthians 3:6). Arguments over disputable matters are hopelessly rooted in a strict adherence to the letter of the law, either an old law that tells people things like, "Don't eat these foods," or an invented law that tells people things like, "Because we are free to eat all foods, that freedom must never be sacrificed even if it brings ruin to the spiritual growth of a fellow Christian." Following the letter of a law, whether it be a new law or an invented one, ultimately brings death.

Kenneth L. Barker and John R. Kohlenberger III: Moreover, even if the strong do not try to convince the weak to change their habits, the practice of the strong can be a stumbling block to the weak, causing distress of soul. Such distress may contain a hint of something tragic, a sorrow of heart induced by following the example of the strong, only to find their consciences ablaze with rebuke and their lives out of fellowship with the Lord. In such a situation, love is not operating.[8]

Peter Stuhlmacher: The freedom of the strong to eat whatever they want can confuse the weak concerning faith in Christ, and this is precisely what ought not to happen in the body of Christ. In order not to offend one's (weak) fellow believers, it is imperative to renounce meat, wine (which has been dedicated to foreign gods . . .) and every other form of nourishment which to the weak can become a hindrance to their faith.[9]

Karl Barth: No triumphant freedom of conscience, no triumphant *faith to eat all things* justifies me, if, at the moment of my triumph, I have seated myself on the throne of God and am myself preparing *stumbling blocks and occasions of falling* instead of making room for God's action. Gone then are my faith and my freedom; and all my knowledge is as though I knew nothing.[10]

> **Romans 14:16** Do not allow what you consider good to be spoken of as evil.

From Good To Bad

The *"good"* spoken of here is the liberty to eat. Persisting in the exercise of one's freedom at the expense of the spiritual formation of others can result in our Christian freedom being *"spoken of as evil."* The word *evil* the apostle Paul uses is *blasphemeistho*, meaning "to blaspheme, to defame, to slander." This is one of the most serious charges in the New Testament.

If we allow that which we know to be good to be blasphemed because of our own stubborn hearts, we have committed a serious evil against God and one another.

> **Romans 14:17–18** For the kingdom of God is not a matter of eating and drinking, but of righteousness, peace and joy in the Holy Spirit, because anyone who serves Christ in this way is pleasing to God and approved by men.

Keep First Things First

The argument about what foods were appropriate and what days were more holy had become an obsession with destructive overtones. Paul brings the discussion to a higher level here. He's taking the focus off externals and zeroing in on what really matters in the kingdom of God.

"Righteousness, peace and joy" characterize the lives of those in whom Christ reigns. The Holy Spirit is always with believers, teaching them righteousness. The result is peace and joy, both of which are fruits of the Spirit.

The apostle directs them to higher and deeper levels of thought. Paul graciously reminds them of their kingdom and of what should be important to them.

What Others are Saying:

James R. Edwards: The reduction of the "kingdom of God" to "eating and drinking" is like playing a Mozart piano concerto with one finger. The reign of God confounds all attempts to reduce it to caricatures and formulas. These are human contrivances designed to serve human ends, but the gospel is a matter of serving Christ.[11]

Adolf Schlatter: But when fellowship results in the destruction of the other's life, there is no upbuilding. This eliminates food from the concerns that are important for the community, for the right to eat meat dare not give rise to an attack on God's work. The work of God is peace and the community's upbuilding. God's work is the individual who is able to believe. To motivate him to sin is to destroy God's work.[12]

Philip Yancey: What does a grace-full Christian look like? . . . The Christian life, I believe, does not primarily center on ethics or rules but rather involves a new way of seeing. I escape the force of spiritual "gravity" when I begin to see myself as a sinner who cannot please God by any method of self-improvement or self enlargement. Only then can I turn to God for outside help—for grace—and to my amazement I learn that a holy God already loves me despite my defects.[13]

> **Romans 14:19–21** Let us therefore make every effort to do what leads to peace and to mutual edification. Do not destroy the work of God for the sake of food. All food is clean, but it is wrong for a man to eat anything that causes someone else to stumble. It is better not to eat meat or drink wine or to do anything else that will cause your brother to fall.

Fostering Fellowship

upbuilding: nurturing, maturing

☞ **GO TO:**

Ephesians 4:11–16 (upbuilding)

Paul is concerned about the peace and **upbuilding** of all believers. His experience has taught him that fellowship is fragile. It takes time and effort to create an environment where fellowship can grow naturally, where the Holy Spirit is free to minister, and where trust abounds so that everyone is comfortable being themselves.

Paul directs his readers' thoughts to principles that could bring about the resolution of the problem. He says, "It's your job to do your best to bring peace and help build up other people" (Romans 14:19). It's our vocation as believer-priests to help each other grow in this holy faith.

Something to Ponder

☞ **GO TO:**

Psalm 34:14; Isaiah 26:3; Ephesians 2:14 (lasting peace)

One could take the word *peace* to mean a number of different things. In the '60s, peace was a state people achieved by going to Beatles concerts and doing lots of drugs. In our modern world, peace is a state of mutual tolerance—the result of a universal attitude that says, "I won't mess with you if don't mess with me." The peace of Christ, however, is quite different from these. The peace of Christ is the result of Christians actively pursuing the edification of other Christians. This is a much more profound, active, and lasting peace.

"*Mutual edification*" implies that the strong may learn something special from the weak, and the weak will be lifted in their spirits and renewed in their faith when they experience acceptance and love from their stronger brethren.

Liberty becomes a dangerous license when we refuse to show honor to our brothers and sisters in Christ. At times when we must make a decision about doing or not doing something, the Holy Spirit will whisper counsel to us. We must be quiet enough to listen.

> **Romans 14:22** So whatever you believe about these things keep between yourself and God. Blessed is the man who does not condemn himself by what he approves.

☞ **GO TO:**

Ephesians 5:13–18; Galatians 5:1 (liberty)

Paul's Beatitude

Chapter 14 ends with a word of clear instruction first for the strong, then for the weak. To the strong he says exercise freedoms associated with disputable matters in privacy. The strong are not to go around setting everyone straight.

Some things need to be kept between us and God. We are not required to go against our convictions if it is not a matter of sin, but we are not to flaunt our freedom either.

Consistency between one's beliefs and one's behavior falls in the area of conscience. When believers are free of condemnation in how they carry out their walk with God, Paul says they are *"blessed."*

KEY POINT

It is possible, by behavior that is contrary to the will of God, to *"destroy the work of God."*

> **Romans 14:23** But the man who has doubts is condemned if he eats, because his eating is not from faith; and everything that does not come from faith is sin.

From Faith

Verse 23 is for the weak. *"Faith"* should be understood here not as that which saves us from hell but as that which guides us in our daily walk with God. When we do something because we are confident that it is right and good, we are acting *"from faith."* When we are not confident about whether or not a certain behavior is right and we do it anyway, what we are doing is *"not from faith."* We ought to be certain that a behavior is right before participating in it.

"Doubt" in Greek means "to be without a way." It means a person does not have the resources to think a matter through. So

doubt is like a red flag. It is a warning, and we need to heed our consciences until we have time for further prayer and research.

Pelagius: What is good is our freedom, which we have in the Lord, so that everything is clean to us. We should not use our freedom in such a way that we appear to be living for the stomach and for feasts.[14]

William S. Plumer: It is not wise equally to press upon young converts and newly formed churches all the truths of Scripture. There is an order of divine instruction; milk for babes, strong meat for men. Let that order be observed. At all events, let us keep the unity of the Spirit in the bond of peace.[15]

Martin Luther: Here the apostle is speaking in a general way regarding faith . . . it is faith in God, faith in one's neighbor, faith in oneself. And by faith in God any person is made righteous, because he acknowledges that God is truthful, in whom he believes and puts his trust.[16]

Study Questions

1. What does the term *disputable matters* mean throughout Romans 14?
2. What does Paul mean when he talks about the strong and the weak believer?
3. According to Paul, judging a fellow believer is wrong. Why?
4. What should we do if we disagree over disputable matters?
5. How might some believers be stumbling blocks to other believers?
6. What does Paul mean when he says, *"Do not allow what you consider good to be spoken of as evil"* (Romans 14:16)?

CHAPTER WRAP-UP

- Acting as the judge of another in disputable matters is contrary to the Word of God. We are not to judge others when it comes to disputable matters. That is God's job. (Romans 14:1–3)
- God accepts both the weak and the strong and commands the strong not to look down on the brother who differs with him. Divergent behaviors exist in the Body of Christ. Whether it is food or drink, sacred days, or the eating of meat, we should all do as unto the Lord and not criticize those who disagree with us. (Romans 14:4–9)

- The strong ought not be a stumbling block to the weak. They should not practice their freedom at the expense of another's spiritual development. (Romans 14:10–18)

- Christians should remember that they are to be loyal to God, not their freedoms. God calls for whatever action will bring peace and mutual edification. (Romans 14:19–21)

- The strong are to be blessed by exercising their freedoms in private. The weak are to act as their consciences direct them. (Romans 14:22–23)

ROMANS 15: COME TOGETHER

CHAPTER HIGHLIGHTS

- Recipe for Unity
- Christ's Example
- Trailblazing
- Paul's Plans
- A Prayer Request

Let's Get Started

The theme of unity looms large in the early part of this chapter with parallel themes of encouragement and endurance. The apostle demonstrates that unity between the strong and the weak, between Jewish converts and Gentile converts, can be achieved in and through the Lord Jesus Christ.

There can be no unity as long as Christians cling to attitudes that cause tension. Paul reminds the Roman Christians that Jesus was one who chose not to go his own way, though he could have, but to serve those around him. Christ is our example for how to nurture unity and peace.

Paul also lifts up the Scriptures as a source of encouragement and hope for the believing community.

The last part of the chapter focuses on personal matters that Paul believes are of interest to the church in Rome.

> **Romans 15:1–2** We who are strong ought to bear with the failings of the weak and not to please ourselves. Each of us should please his neighbor for his good, to build him up.

Burden Bearing

Paul's use of *"we"* indicates again that he counted himself among "the strong." The strong are the ones with the ability to resolve the differences between themselves and the weak. It is up to them.

In one sentence the second verse of chapter 15 sums up a crucial precept for any body of believers. Paul is clear. Every Christian's life should be characterized by a refusal to be self-interested and a resolution to look after others in the fold.

Something to Ponder

If Christians were successful at doing what Paul says they should do in Romans 15:2, ponder the difference it would make in your church.

> **Romans 15:3** For even Christ did not please himself but, as it is written: "The insults of those who insult you have fallen on me."

Born To Serve

Paul's expression, *"for even Christ did not please himself,"* sets the tone for this section, if not for the whole chapter. Christ is our chief example. The phrase *"for even Christ"* reveals that Christ was the only one who had the right, the godly right, to please himself. His motive would have been absolutely pure if he had chosen to look out for himself, but Christ chose to look out for other people, who were fallen. He chose to respect their obvious limitations and their vast needs.

Paul's spirit had been touched by Jesus on the road to Damascus. In an instant he knew the heart of his Savior. Now having fellowshiped with and served the risen Lord faithfully for years, Paul reminds the troubled church that they needed to change their perspective and listen to Christ their leader.

Jesus preached, *"If anyone would come after me, he must deny himself and take up his cross and follow me"* (Matthew 16:24). (See GWLC2, page 10 for more about these words.) This is the spirit of the apostle's heart as we enter Romans 15.

Remember This . . .

Everyone wants to be considered strong. Boys flex their muscles to see who has bigger biceps. We play sports to see who has the stronger team. We want to be strong. We often fail to remember, however, that the strong have a responsibility to be leaders, to act as models, and to show compassion.

As a boy, I was often the last to be picked for baseball teams. No one picked me because I could never get a hit. As a member of the weak in the sport of baseball, I keenly felt the power of the strong. As I stood in front of the two captains and the boys who had already been picked, I knew that they had the power to accept or reject me. Rejection was not a fun feeling. Similarly in the spiritual realm, God has called upon the strong to bear the failings of the weak and not to reject them. Strength is a privilege, and with privilege comes responsibility.

Something to Ponder

If we live only *"to please ourselves,"* our lives will wither. Paul is not suggesting that personal pleasure is bad, but so often it's all people think about—the next meal, the next movie, the next trip to Europe, the next cruise, the next sports event.

There has to be room somewhere in our minds for Paul's direction: *"Each of us should please his neighbor for his good, to build him up."* Being selfish leaves no room for fellowship, prayer, or worship. Self-centeredness blinds us to the needs of others.

If we fail to love others, we will seriously hinder the growth of the Body of Christ.

When we please ourselves we do what comes naturally, but that is not the way of <u>Christ</u>. This is the first time in his letter that Paul uses Christ as an example. Earlier Paul refers to Jesus as our Lord and Savior, as the Son of God, and as Christ. Now Paul wants to focus on Jesus' behavior, not his lordship.

Take It to Heart

☞ **GO TO:**

1 Peter 2:18–21 (Christ)

John 8:29 (Father)

We say we believe in Christ, but we often live the way we want, which means we abandon Christ. By contrast Christ calls us to suffer with him. That's why Paul quotes from Psalm 69:9 saying, *"For even Christ did not please himself, but, as it is written: 'The insults of those who insult you [God] have fallen on me.'"*

Jesus went to great lengths to serve others. Despite insults, rejection, beatings, and death on the cross, Jesus remained focused on obeying his <u>Father</u> and acting for our good. We need to do the same. Make it your goal to give the world a daily glimpse of Jesus.

Matthew Henry: The self-denial of our Lord Jesus is the best argument against the selfishness of Christians. Christ pleased not himself. He did not consult his own worldly credit, ease, safety, nor pleasure; he emptied himself, and made himself of no reputation; and all this for our sakes, and to set us an example. His whole life was a self-denying, self-displeasing life.[1]

John Chrysostom: What Paul says is this: If you are strong, then let the weak test your strength.[2]

> **Romans 15:4** For everything that was written in the past was written to teach us, so that through endurance and the encouragement of the Scriptures we might have hope.

The Role Of The Scroll

To the apostle Paul, the Scriptures were authoritative. He did not take a mere Bible-as-literature approach to the Word of God. He discovered in them a source of wisdom, knowledge, encouragement, and hope.

The apostle's mind and heart were saturated with its truth. Paul's teaching flowed out of his study and research of the *"whole will of God"* (Acts 20:27), and out of his personal experience. What he shared was a careful presentation of the passions in his heart and life.

Meet Paul—A key to understanding Paul is understanding his conversion encounter with Christ on the **road to Damascus**. A bright light shone from heaven, temporarily blinding him, and Jesus' voice called to him from heaven, telling him to stop persecuting Christ. Paul's spiritual eyes were opened.

road to Damascus: road north from Jerusalem through Galilee

From that moment on God's grace guided his path. God used his years of professional study as a Pharisee in ways he never anticipated, and he discovered new meaning in the writings he had studied.

Remember, as a Pharisee, Paul showed violent hostility toward anyone, Jew or Gentile, who threatened to cause a breach in the **palisades of the Torah** given to safeguard and uphold his beloved nation Israel.

palisades of the Torah: protection of the law

After his conversion Paul saw the Scriptures not as containing theoretical or historical documents, but as a book filled with instructions from God, bringing encouragement and assurance to those who choose to follow Christ. Paul spent the rest of his days trying to pass this truth on to the world.

> **Romans 15:5–6** May the God who gives endurance and encouragement give you a spirit of unity among yourselves as you follow Christ Jesus, so that with one heart and mouth you may glorify the God and Father of our Lord Jesus Christ.

One Heart And Mouth

Having elevated the Scriptures to their holy purpose, one of Paul's greatest contributions to the historical faith, he now offers a prayer on behalf of the church that expresses Paul's desire for a spirit of oneness.

This prayer is authentication of Paul's personal experience with God. What God had given to the apostle he would surely give to others who believed. There is a constant need for hope, strength, and assurance in a world that leeches our human and spiritual potential. Knowing our daily need, God has given the Body of Christ a teacher and <u>counselor</u> in the person of the Holy Spirit.

☞ **GO TO:**

John 14:26; 15:26; Acts 1:4–5 (counselor)

When Paul says, *"so that with one heart and mouth you may glorify . . . God,"* he is not expressing a hope that all Christians will be exactly the same. Rather, he is expressing his hope that Christians will with all their different gifts and talents come together in a harmonious unity, like that of many instruments in an impressive orchestra.

Something to Ponder

What Others are Saying:

John Murray: They [Romans 15:5–6] are in the form of a wish addressed to men that God would accomplish in them the implied exhortation, an eloquent way of doing two things at the same time, exhorting men and prayer to God. Without the enabling grace of God exhortation will not bear fruit. Hence the combination. No form of exhortation is more effective in address to men than this.[3]

Henri Nouwen: The authority of Christ is an authority based on humility and obedience and received by experiencing the human condition in a deeper, broader, and wider way than any person ever did or ever will do.[4]

> **Romans 15:7** Accept one another, then, just as Christ accepted you, in order to bring praise to God.

As Christ, So You

☞ **GO TO:**

Romans 5:8; 1 John 3:16–18 (example of love)

Remember This . . .

Paul is not asking the Roman Christians to give anything more than what they themselves had received. They were recipients of Christ's unconditional love. Paul told them to show the same love to their fellow Christians. He hopes the message he has delivered will enable both the strong and the weak to put their differences behind them so they can follow the <u>example of love</u> set by Jesus.

It is good for us to reflect on all that we have received from Christ. We spit on Christ with our sins, and he accepted us. With our sins we slapped Christ in the face, and he turned to us his other cheek. Finally, our sins nailed Christ to the cross, and what did he do in response? He asked God to forgive us because we knew not what we were doing. Filled with such a bounty of love and forgiveness, have we any excuse for failing to show love and forgiveness to those around us?

> **Romans 15:8** For I tell you that Christ has become a servant of the Jews on behalf of God's truth, to confirm the promises made to the patriarchs.

A Model Of Servanthood

Paul begins to build on his discussion of the example of Christ by explaining that Christ was first and foremost a servant of the Jews. Jesus directed almost all of his earthly ministry toward the nation of Israel and limited the ministry of the original twelve disciples to their own people. This was to fulfill the promises made to the patriarchs.

Paul's words would have reminded the Gentiles not to look down on the Jews. Indeed, salvation was from the Jews!

> **Romans 15:9–12** So that the Gentiles may glorify God for his mercy, as it is written: "Therefore I will praise you among the Gentiles; I will sing hymns to your name." Again, it says, "Rejoice, O Gentiles, with his people." And again, "Praise the Lord, all you Gentiles, and sing praises to him, all you peoples." And again, Isaiah says, "The Root of Jesse will spring up, one who will arise to rule over the nations; the Gentiles will hope in him."

He's God Of The Gentiles Too

Having explained Christ's focus on the Jews, Paul is quick to point out that God always had the Gentiles in mind. He proves this point by quoting from three Old Testament passages that present the Gentiles as giving praise to a God who saved them.

Keep in mind the Gentile church was in its early stages. It began at **Pentecost**, and this letter was written only about twenty-two years later. A great deal of teaching and dialogue needed to take place so both the Jews and the Gentiles would appreciate what God had accomplished in sending Christ. With Christ two very different worlds were brought together. It's not surprising that the bulk of Paul's letter is an effort to iron out the wrinkles of a union that, before Christ, neither group dreamed possible.

Meet Paul—Paul's call to be an <u>apostle to the Gentiles</u> involved giving the Gentiles a solid theological foundation. If we think of the early church as a ship floating aimlessly on the waters of ignorance and youth, Paul's job was to steer the vessel on a straight course to knowledge about God and about God's relationship to humans.

Pentecost: during a Jewish celebration, the Holy Spirit came on believers, enabling them to speak foreign languages

☞ **GO TO:**

Acts 2:1–4 (Pentecost)

Acts 9:15; Romans 11:13; Galatians 1:16–17; 2:8; 2 Timothy 4:17 (apostle to the Gentiles)

Paul's Scripture Quotes

Verse in Romans	Title of Selection	Quoted from:	Words Quoted:	Expected Result:
Romans 15:9	A Song of David	2 Samuel 22:50	Praise among the nations; hymn to the name of God	Praise
Romans 15:10	The Song of Moses	Deuteronomy 32:43	Rejoice, O nations (Gentiles), with his people	Rejoice
Romans 15:11	Psalm of David	Psalm 117:1	Praise the Lord, all you nations (Gentiles), extol him	Extol
Romans 15:12	Isaiah: Song of Messiah	Isaiah 11:10	Root of Jesse will stand like a banner, the people of the nations will rally	Rally for action

The God who made a Covenant of Promise with Abraham is the same God who chose Mary and Joseph to parent the Christ child. They were the instruments God used to begin the New Covenant. God's love for the world stretches over all of time.

> **Romans 15:13** May the God of hope fill you with all joy and peace as you trust in him, so that you may overflow with hope by the power of the Holy Spirit.

Hope For All

All that God accomplished in sending the Messiah to the Jews was glorious in and of itself, but God had an additional purpose in mind. He was going to keep his <u>promise to Abraham</u> so that *all* the **nations** of the world would be blessed through him. This blessing would result in the Gentiles giving glory to God. The overflow of his mercy to the Gentile world would bring millions into his kingdom.

We should never trivialize or belittle our Jewish heritage. God has richly blessed the nations of the world because of his promises to Israel. We must always obey the Word and *"pray for the peace of Jerusalem"* (Psalm 122:6). God still has a <u>glorious day</u> in store for the nation of Israel.

Both Jews and Gentiles should be eternally grateful that God chose to love us by giving us the gift of his Son. This is why the apostle closes this section of his discussion with a brief, but appropriate, benediction. Paul wants his readers to feel joyful and peaceful. In this way the apostle closes his discussion of the conflict in Rome and is ready to move on to other matters.

nations: the world's Gentiles

☞ **GO TO:**

Genesis 12:1–3;
    Numbers 14:2; 15:7;
    Acts 7:1–8
    (promise to Abraham)

Zechariah 2:11–12;
    Matthew 25:32; Acts
    10:35 (nations)

Romans 11:25–27
    (glorious day)

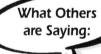

**What Others
are Saying:**

C. S. Lewis: "God is easy to please, but hard to satisfy" (George MacDonald). The practical upshot is this. On the one hand, God's demand for perfection need not discourage you in the least in your present attempt to be good, or even in your present failures. Each time you fall he will pick you up again. And He knows perfectly well that your own efforts are never going to bring you anywhere near perfection. On the other hand, you must realize from the outset that the goal towards which He is beginning to guide you is absolute perfection.[5]

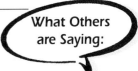
Elizabeth O'Connor: Everywhere we look there is need, and as we understand the Christian Church, this is the way it is always going to be. The church which ignores need, ignores Jesus. We are probably never so much aware of how weak we are as when we pray for each other in the membership of the church. We know the uprisings and the downsittings of one another well enough to make us aware . . . that the transcendent power belongs to God and not to us.[6]

Take It to Heart

When we are involved in one of life's battles, it's easy to become pessimistic, unhappy, and anxious. By remembering all Christ has done for us on the cross, we will get our minds back on the right track. The Holy Spirit can give us the power to hope when we have no strength.

> **Romans 15:14** I myself am convinced, my brothers, that you yourselves are full of goodness, complete in knowledge and competent to instruct one another.

Kudos!

Having finished his explanation for how the weak and the strong can live harmoniously, Paul now turns to encourage his readers. Much of what preceded this passage had to do with making right decisions so *"goodness"* is probably a reference to moral excellence here, but Paul doesn't stop there. He tells them he thinks they are *"complete in knowledge and competent to instruct one another."* Paul may have wanted to silence any doubts the relatively new converts had about whether they were wise or knowledgeable enough to continue their community. It would have been a big boost to hear the great apostle speak of them in this way.

Take It to Heart

While it's necessary to address problems that exist in a fellowship, we also need to appreciate the good things that are happening. We need to monitor the negative or it will devour whatever gets in its way.

> **Romans 15:15–16** I have written you quite boldly on some points, as if to remind you of them again, because of the grace God gave me to be a minister of Christ Jesus to the Gentiles with the priestly duty of proclaim-

> ing the gospel of God, so that the Gentiles might be-
> come an offering acceptable to God, sanctified by the
> Holy Spirit.

Just Doing My Job

Paul's letter is assertive and to the point. In this passage it sounds as though he wanted to prevent any hurt feelings on the part of his readers. He tells the Romans that though he has been bold in some places, he was bold only because being bold is part of his God-given calling as a minister to the Gentiles.

No doubt Paul hoped the Roman Christians would join him in his ardent pursuit to spread the good news of God's salvation through Christ.

Meet Paul—The apostle was not just the church's first theologian; he was a passionate missionary. He showed heartfelt concern for the feelings of others and was blessed with effective communication skills. We know this from his actions and words that we read in the Book of Acts, as well as in the fourteen books he authored in the New Testament. He was faithful to his calling and impressive in his giftedness.

Grabbed by Grace

priestly duty: *every believer is a priest and is on duty at all times*

Paul had received God's saving grace, and he was continually receiving God's grace to enable him to do the work God wanted him to do. Paul's **"*priestly duty*"** was to proclaim "*the gospel of God.*" Paul knew that for his ministry to be fruitful, he had to do his work in the power given to him by the Holy Spirit.

When Paul became a Christian, he understood for the first time that a person is saved by grace and not by works. Grace eliminated the need to work one's way to heaven. But Paul also saw his own sinfulness. He never claimed to be worthy of his high calling to minister to others. In fact, he called himself the chief of sinners.

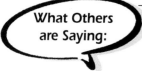

What Others are Saying:

Elizabeth O'Connor: We are seeking to bring people into the Christian community. . . which can mature them and bring them to a point of ministry; so that their belonging to the people of God takes precedence over every other loyalty, over every other group in which there is a belonging. This is how our time is to be spent, being the channel of God's grace to bring into being a corporate existence so that people can see the gospel concretized.[7]

Henri Nouwen: God's grace is indeed like a gentle morning dew and a soft rain that gives new life to barren soil. Images of gentleness. My call is indeed to become more and more sensitive to the morning dew and to open my soul to the rain so that my innermost self can bring forth the Savior.[8]

Saint Augustine: The Gentiles are offered to God as an acceptable sacrifice when they believe in Christ and are sanctified through the gospel.[9]

> **Romans 15:17–19** Therefore I glory in Christ Jesus in my service to God. I will not venture to speak of anything except what Christ has accomplished through me in leading the Gentiles to obey God by what I have said and done—by the power of signs and miracles, through the power of the Spirit. So from Jerusalem all the way around to Illyricum, I have fully proclaimed the gospel of Christ.

So The World May Know

Paul proved to be a useful servant for a very special reason. Professor James R. Edwards writes that both Paul's "usefulness to God and his greatness in history are due to the fact he did not confuse the servant of the mission with the Lord of the mission."[10]

It's hard to talk about your successes without drawing too much attention to yourself and giving too little glory to God. The apostle was aware of this problem and handled it carefully.

Paul acknowledged that all credit must go to Christ. It was Christ who called him, ordained him, and equipped him for the work of ministry. A true servant knows that every success is simply a manifestation of the grace of God.

Paul is a humble man. Real humility was destroyed when sin entered into man's experience. With godly humility removed, godly restraints on man's behavior were also removed. Man's appetite for self-fulfillment had no limits. Good things were taken to the extreme and man's unbridled pleasures destroyed him. So Paul's refusal to take credit was due to God living in and through him.

Philip Yancey: One who has been touched by grace will no longer look on those who stray as "those evil people" or "those poor people who need our help." Nor must we search for signs of "loveworthiness." Grace teaches us that God loves because of who God is, not because of who we are. Categories of worthiness do not apply.[11]

IN OTHER LETTERS Paul expresses the mystery of godliness this way: *"I have been crucified with Christ and I no longer live, but Christ lives in me. The life I live in the body, I live by faith in the Son of God"* (Galatians 2:20). The apostle shows that the believer's identity with Christ is the key to true spirituality. It is faith in Jesus as God's Son that opens our understanding and allows us to perceive God's work of grace in our lives.

Meet Paul—Paul's glory was in Christ and in him alone. Understanding this, he was now at liberty to share the rest of his experience as a servant of Christ. The Spirit had empowered him to accomplish much in the Gentile world. He used both signs and miracles.

The apostle's only tool was the Gospel of Jesus Christ. He had no programs, no balloons, and no door prizes. What he did was done through the grace of the Holy Spirit and the power of the Gospel. You recall in the beginning of this epistle that Paul demonstrated perfect confidence in the Gospel and wrote, *"For in the gospel a righteousness from God is revealed"* (Romans 1:17). This is all Paul had, and it is all he needed.

> **Romans 15:20–22** It has always been my ambition to preach the gospel where Christ was not known, so that I would not be building on someone else's foundation. Rather, as it is written: "Those who were not told about him will see, and those who have not heard will understand." This is why I have often been hindered from coming to you.

Trailblazer

The Gospel had transformed Paul, and he was confident it would transform others as well. The Spirit had placed in Paul's heart a desire to go to places where the Gospel had never been preached.

He wanted to be a trailblazer. He took his directive from Isaiah 52:15: *"For what they were not told, they will see, and what they have not heard, they will understand."*

It was because of Paul's commitment to bring the Gospel to new places that he hadn't made it to Rome yet. Paul explained to the believers in Rome that because he had been faithful to the mission God placed in his heart, he had *"often been hindered from coming to* [them].*"* Rather than being with them, he was preaching the Gospel to those who didn't know Christ.

Paul loved serving the Lord in spite of the <u>hardship and persecution</u> he endured. As the apostle to the Gentiles, he championed the first great missionary movement. His approach to evangelism and church planting has been studied by students and scholars ever since his writings were circulated. Many of his principles are used today by missionary organizations all over the world.

Elizabeth O'Connor: If we are to accept the challenge of the crisis of our times, we, as Christians, must know that the world's deepest need is for saints. These are people who can give themselves in ways that seem fanatical to those who live by the usual ethical and moral norms. These are people who live normally by the second mile. It is not sporadic with them. They have thrown the familiar "duty" maps away. They are utter fools for Christ's sake. They are always finding some cruel little cross to climb up on.[12]

> **Romans 15:23–27** But now that there is no more place for me to work in these regions, and since I have been longing for many years to see you, I plan to do so when I go to Spain. I hope to visit you while passing through and to have you assist me on my journey there, after I have enjoyed your company for a while. Now, however, I am on my way to Jerusalem in the service of the saints there. For Macedonia and Achaia were pleased to make a **contribution** for the poor among the saints in Jerusalem. They were pleased to do it, and indeed they owe it to them. For if the Gentiles have shared in the Jews' spiritual blessings, they owe it to the Jews to share with them their material blessings.

☞ **GO TO:**

2 Corinthians 4:7–18 (hardship and persecution)

Something to Ponder

What Others are Saying:

contribution: money gift

Leave The Light On For Me

Paul was a gifted, pioneer-spirited servant of Christ. He believed that he had worked in the regions of the two Antiochs, Cappadocia, Galatia, Phrygia, Achaia, and Macedonia as long as was spiritually profitable. His years of labor in these territories that lay south and west of the Black Sea represent a life well lived for the Lord.

It was now time for him to move on. The Spirit of God was urging Paul to complete a number of other missions, to take an offering to assist the poor *"among the saints in Jerusalem,"* and to travel to Rome where he would face the conclusion of his unique service to the church.

For many years Paul had wanted to visit the church in Rome. With a number of trained servants in place carrying out their ministerial duties faithfully, a trip to Rome now seemed possible. Of equal if not greater importance was Paul's burden for Spain, the frontier of the empire in the West. Spain was a Roman colony where many Jews had migrated. His heart was drawn both to his people and to a territory that did not have a Christian church.

Paul seeks the Roman believers' prayer support. He needs protection from the hostile, nonbelieving Jewish community. They had <u>forced</u> his departure from Jerusalem at an earlier time in his ministry. It is only *"by God's will"* that he hopes to go to Rome and *"be refreshed"* in the fellowship of these dear brethren.

Meet Paul—At this point in Paul's life and service he had been traveling for a long time with very little except his **scrolls and parchments**. His journey had begun with the martyrdom of <u>Stephen</u> in A.D. 36 when he consented to this young evangelist's death. A year later he was <u>converted</u> (see GWMB, pages 227–229). Paul's first missionary tour (see illustration, page 81) had been with **Barnabas**, sent out by the church at Antioch in A.D. 45–50.

Now some twenty years later, having completed two additional mission tours (see illustration, page 233), he is writing the church at Rome, presenting them with a major document on the foundations of the Gospel and an explanation of the relationship between Jew and Gentile in God's overall plan of redemption.

☞ **GO TO:**

Acts 9:26–30 (forced)

scrolls and parchments: papyrus copies of parts of the Old Testament

Barnabas: name means *"son of encouragement";* a Jewish Christian

☞ **GO TO:**

2 Timothy 4:9–18 (scrolls and parchments)

Acts 7:1–8:1 (Stephen)

Acts 9:1–15 (converted)

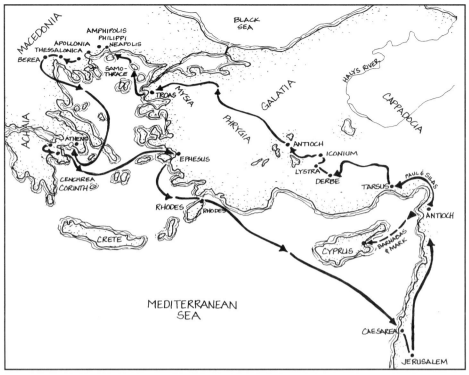

Paul's Second and Third Missionary Journeys

The top map shows the route of Paul's second missionary journey. The bottom map shows his third trip through the area. He covered a wide territory and established many groups of believers throughout his lifetime. Often, he traveled with companions, training them to follow his example in teachings and lifestyle.

Remember, Paul is writing this letter from Corinth. He could have made a trip from Corinth to Rome in a relatively short amount of time, but instead he explains, *"Now, however, I am on my way to Jerusalem in the service of the saints there."* The purpose of the Jerusalem trip? *"To make a contribution for the poor among the saints in Jerusalem."* Paul puts duty before pleasure.

The financial gift Paul refers to was a collection made during Paul's third missionary journey. Paul mentions the churches are pleased to address this need, but he also points out that the Gentiles owe it to the Jews to share with them their material blessings, because the Jews shared with the Gentiles their spiritual ones. Here is a wonderful example of the strong bearing the burdens of the weak.

Saint Jerome: Mark well the swiftness of the Word. It is not satisfied with the East but desires to speed to the West as well![13]

James Montgomery Boice: Some Christians act as if believers should sail through life on automatic pilot, expecting God to direct their lives in a supernatural way apart from any direct involvement from them. . . . Paul did not think like that. He was open to God's special guidance, as we learn from the accounts of his missionary journeys in Acts. He obeyed God's leading. But he also made plans, and one of those plans, which was quite important in his thinking, was to carry the gospel to the far corners of the known Roman world—to Spain.[14]

this fruit: the collection of money from the Gentile churches

> **Romans 15:28–29** So after I have completed this task and have made sure that they have received **this fruit**, I will go to Spain and visit you on the way. I know that when I come to you, I will come in the full measure of the blessing of Christ.

Looking Forward To It

"Work is work," Paul explained. He had to visit Jerusalem first, there was no getting around it, but as soon as his work was completed there, he would board the first ship to Rome. This is at least the third mention of his desire to visit the Roman believers. He knew that visiting them would be the occasion of one of Christ's more abundant blessings.

Like Paul, many of us long to do things that we know would enrich our lives extravagantly, but duty has a way of calling and often we must postpone the fulfillment of our heart's longings. Let's remember that God knows what we long for, and he is sovereign. The Lord of all will bring you the fulfillment of those longings, provided such would be the very best thing for you and the whole universe. Let us also remember that the final destination of our lives will be so glorious that no matter what we endure, all our suffering will seem like nothing in the end.

Take It to Heart

> **Romans 15:30–33** I urge you, brothers, by our Lord Jesus Christ and by the love of the Spirit, to join me in my struggle by praying to God for me. Pray that I may be rescued from the unbelievers in Judea and that my service in Jerusalem may be acceptable to the saints there, so that by God's will I may come to you with joy and together with you be refreshed. The God of peace be with you all. Amen.

Let Us Pray

Paul is realistic about the dangers he faces, but his obedience to the Spirit's leading must have kept his natural fears in check. He asks the Romans to pray for his safety from those who don't believe and that what he does in Jerusalem will go well with everyone. This is a wonderful example of courage and humility that is frequently apparent in Paul's writings.

From a purely human perspective, the events in Jerusalem went from bad to worse. In Acts 21–27 Luke offers a full account (see illustration, page 236). Paul was nearly beaten to death by an out-of-control <u>mob</u>. Then he languished for two years in a Caesarean jail, which may have been worse than the beating. Paul arrived in Rome not as a pioneer missionary, but as a prisoner of the Roman government.

Paul died in Rome during the latter years of Nero's reign, about A.D. 68 (see GWMB, pages 234–235). According to Scripture, Paul never experienced the sense of joy and intimacy with the Roman church that he longed for, but God's servant, Paul the apostle, was nevertheless <u>faithful</u> until the Lord called him home.

He closes the chapter with his third benediction: *"The God of peace be with you all. Amen."* Paul wishes that all the believers in Rome would live together in a spirit of peace.

☞ **GO TO:**

Acts 21:30 32 (mob)

Acts 28:30–31 (faithful)

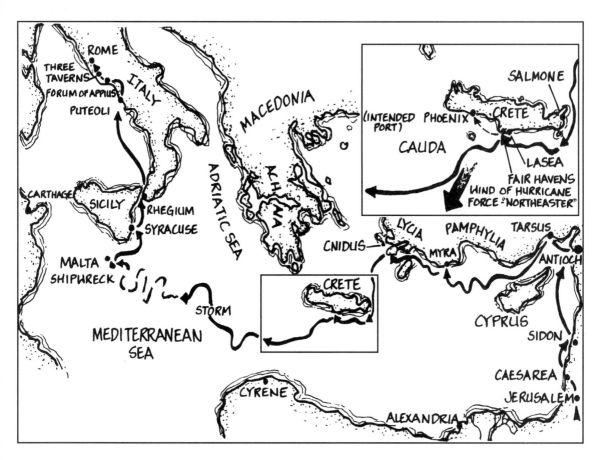

Paul's Final Journey

This map shows the route of Paul's last journey from his capture in Jerusalem to his imprisonment in Caesarea and his final imprisonment and death in Rome. The inset area shows where a storm blew the ship carrying Paul off course (Acts 27:7–28:1).

benedictions: *a blessing*

Take It to Heart

☞ **GO TO:**

Acts 15:5, 13, 33
(benedictions)

God intends for our lives to be **benedictions**, regardless of the trials and tests we are called to bear. The God of peace guided the path that his servant Paul walked. The same God will guide the paths of our lives if we, like Paul, *"offer [our] bodies as living sacrifices, holy and pleasing to God"* (Romans 12:1). Paul's life was so deeply touched by God that his benedictions overflowed with references to God's grace and love. Our gratitude to God ought to manifest itself in similar expressions of praise, in worship, and in communion with other believers.

Kenneth L. Barker and John R. Kohlenberger III: At the time of writing, Paul was aware of stubborn Jewish opposition to him and his work. The attempt on his life when he was about to leave Jerusalem (Acts 20:3) clearly shows that his apprehension was justified . . . so he requests prayer now, the kind involving wrestling before the throne of grace that the evil designs of other people may be thwarted (Ephesians 6:18–20).[15]

Theodoret of Cyr: Paul called God the *God of peace* here for a reason, because he was concerned about those at Rome who were battling one another or at least who were suspicious of one another. He wanted them to be at peace with each other because of the controversy which they were having over the observance of the law.[16]

Study Questions

1. Why should the strong bear the shortcomings of the weak? Whose is the example to follow?

2. The Gentiles were always a part of God's plan. How do the quotes from verses 9–12 prove this point?

3. Paul's guiding precept was, *"I glory in Christ Jesus in my service to God"* (verse 17). How did that help him to be a profitable servant?

4. Paul had a longing to visit Rome, but his trip there had to be postponed. What are some good things to keep in mind when it comes to the postponed fulfillment of deep longings?

5. Why did Paul say the Gentiles of Macedonia and Achaia owed an offering to the Jewish believers in Jerusalem?

CHAPTER WRAP-UP

- Unity is a significant part of the Gospel message. We are called to bear the burdens of the weak. (Romans 15:1–2)

- Christ Jesus is the way to perfect unity. We should follow the example of Christ. He will give us power to control our mouths and believe with our hearts. (Romans 15:3–6)

- If Christ could accept us while we were still in our sin, then we too must accept sinners in a like manner. Whether we are Jews or Gentiles, God's mercy has made a way for us. (Romans 15:7–13)

- Paul longs to visit Rome but must first journey to Jerusalem to deliver a relief offering to the poor there. (Romans 15:14–22)

- Paul commends the Romans and attributes the boldness of his letter to his calling as Christ's ambassador. He has been about the business of trailblazing for the sake of Christ. (Romans 15:23–29)

- In closing, Paul asked the Romans to pray for him, that he would persevere through the trials before him. (Romans 15:30–33)

ROMANS 16: A FOND FAREWELL

CHAPTER HIGHLIGHTS

- Commendation and Appreciation
- Greetings and Affirmations
- Affection and Ambassadorship
- A Gracious Warning
- Greetings from Friends
- A Concluding Doxology

Let's Get Started

Dr. Larry Richards writes, "In some circles it remains popular to portray Paul as a narrow, chauvinistic zealot, an ideologue more concerned with theology than with people. The image could hardly be more distorted . . . in fact, among the people Paul asked to be remembered to are many women—a rather strange thing if Paul were the confirmed chauvinist many suppose."[1]

It is beyond question. Paul loved *all* people enough that he diligently worked to bring them the truth of God, regardless of what that mission cost him.

Romans 16, the concluding chapter in Paul's Epistle to the Romans, allows the reader to see his heart. We observe these:

- A heart for the church as people
- An appreciation for believers as fellow servants
- A concern for protection from false teachings and teachers
- Skills as a master teacher
- An understanding of spiritual warfare
- An understanding of community in the Body of Christ
- Thankfulness to God, who establishes all believers in the truth

The apostle's grasp of **ecclesiology** was both multifaceted and deep, as his letters to the churches demonstrate. Though the church is complex, Paul believed her to be at the core an embodiment of

ecclesiology: theological doctrine of the church

people who belong to God and to one another. Therefore, the church was a mosaic made up of faces reconciled to God through Jesus Christ.

Paul greets people by name, acknowledging their giftedness and service in Christ's name. This was more than doctrinal theory to the apostle; it was reality. Paul had been shoulder to shoulder in the trenches with a number of these folks and, directly or indirectly, he knew each one. Together they had served the Lord Christ. Together they had worked to advance the Gospel.

Paul, their brother and friend, was immeasurably grateful for their prayers, their teamwork, and their fellowship. He highly valued each person. Each had become special to him, and he wanted them to be recognized and received by their brethren in Rome.

> **Romans 16:1–2** I commend to you our sister Phoebe, a **servant** of the church in Cenchrea. I ask you to receive her in the Lord in a way worthy of the saints and to give her any help she may need from you, for she has been a great help to many people, including me.

Meet Phoebe

The first on Paul's list of people to greet is a woman by the name of Phoebe, a Gentile Christian. She lived in Cenchrea, a little port town just southwest of Corinth. Since Paul wrote this letter from Corinth, most believe Phoebe was Paul's **emissary** to deliver the letter.

emissary: personal representative

deaconess: female officer in the church who cared for the needs of women

There is sufficient information to support the idea that Phoebe was accustomed to serving. She was a **deaconess** in her church in Cenchrea (see GWWB, page 283). Paul refers to her as *"sister"* and *"servant"* and asks the Roman believers to *"receive her in the Lord in a way worthy of the saints."* This is a woman of high standing. She has been *"a great help to many people, including me,"* concludes Paul (see WBFW, page 204).

☞ **GO TO:**

1 Peter 4:8–10
(hospitable)

Grabbed by Grace

Paul asked the church, the entire body, *"to receive her [Phoebe] in the Lord."* Just as we show honor and deference to the Lord, so he was asking the brethren to please exercise graciousness to this valuable servant of Christ. It was an appeal to be <u>hospitable</u>, a common grace among believers.

Once we have experienced Christ's kindness to us, we are to show the same to fellow believers. Our unity in Christ binds us all together.

> **Romans 16:3–5a** Greet Priscilla and Aquila, my fellow workers in Christ Jesus. They risked their lives for me. Not only I but all the churches of the Gentiles are grateful to them. Greet also the church that meets at their house.

Hi Priscilla And Aquila

Having introduced Phoebe, Paul turns his attention to greeting a number of old friends. First, he sends special greeting to <u>Priscilla and Aquila</u>, a couple who were fellow workers in the ministry of the Gospel. His friendship with them had been a long and appreciated relationship. They first met in Corinth where Paul teamed up with them. They were fellow tentmakers who had been driven out of Rome by Claudius in A.D. 49 when he expelled the Jews (see GWWB, pages 284).

Priscilla and Aquila, like Phoebe, were people of a deep, consistent faith. Paul tells the church in Rome *"all the churches of the Gentiles are grateful for them."*

Priscilla and Aquila also had a **house church** (see illustration, page 242). Paul wanted to send his greetings to all of the people that gathered there. This gives you a sense of Paul's love for the church. Paul had been involved in planting many fellowships of believers, but here was a church that had been started by his dear friends, a Jewish couple.

☞ **GO TO:**

Acts 18:1–4
    (Priscilla and Aquila)

house church: group of believers who gathered regularly in a home to worship

> **Romans 16:5b–7** Greet my dear friend Epenetus, who was the first convert to Christ in the province of Asia. Greet Mary, who worked very hard for you. Greet Andronicus and Junias, my relatives who have been in prison with me. They are outstanding among the apostles, and they were in Christ before I was.

Hi Y'all

Paul sends a special word of greeting to Mary, *"who [had] worked very hard"* for the Roman believers. Paul saw her work as significant. There are six persons known as Mary in the New Testament,

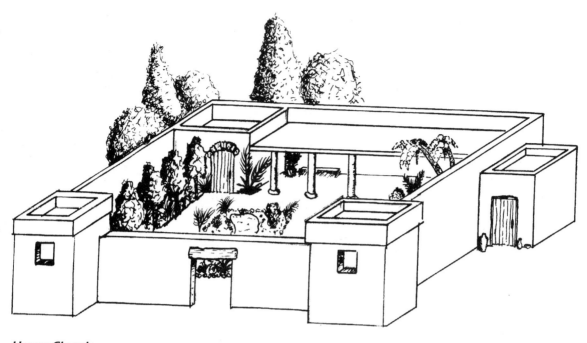

House Church

Priscilla and Aquila may have been wealthy and may have lived in a house such as this one with an inner courtyard suitable for holding large gatherings.

and this one is unknown apart from this text. But God knows who she is. And God knows each one of us—all of us whose names are *"written in the Lamb's book of life"* (Revelation 21:27). (For more about the Lamb's book of life, see GWRV, page 48.)

Four of the first seven names in Paul's list belong to women, and of the twenty-nine names in the total collection, one-third are women. This is evidence that Paul was not a chauvinist. In fact, he shows great respect for the women he knew and with whom he served.

relatives: *fellow countrymen*

Paul asks the believers in Rome to *"Greet Andronicus and Junias, my **relatives** who have been in prison with me."* Andronicus and Junias were another husband and wife team who were highly respected as leaders among the apostles. (Paul is using the word "apostles" here in the general sense, meaning "those who are sent," as with missionaries.) Since Adronicus and Junias were brought to Christ before Paul, it is likely they were among the Roman visitors who had come to Jerusalem and were a part of the Pentecost experience. To be well known by the apostles suggests they had spent time in Israel.

The Mary that Paul mentions serves as a reminder of God's grace in all who believe. For most of us, stardom comes after this life, not during it. And that was the case for this Mary too. She lived for Jesus. Paul was led to shine a spotlight on her efforts, and now her name and her hard work live on in the pages of Scripture.

Something to Ponder

What Others are Saying:

James Montgomery Boice: One fascinating thing about Romans 16 is what it reveals about Paul. Some have the idea that people who are interested in ideas—in this case those who study Christian theology—are not interested in people. They are supposed to immerse themselves in books. They are not "relational," as we say. There are people like this, of course. But Paul is a refutation of the idea that those who are interested in doctrine cannot be interested in those for whom the doctrine has been given.[2]

John Chrysostom: I think there are many, even some apparently good commentators, who hurry over this part of the epistle because they think it is superfluous and of little importance. They probably think much the same about the genealogies in the Gospels. Because it is a catalog of names, they think they can get nothing good out of it. People who mine gold are careful even about the smallest fragments, but these commentators ignore even huge bars of gold.[3]

> **Romans 16:8–12** Greet Ampliatus, whom I love in the Lord. Greet Urbanus, our fellow worker in Christ, and my dear friend Stachys. Greet Apelles, tested and approved in Christ. Greet those who belong to the household of Aristobulus. Greet Herodion, my relative. Greet those in the household of Narcissus who are in the Lord. Greet Tryphena and Tryphosa, those women who work hard in the Lord. Greet my dear friend Persis, another woman who has worked very hard in the Lord.

Good Job, Friends!

In this next group of people, Paul shifts gears from expressions of appreciation to expressions of affirmation. Paul expresses a personal attachment to Ampliatus, a converted Roman slave. Ampliatus as well as Urbanus are common slave names according to historical research.

Paul's expression of love to Ampliatus is a clear demonstration of how honest Paul was in his relationships. Paul was a man who was free in Christ to give himself to the people he served. We also see Paul was more intimate with some than with others, as was Jesus when he was on earth, and it wasn't a problem. It is never a problem when all parties are mature.

Urbanus had assisted the apostle sometime in the past and was also a blessing to others. Paul calls him *"our fellow worker in Christ."* Urbanus was no sloth.

Paul uses the loving expression *"my dear friend"* when mentioning Stachys. This suggests a bond of affection between them. Stachys was also a common slave name during that period of history. Paul had a special love for those who had a hard life in that pagan society.

Apelles was a fairly common name in the middle of the first century; it was even known among the imperial household. His name was common, but he was a man with an uncommon soul for God. Paul says Apelles was *"tested and approved in Christ."* This indicates what God takes note of in the lives of his children. God never overlooks righteousness.

The next group that Paul greets seems to be more distant, but not less important. Aristobulus is a name that was common among the **Herodian** dynasty. Paul's greeting is to the Christians within the household. Most things scholars say about Aristobulus are still conjecture, but the believers—most likely slaves—within the household were on Paul's heart and no doubt in his prayers.

Herodion was a Hebrew Christian. Beyond that we know nothing about him. Paul's greeting was surely brief, but Herodion was probably a distant relative. Paul may not have known him well. Once he remembered him, Paul felt compelled to mention his name.

It is suggested that those in the Narcissus household were probably the Christian slaves of the well-known Tiberius Claudius Narcissus, a wealthy **freeman** of the Roman Emperor Tiberius. We cannot be absolutely sure they are the same person. Nevertheless, Paul was concerned about those in this household who were believers.

It is significant to note that Paul greets three women—Tryphena, Tryphosa, and Persis—who *"worked hard"* (see GWWB, page 285). Paul knows that God honors hard work, and he wants to give honor to these dear sisters in Christ. In Romans 13:7, Paul says, *"Give everyone what you owe . . . if respect, then respect; if honor, then honor."* Paul is practicing what he preached.

Herodian: *relatives of King Herod the Great and his family*

freeman: *a former slave; took their patron's name*

Craig S. Keener: "Tryphaena" and "Tryphosa" are Greek names sometimes used by Jewish as well as Greek women. One scholar, noting that both names come from the same root meaning "delicate," thinks that Paul may be playing on their names ironically when he says they "labor hard."[4]

What Others are Saying:

Kenneth L. Barker and John R. Kohlenberger III: Similar in name Tryphena and Tryphosa [Romans 16:12] were likely sisters. It was not uncommon then, as now, to give daughters names with a certain resemblance. Since their names mean "dainty" and "delicate," their Christian convictions led them to put aside any tendency to live a life of ease. They are given an **accolade** for being hard workers in the Lord's cause.[5]

accolade: a sign of great respect, approval, or appreciation

> **Romans 16:13–16** Greet Rufus, chosen in the Lord, and his mother, who has been a mother to me, too. Greet Asyncritus, Phlegon, Hermes, Patrobas, Hermas and the brothers with them. Greet Philologus, Julia, Nereus and his sister, and Olympas and all the saints with them. Greet one another with a holy kiss. All the churches of Christ send greetings.

Say Hi To The Whole Gang

Paul continues his greetings. It's as if he wants to make certain he doesn't overlook anyone who has touched his life in a significant way. His love isn't self-promoting, but thoughtful, genuine, and Christ-oriented.

All of those whom Paul mentions are ambassadors for Christ. Their history is our history. They carried the flag in their generation. They fulfilled the admonitions of their teacher and friend, Paul, who taught: *"Love must be sincere. Hate what is evil; cling to what is good. Be devoted to one another in brotherly love. Honor one another above yourselves. Never be lacking in zeal, but keep your spiritual fervor, serving the Lord"* (Romans 12:9–11).

The church in Rome represented a number of house churches. There were many slaves finding their freedom in Jesus Christ, while still in bondage to the imperial authority. A few Christians came from nobility and the ruling classes, but the majority were the world's outcasts, and they grew and became healthy, profitable servants of the Lord.

Paul greets Asyncritus, Phlegon, Hermes, Patrobas, Hermas,

and the brothers with them; he greets Philologus, Julia, Nereus and his sister, and Olympas and all the saints with them. Paul concludes his greetings by telling them to *"Greet one another with a holy kiss."*

Kissing was a cultural act that signified acceptance and heartfelt brotherly love. As Paul suggests, a holy kiss is a formal, godly greeting.

Something to Ponder

☞ **GO TO:**

Mark 15:21
(in Jerusalem)

Paul says to *"Greet Rufus, chosen in the Lord, and his mother, who has been a mother to me, too."* A man with the name Rufus is reported to have been <u>in Jerusalem</u> on the day of the Lord's crucifixion. He was with his father, Simon, and his brother Alexander. They were a Jewish family from Cyrene, an important city of Libya in North Africa. They were in the Holy City celebrating the Passover.

Many theologians and historians believe that this Rufus in Romans 16 is likely to have been the young lad that was in Jerusalem on that fateful day. The expression, *"chosen in the Lord,"* surely lends itself to this speculation.

When Paul thinks of Rufus, he is also reminded of his mother, who has a special place in his heart. For Paul to address her as "mother" suggests a close friendship.

Remember This . . .

We have observed the apostle's demeanor toward his relatives and friends. Paul refers to them as *"dear friend,"* *"relatives who have been in prison with me,"* *"tested and approved,"* "hard workers," "fellow workers in Christ," and *"chosen."* These were men and women who were obedient in planting seeds of the faith that have been passed along one person at a time to the present day. If this is but a sampling of the early church, we can conclude that this church was distinguished by its faithful workers and their brotherly love.

What Others are Saying:

Brennan Manning: What makes authentic disciples is not visions, ecstasies, biblical mastery of chapter and verse, or spectacular success in the ministry, but a capacity for faithfulness. Buffeted by the fickle winds of failure, battered by their own unruly emotions, and bruised by rejection and ridicule, authentic disciples may have stumbled and frequently fallen, endured lapses and relapses, gotten handcuffed to the fleshpots and wandered into a far country. Yet, they kept coming back to Jesus. . . . I am still a ragamuffin, but I'm different . . . where sin abounded, grace has more abounded.[6]

James R. Edwards: First, despite the uncertainty about many of them, the names reveal a remarkable diversity in early Christianity. Paul mentions twenty-nine persons, twenty-seven of them by name, a full third of whom are women. There are Jewish, Greek, and Latin names. A few stem from the nobility and ruling classes, but the majority are names of slaves or freed persons. The Roman churches appear to have been cross-class churches, with membership predominantly from the lower strata of society.[7]

> **Romans 16:17–20** I urge you, brothers, to watch out for those who cause divisions and put obstacles in your way that are contrary to the teaching you have learned. Keep away from them. For such people are not serving our Lord Christ, but their own appetites. By smooth talk and flattery they deceive the minds of naive people. Everyone has heard about your obedience, so I am full of joy over you; but I want you to be wise about what is good, and innocent about what is evil. The God of peace will soon crush Satan under your feet. The grace of our Lord Jesus be with you.

Watch Out For The Troublemakers

Paul had a good eye. He had worshiped Jesus so long that he had gained wisdom. As a church planter, he had the heart and gifts of a pastor and teacher. Beyond the obvious expression of love and appreciation, Paul is rightly concerned for the believers' protection from **false teachers** who introduce division and pollute biblical teaching on the grace of God.

The apostle never loses sight of the fact that believers are engaged in spiritual warfare. In other epistles, he gives instruction on how to prepare for battle. In Romans 16, Paul is simply sounding the alarm and reminding these servants to be on the alert, not to tolerate *anything* that pollutes the faith.

We cannot escape doing spiritual battle, but if we put on the full armor of God, we can win, and in this way serve our Savior. There will be peace in the battle, if we are fighting with the right weapons. This is why Paul says, *"The God of peace will soon crush Satan under your feet"* (Romans 16:20). If he is going to be crushed under the feet of believers, that means we are to get in the fight now.

God, for Paul, was not some abstract, impersonal concept, nor was he some absentee clockmaker who designed life and expected

false teachers: those who pretend to be Christians and teach falsehoods rather than God's truth

 GO TO:

1 Peter 5:5–11 (spiritual warfare)

Ephesians 6:10–19 (armor of God)

it to work automatically on its own. Rather, Paul discovered God was ever present and personally involved in the lives of each believer.

Paul closes this section with a blessing, *"The grace of our Lord Jesus be with you."* The apostle of the grace of God focuses our attention back where the power of our faith rests—on the Gospel of God's grace in Christ Jesus.

Something to Ponder

☞ **GO TO:**

Matthew 24:3–25;
2 Timothy 3:1–9;
Titus 1:10–16
(division)

1 Timothy 2:2
(stay away)

What Paul was concerned about in his day, we are still concerned about today. Times have changed. Cultures are different. But the attacks on God's truth are the same. Paul warns the church in Rome to be alert for people who want to cause <u>division</u>. He tells the Romans to <u>stay away</u> from them.

In spite of the warnings, the apostle affirms his confidence in them. He says, *"everyone has heard about your obedience, so I am full of joy over you."* Obedience is faith in action and it keeps the enemy on the defensive.

IN OTHER LETTERS The spiritual battle must be fought with spiritual weapons. Paul told the Corinthians, *"The weapons we fight with are not the weapons of the world. On the contrary, they have divine power to demolish strongholds. We demolish arguments and every pretension that sets itself up against the knowledge of God, and we take captive every thought to make it obedient to Christ"* (2 Corinthians 10:4–5)

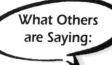

What Others are Saying:

Craig S. Keener: Genesis 3:15 promised that the serpent who deceived Adam and Eve to partake of the fruit (cf. Romans 5:12–21) would ultimately be crushed beneath the feet of Eve's seed. . . . Here Paul applies it more broadly to the Messiah's followers as well. His point is that they should persevere to the end, and their opposition will be defeated.[8]

> **Romans 16:21–24** Timothy, my fellow worker, sends his greetings to you, as do Lucius, Jason and Sosipater, my relatives. I, Tertius, who wrote down this letter, greet you in the Lord. Gaius, whose hospitality I and the whole church here enjoy, sends you his greetings. Erastus, who is the city's director of public works, and our brother Quartus send you their greetings.

So Long, Farewell, Auf Wiedersehen, Good-bye

Paul has a number of other greetings he wants to share with these dear friends. He wants them to know that they are in the hearts and prayers of the people with whom he has spent years serving the kingdom of God.

Paul writes, *"Timothy, my fellow worker, sends greetings to you."* Timothy and Paul were companions on the second and third missionary journeys (see illustration, page 233). Paul viewed Timothy as his <u>spiritual son</u>, so it makes sense that Paul would include his greeting.

Tertius, mentioned in verse 22, is Paul's faithful **amanuensis** who transcribed this letter. Paul often used the services of a secretary. Tertius would have done this duty for Paul as though he were doing it for the Lord himself. He would have asked Paul to be allowed to include his own greeting.

Finally, three others send their best wishes to the Romans.

As we look at the list of Paul's ministry partners, Timothy, Lucius, Jason, Sosipater, Gaius, Erastus, and Quartus, it's amazing to observe how God surrounded Paul with great men and women. They helped, through their good service, to enlarge on the use of Paul's gifts and expand the kingdom of God.

Silas, Titus, Barnabas, and Sosthenes, who are not mentioned in this letter, were among the other faithful workers with whom Paul had frequent contact and fellowship. Paul was a team player; he didn't try to reach the world for Jesus alone. He learned the art of receiving others whom the Spirit of God called. By observing Paul and those around him, we see how valuable it can be to offer our humble support wherever a need surfaces and our talents coincide.

These brethren who preceded us by nearly two millennia sent their greetings to people they had never met. Yet in the mystery of godliness, they experienced love in their hearts for the believers in Rome.

> **Romans 16:25–27** Now to him who is able to establish you by my gospel and the proclamation of Jesus Christ, according to the revelation of the mystery hid-

☞ **GO TO:**

Philippians 2:20–22;
1 Timothy 1:2, 18
(spiritual son)

amanuensis: *one who transcribes from another's dictation*

Something to Ponder

Remember This . . .

> den for long ages past, but now revealed and made known through the prophetic writings by the command of the eternal God, so that all nations might believe and obey him—to the only wise God be glory forever through Jesus Christ! Amen.

"To God Be The Glory" And Then Some

Paul ends this theological treatise with a flourish. In its simplest form this doxology says, "To God be the glory," but Paul packs a lot more into it than that.

He points out that what had long been a mystery—God's plan for saving humankind—had finally been revealed in Jesus Christ. Why? *"So that all nations might believe and obey him. . . ."* This is a reference to the Great Commission, the responsibility of all Christians to preach the Gospel.

Lastly, Paul describes God by using two adjectives. The first is *"only,"* meaning there is but one God, for Jew and Gentile alike. The second adjective is *"wise,"* meaning God's ways are not our ways, that if we are faithful in looking to him for guidance, he will make us the people he wants us to be. Glory be to God!

What Lay Ahead?

A fire raged throughout the city of Rome in A.D. 64, seven years after Paul's epistle was written. When people saw how quickly Emperor Nero rebuilt the city in his honor, many blamed him for setting the fire. Needing a scapegoat, Nero blamed Christians and initiated widespread execution of them. Christians were torn to death by dogs and used as torches to light Nero's gardens and parties.

Although Nero's reign ended in 68, the persecution of Christians continued. The great colosseum (see illustration, page 251) was built between 75 and 80. Built for sportive entertainment, the colosseum showcased gladiatorial combats, but was also where many Christians were thrown to beasts.

There is little doubt the Christians in Rome looked to Paul's letter as a source of continual instruction and solace. *"Bless those who persecute you,"* he wrote (Romans 12:14), and, *"Who shall separate us from the love of Christ? Shall trouble or hardship or persecution or famine or nakedness or danger or sword? . . . No, in all these things we are more than conquerors through him who loved us. For I am convinced that neither death nor life, neither angels nor demons, neither the present nor the future, nor any powers, neither*

Colosseum

Ruins of the great Roman colosseum are still standing, a present-day reminder of the brave faith of Christians who were willing to give up their lives for the sake of Christ.

height nor depth, nor anything else in all creation, will be able to separate us from the love of God that is in Christ Jesus our Lord" (Romans 8:35, 37–39).

Likewise, Paul's assurance that all Christians were saved by grace through faith would have comforted those who suspected death was near. It is likely this epistle helped many Christians resist the temptation to turn away from Christ in the face of persecution and rather to press on toward the goal for which God called them.

Study Questions

1. How did Phoebe come to know the apostle at a level as personal as the text reveals?
2. How were Priscilla and Aquila involved in the church at Rome?
3. Paul extended sixteen special greetings to individuals and groups of Christians. How might a greeting from Paul have encouarged them?
4. How do false teachers create divisions in the church?
5. How does the church go about crushing Satan under its feet?

- Paul commends Phoebe to the Romans and asks that they welcome her. (Romans 16:1–2)

- Paul sends a special greeting to Priscilla and Aquila, his fellow workers and a highly respected husband and wife team. Even though they were Jewish Christians, all the Gentile churches were grateful for their service. In addition, Paul sends greetings to twenty-nine people, twenty-seven by name, and also greetings to house churches. (Romans 16:3–15)

- Paul was God's ambassador of the grace of God in his generation. He sought to encourage godly and affectionate relationships. (Romans 16:16)

- Paul issues a warning about those who teach what is contrary to truth. He knows they have power over certain people, and this weakens the whole church by creating divisions. (Romans 16:17–20)

- Paul's team members, like their leader, want to greet the believers in Rome, so Paul includes their greetings at the end of his letter. (Romans 16:21–24)

- Paul concludes his writing with a beautiful doxology. His faith is bold and far reaching. He wants all nations to come to faith in the Lord Jesus Christ. (Romans 16:25–27)

THE ROMANS RECAP

CHAPTER HIGHLIGHTS

- Everybody's Gospel
- Romans The Short Way
- Romans on Being Human
- Romans on God
- Romans on Believers
- Romans Packs a Punch

Let's Get Started

In the four brief decades following the resurrection of Jesus, the Gospel burst out of tiny Palestine and spread across the Roman world. The story of the love of God expressed in Jesus Christ, and the promise of salvation for all who believe, shook the foundations of both Jewish and pagan belief. Christianity was truly a revolutionary faith, welcomed by millions.

While Christianity was firmly rooted in God's Old Testament revelation to the Jewish people, it seemed to Jew and Gentile alike to be a radical departure. In the first century some 10 percent of the population of the Roman Empire was Jewish. While that people was commonly misunderstood and ridiculed, there was still a significant group of Gentiles who were drawn to the Old Testament's high moral vision and its revelation of one God who created all things. The first Christian converts were drawn from this pool of Jewish believers and Gentile "god fearers" who were familiar with the Old Testament, and who acknowledged Jesus as the Messiah promised by the Old Testament prophets.

KEY POINT

The first Christians were Jewish believers and Gentile "god fearers."

Yet how were these early Christians to reconcile their faith with the older revelation? What, really, was Christianity all about?

More than any book in the New Testament, the Book of Romans clearly defines the core teachings of Christianity, and shows the harmony of the new faith with God's revelation of himself in the Old Testament. And the key to understanding both the link between old and new and the stunning impact of the Gospel is to understand that Romans universalizes the message of the Old Testament.

Everybody's Gospel

When we look at the Old Testament we notice a striking fact. The first eleven chapters of the Old Testament are about God's dealings with the whole human race. The next 905 chapters focus on God's special relationship with a single family—that of Abraham and his descendants, the Jewish people. The new focus begins in Genesis 12, as God chooses a man named Abram and makes him a series of promises. The Old Testament then traces the expansion and fulfillment of these promises through some two thousand years of history, up to the birth of Jesus Christ. It's no wonder then that first-century Jews saw themselves as God's chosen people, uniquely his, with little or nothing in common with the Gentiles all around them.

As the story of a crucified and risen Savior spread across the empire, thousands upon thousands of Gentiles became worshipers of the Jewish Messiah. Suddenly and unexpectedly the faith that had just been birthed in the Holy Land had become a universal faith, good news for all!

At first neither Jewish nor Gentile Christians grasped what was happening nor how to explain it. Then the apostle Paul, who had been largely responsible for stimulating the missionary movement that carried the Gospel message to the first-century Roman world, wrote a letter to the Christians in Rome. In this letter Paul carefully explained the universal Gospel of Jesus Christ—God's good news for all human beings—and showed that it is in complete harmony with the basic teachings of the earlier revelation.

Remember This . . .

treatise: a speech or written work including facts and principles that lead to conclusions

There can be no doubt that the Book of Romans, this letter that Paul wrote to Christians living in Rome, is the key document in our New Testament. When we understand its teachings, we truly understand what Christianity is all about.

Romans The Short Way

Paul's letter to the Romans is a carefully reasoned **treatise**. Each chapter flows logically and naturally into the next. Let's look at Romans section by section and follow Paul's reasoning.

Romans 1–3. The theme of Romans is righteousness (see table, "Charting Righteousness in Romans," page 256), not as mere human goodness, but as absolute moral perfection. In the first three chapters of Romans Paul shows that Jew and Gentile alike lack this absolute righteousness. In fact both Jews and Gentiles are sinners. They are all under the wrath of God, and are doomed. But at the end of chapter 3 there's good news. Christ's death satisfied justice's demand that God punish sin. The death of Jesus as mankind's substitute revealed how God could be righteous and still offer forgiveness to Old Testament sinners, as well as to contemporary believers in Jesus.

Romans 4–5. In chapters 4 and 5 Paul goes on to show that God has always accepted faith in his promises in place of that perfect righteousness that no human being possesses. God accepted Abraham's faith in place of the righteousness Abraham lacked, and God accepts a believer's faith in Jesus in place of the righteousness he or she lacks. The principle of faith, so deeply rooted in the Old Testament, has been universalized, and applies to Jew and Gentile alike. And why did God choose to give his Son for us? God acted because he loves all human beings, despite the fact that all have made themselves his enemies. If we were to be saved, God had to act, because by nature all human beings are spiritually dead and thus we are unable to help ourselves.

Romans 6–8. Then in chapters 6 to 8 Paul unveils a stunning truth. God isn't satisfied to forgive sinners and credit them with righteousness. God intends to actually make righteous those who believe in Jesus! Paul explains that the Holy Spirit unites those who believe in Jesus to the Savior. This means when Jesus died on the cross, those who believe died with him. It also means that when Jesus was raised from the dead, believers were raised too and infused with spiritual life! Salvation involves an inner transformation so that, empowered by God's Holy Spirit, Christians can actually live a righteous life here and now! And our union with Jesus also means that in the resurrection we will become perfectly righteous, through and through, as Jesus himself is!

Romans 9–11. In chapters 9 to 11 Paul answers troubling questions that might be raised by those steeped in the Old Testament. Does the universalizing of the Gospel mean that God has abandoned the Jewish people? Is what God has done for all fair to Israel? Paul's answer is, first, that God is free to act as he chooses, as God's initial choice of Israel illustrates. Second, Paul points out that thousands of Jews have become Christians, so one can hardly say the Jews have been abandoned. And finally, Paul states that the promises in the Old Testament made to national Israel will be kept in the future, at history's end.

Romans 12–16. In the last chapters of Romans Paul returns to the theme of practical righteousness. But now, rather than focus on how individuals are enabled by God's Spirit to live righteous lives, Paul draws a powerful portrait of Christians living together as a righteous community—a community that demonstrates to all the world the blessings God has always desired for humankind.

Charting Righteousness in Romans

Reference	Theme
Romans 1–3	Righteousness needed
Romans 4–5	Righteousness given
Romans 6–8	Righteousness experienced
Romans 9–11	Righteousness of God's choices
Romans 12–16	Righteousness worked out in community

Critical Truths

Paul's argument in Romans rests on several critical truths, or beliefs, that are central to Christianity. When we understand these truths we'll not only better understand the significance of Romans, but we will also better understand our Christian faith. Let's look at these critical beliefs and track their implications as Paul develops them in the Book of Romans.

Romans On Being Human

Human Beings Are Spiritually Dead

Looking back to the fall of Adam described in Genesis 3, Paul writes, *"in this way death came to all men, because all sinned"* (Romans 5:12).

☞ **GO TO:**

Psalm 88:3–5, 9–12 (biological)

Ephesians 2:1–3 (spiritual)

Revelation 20:7–14 (eternal)

In Scripture *"death"* can mean three different things. It can mean <u>biological</u> death, the end of a person's life on earth. It can mean <u>spiritual</u> death, the end of a living person's link with God. Or it can mean <u>eternal</u> death, separation from God throughout eternity. In Romans Paul is primarily concerned with spiritual death, the end of a living person's link with God.

The Book of Genesis reports that God warned Adam against eating fruit from one forbidden tree. God said, *"When you eat of it you will surely die"* (Genesis 2:17). Adam ate, and in addition to dying biologically years later, he died spiritually the moment he disobeyed. Paul reminds us the state of spiritual death was passed on to Adam's offspring (Romans 5:12–21), Jew and Gentile alike.

Even before going on in Romans to speak of sin, Paul establishes the fact that all human beings are spiritually dead. In Romans 1 Paul notes that God has revealed himself to every human being who has ever lived through his creation. *"What may be known about God is plain to them,"* Paul says. *"For since the creation of the world God's invisible qualities—his eternal power and divine nature—have been clearly seen, being understood from what has been made"* (Romans 1:19–20; see also Psalm 19:1–4). Man's reaction to God's revelation of himself has been to *"suppress the truth by their wickedness"* (Romans 1:18). Rather than thank and worship the Creator, human beings have invented their own deities and refused to acknowledge him. This, Paul argues, is clear evidence of the spiritual deadness of humankind.

Human Beings Are Sinners

The Old Testament uses three different words for *"sin."* The principle Hebrew word for sin is *ḥāṭā'*, meaning "to miss the mark" or "to fall short of the standard" that God sets for humankind. This implies that a moral standard established by God exists, and that it is known by human beings. In Romans 2 Paul universalizes this principle. He notes that the Jews have been given a special revelation of the divine standard of right and wrong in Old Testament law (2:17–28). But the Gentiles possess an internal, general revelation of the divine standard! Paul points out that all people have a moral sense. This is shown by the fact that when any individual, Jew or Gentile, violates his own standards his conscience accuses him. And Paul goes on to point out that no human being has ever lived up to his or her convictions about what is right, whether that conviction was shaped by God's revealed law or by the standards of his or her society. All have fallen short of their own standards of right and wrong, and in the sense of *ḥāṭā'*, all are sinners.

But mankind's condition as sinners is far more serious than "missing the mark" might suggest. Another basic word for sin in Hebrew is *peša'*, a word that describes a rebellion or revolt against the standard. Human beings not only fall short of doing what they know is right, they consciously choose to reject and rebel against known moral standards.

A third word in the biblical vocabulary of sin is *'āwōn*, which is often rendered "iniquity" and which implies a twisting of the standard. Whether or not a person rebels against known standards of right and wrong, twists and distorts them, or simply falls short of them, he or she is guilty of sin. And this is the universal condition of humankind.

What is significant in Romans is that Paul shifts the focus from acts of sin to the fact that fallen human beings are sinners by nature. We do fall short of God's revelation of righteousness, and moreover we rebel against what we believe is right and we twist and distort God's standards for our own selfish ends. The fault is rooted in the fact that we are spiritually dead, unresponsive to God and, indeed, in rebellion against him.

The consequences of being sinners are traced in Romans 1:21–32. There Paul shows that sin has an impact on interpersonal morality and on individual personalities as well. As sinners human beings are vulnerable to *"every kind of wickedness, evil, greed and depravity."* Sin's grip on us is shown in our gossip, slander, envy, insolence, and arrogance. It is shown in our faithlessness, heartlessness, and ruthlessness. And while some human beings are "better" than others, there is <u>none</u> that is righteous as God calls us to be righteous.

Human Beings Are Under God's Wrath

Paul also argues that as spiritually dead sinners, all human beings are under the wrath of God. In fact, Paul indicates that the devastating effects that sin has on individuals, families, and society are evidence of God's wrath. The fact that God hates sin and will not let it go unpunished is underlined by our everyday experience!

The anguish caused by divorce, the violation felt by victims of crime, the hurt that even an unkind word can cause, are constant reminders that sin has terrible consequences. Thus, Paul tells us, *"the wrath of God* is being revealed *from heaven against all the godlessness and wickedness of men"* (Romans 1:18, emphasis added).

The message of Scripture and experience is that sin will not go unpunished. Every human being stands guilty before God, already judged by him to be a sinner deserving of eternal punishment. This is the terrible condition of all humankind, Jew and Gentile alike.

Human Beings Need A Righteousness That Comes From God

By the first century the concept of righteousness had been distorted in Judaism. The Old Testament calls God *"<u>righteous</u>,"* and says that whatever God does is *"<u>always righteous</u>."* Simply put righteousness is defined by God's character, and ultimately his

Something to Ponder

☞ **GO TO:**

Romans 3:9–20 (none)

KEY POINT

Nobody gets away with sin. All sinners deserve punishment.

☞ **GO TO:**

Psalm 4:1; Isaiah 45:21 (righteous)

Psalm 71:24 (always righteous)

character is the standard by which all are measured. While the Old Testament speaks of righteous men and women, it also makes it clear that *"no one living is righteous before you"* (Psalm 143:2). In a relative sense those who trusted in God and sought to obey his law were identified as righteous. But in an absolute sense no human being is righteous as God is righteous. Yet God did command Israel to *"be holy, because I am holy"* (Leviticus 11:44, 45), thus establishing perfection as the ultimate standard by which all human beings would be judged.

Paul points out that the Jews had lost sight of this reality and were attempting to establish their own righteousness by trying to keep Old Testament law. Yet only a righteousness which came from God could be as perfect as the righteousness of God. Rather than being acceptable to God based on their efforts to be good, all human beings have fallen short of perfection and as such are subject to the wrath of God.

Nor is there one thing that a human being can do to make a difference! Even the law, which the Jews mistakenly viewed as a guide to perfection, condemned them. For *"whatever the law says, it says to those who are under the law, so that every mouth may be silenced and the whole world held accountable to God. Therefore no one will be declared righteous in his sight by observing the law; rather through the law we become conscious of sin"* (Romans 3:19–20).

This dark and pessimistic view of human nature has universal application to all, Jew and Gentile alike. Yet in Romans Paul sees this as good rather than bad news! If salvation depended on human effort, all would be lost. But salvation is offered to lost human beings as a free gift by a loving deity. Humankind has hope because our deliverance from the power of sin and death does not depend on what we can do for God, but rather on what God has done for us!

Origen: Let us see in what way knowledge of sin comes through the law. It comes insofar as we learn through the law what to do and what not to do, what is sin and what is not sin. The law is like medicine through which we perceive the true nature of our disease. . . . The medicine itself is good, not least because it enables us to isolate the disease and seek to cure it.[1]

What Others are Saying:

Paul's dark view of humanity reflected in Romans is good news, for those who take it to heart and who abandon all hope in themselves may choose to throw themselves entirely on the mercy of God.

Remember This . . .

Romans On God

The Jews thought of themselves as the unique people of God. In Romans Paul draws on Old Testament teachings to show that all human beings, Jews and Gentiles alike, share the same spiritual condition and have the same desperate need of God. In Romans Paul also counters the view that God is God of the Jews only, to show that he is the God of all.

God Speaks To All

One of the things that set the Jewish people apart was possession of the Old Testament Scriptures. God had revealed himself to the Jews! But Paul shows in Romans 1 that God has always spoken to all people, and while the revelation to Israel is far more clear and definitive, all people everywhere have heard <u>his voice</u>. Thus the fact the Gospel is for everyone, *"first for the Jew, then for the Gentile"* (Romans 1:16), is not new. God is the God of all, and from the beginning God has revealed himself to all.

☞ **GO TO:**

Romans 1:19–20
(his voice)

God Gives Righteousness To All Who Believe

Paul has shown that all human beings are sinners, spiritually dead and under God's wrath. In Romans 4 Paul looks back into the Old Testament and demonstrates that God has always accepted faith in his promises in place of the righteousness that no human being possesses. In a key verse in Romans 4 Paul introduces several critical theological concepts. Paul writes that *"to the man who does not work but trusts God who justifies the wicked, his faith is credited as righteousness"* (Romans 4:5). Let's look at some very important phrases in this verse.

Trusts God. In the New Testament a single Greek word group communicates the idea of faith, belief, and trust. The range of meanings carried by this word group are illustrated by English terms that are used to translate its various forms: "to rely on," "to commit oneself to," "to trust," "believe," "faithful," "reliable," "trust," and "faith."

In the New Testament Jesus Christ is set forward as the object of this kind of trust. There is a great gap here between biblical faith and intellectual assent or agreement. We may believe that George Washington was the first president of the United States, or that the earth is round rather than flat. We may believe that God exists, and that Jesus Christ was a real person who lived in the first century. But we do not have faith in the biblical sense until we have put our trust in Jesus and claimed the promise that God will forgive our sins for Jesus' sake. The person who trusts God does not rely for salvation on his or her own efforts to do good, but has come to rely completely on Jesus' sacrifice of himself on the cross to establish and maintain a personal relationship with God.

Justifies the wicked. The Hebrew root translated "justify" has important judicial meaning. In law a person's actions are called into question and examined. If found innocent the person is "justified"; he or she is vindicated.

The Old Testament presents God as the judge who evaluates human actions. Because he is righteous, he does not clear the guilty. Yet in Psalm 51 David calls on God to justify him—to declare him innocent—despite the fact that he is guilty of sin! The Old Testament hints at how God can do this. But it is the New Testament that unveils the plan God intended to put into effect from before the creation of the material universe. As Romans 3:21–26 explains Jesus died as an atoning sacrifice. That is, Jesus took our sins upon himself and paid the penalty that sin requires. With the penalty paid God justifies—declares innocent—all who believe in Jesus. These words recorded in Romans are undoubtedly some of the most significant in the entire Bible.

☞ **GO TO:**

Isaiah 53:11–12 (Old Testament)

> For all have sinned and fall short of the glory of God and are justified freely by his grace through the redemption that came by Christ Jesus. God presented him as a sacrifice of atonement, through faith in his blood. He did this to demonstrate his justice, because in his forbearance he had left the sins committed beforehand unpunished—he did it to demonstrate his justice at the present time, so as to be just and the one who justifies those who have faith in Jesus. (Romans 3:23–26)

Faith credited as righteousness. Paul points out God has shown from the beginning that he will accept faith in place of that perfect righteousness which no person possesses. He did this for Abraham, the forefather of the Jewish people, before there was a Jewish people. In fact, God pronounced Abraham innocent and credited him with righteousness because of his trust in God before Abraham was circumcised. As circumcision was the sign that marked an individual off as a Jew, Paul argues that Abraham was declared righteous as a Gentile!

☞ **GO TO:**

Genesis 15:6 (Abraham)

It follows that the principle of justification by faith—being declared innocent by God on the basis of trust in God rather than on the basis of what a person has actually done—is a universal principle, not a truth for Israel alone. Thus Paul concludes in Romans 4, *"The words 'it was credited to him' were written not for [Abraham] alone, but also for us, to whom God will credit righteousness—for us who believe in him who raised Jesus our Lord from the dead. He was delivered over to death for our sins and was raised to life for our justification"* (Romans 4:23–25).

What Others are Saying:

John Chrysostom: Whoever has become righteous through faith will live, not just in this life but in the one to come as well. This righteousness is not ours but belongs to God, and in saying this Paul hints to us that it is abundantly available and easy to obtain. For we do not get it by toil and labor but by believing.[2]

God Has Shown Love For All

In Romans the apostle has shown all human beings are helpless in the grip of sin and death. But then Paul presents the good news. God has chosen to freely forgive human beings! God in the person of Jesus Christ stepped into history to pay the penalty justice demands. In a great and stunning transaction Jesus took on himself the sins of the world, and Christ's own righteousness is credited to anyone who trusts in him.

The great mystery here is not what God has done for us in Christ, but why? Paul's answer is simple. *"God demonstrates his own love for us in this: While we were still sinners, Christ died for us"* (Romans 5:8).

KEY POINT

The reason God sacrificed Christ for our salvation is because he loves us.

Romans On Believers

In the first chapters of Romans the apostle Paul has described the universal condition of humankind, and the universal offer of salvation to all who will trust in Jesus Christ. In chapter 6 of Romans the focus shifts to believers. Here again, however, the message is universal in one vital respect. While the Old Testament made a distinction between Jew and non-Jew, Paul no longer makes that distinction. All Christians, whatever their ethnicity, race, gender or other differences are one now in Christ. What God intends to do for and in those who have come to him through Jesus is for all, without any of the old distinctions.

What then are the great contributions of Romans to our understanding of what God does for all believers?

God Enables Believers To Live Righteous Lives

Romans 6 introduces the stunning truth that Christians are *"united with"* Jesus Christ. God not only forgives the sins of those who believe in Jesus but also pronounces them innocent. God establishes a living link—a bond—between the individual believer and the Lord. Because of this bond we were, spiritually speaking, present at the cross and died with Jesus. We were also present at Jesus' resurrection and were raised to new life with him. Through this union that God established when we believed, Jesus' own power flows to us and enables us to live the righteous life that is impossible for sinners to achieve!

Paul is very careful to distinguish what we are able to do by our own efforts from what God is able to do in and through us. We do not achieve a righteous life. We *are enabled* as Christ's life is lived out through us. And here the apostle identifies clearly a truth implied but not defined in the Old Testament. For in Romans Paul speaks not only of *"God,"* but also of *"Jesus Christ,"* and of *"the Holy Spirit."*

Cyril of Alexandria: As we have died a death like his, so we shall also be conformed to his resurrection, because we shall live in Christ. It is true that the flesh will come to life again, but still we shall live in another way, by dedicating our souls to him and by being transformed into holiness and a kind of glorious life in the Holy Spirit.[3]

The Trinity In Scripture

The word *trinity* isn't found in the Bible. It's an invented theological term, used to express the conviction that the Bible's one God exists in three Persons. We see hints of this in Genesis 1:1, where the Hebrew name of God, Elohim, is a plural rather than singular noun. We see it in Genesis 1:26, which reports that God said, *"Let us make man in our image."* And we see it in frequent references to the *"Spirit of God."* Even the great affirmation of faith recited by Jews from ancient times, *"the Lord our God, the Lord is one"* (Deuteronomy 6:4), hints at trinity, for the word *"one"* is a Hebrew term that emphasizes plurality in unity, as in referring to one bunch made up of many grapes.

It is not until the New Testament however that a clear image is drawn of Scripture's one God existing in three persons. We see Jesus speak of the Father as *"the only true God,"* and yet affirm that, *"I and the Father are one"* (John 17:3; 10:30). The Bible clearly speaks of Jesus as God come in the flesh, one with and yet distinct

KEY POINT

Christians are united with Christ in his death and resurrection, enabling us to live righteously by the power of the Holy Spirit.

What Others are Saying:

☞ GO TO:

John 1:1–14; Philippians 2:5–11; Colossians 1:15–20 (Jesus)

☞ **GO TO:**

John 14:15–17
(Holy Spirit)

2 Corinthians 2:1–11;
Hebrews 9:14 (God)

Ephesians 1:1–14
(Father, Son, and
Spirit)

**Remember
This . . .**

from God the Father. In the same way Jesus identifies the Holy Spirit as one exactly like himself, and in other passages the Spirit is unmistakably identified as God. In another of Paul's letters, Ephesians, the apostle defines the roles of Father, Son, and Spirit in our salvation, acknowledging each as God.

The Role Of The Spirit In Romans

Understanding the fact that God exists in three Persons is important background for Romans. As we reach Romans 7 and especially Romans 8, we are introduced to the Holy Spirit as the person who is himself our living link with Jesus, and through whom flows the power that enables us to live godly and holy lives.

Romans teaches us that all Christians are linked individually to Jesus by the Holy Spirit. It is because of our union with Jesus that God can lift us beyond ourselves, enabling us to live righteous lives that it would be impossible for us to live on our own. God not only declares us to be righteous because of what Jesus did for us, but he also intends to actually make us righteous people here and now! And the key to living righteous lives is the fact that we are united to Jesus, so that his power can flow into and through us.

God Will Ultimately Make All Believers Like Jesus

As long as we live here on earth we will be torn between the pull of our old, sinful selves and the new creations we've become in Jesus. At times we'll respond to God's inner promptings and, in Paul's words, find that *"the righteous requirements of the law"* are being fully met in us. We'll freely, gladly, and spontaneously do the right thing, lifted up and enabled by the Holy Spirit within us.

All too often, however, we'll give in to the pull of sin, or try to do right in our own strength and fail. But a day is coming when God will make us totally righteous, purging from us the last vestiges of sin and making us like Jesus himself. Paul looks forward to this day, the day of our resurrection, and says that the Spirit who now lives within us is the down payment that guarantees our ultimate deliverance. In Paul's words, we *"have been called according to [God's] purpose,"* and this means that we have been *"predestined to be conformed to the likeness of his Son, that he might be the firstborn among many brothers"* (Romans 8:29).

God *guarantees* that those who have trusted Jesus as Savior, who have been united with Jesus by faith, and who are linked to

☞ **GO TO:**

Romans 8:23
(down payment)

Jesus even now by the Holy Spirit, will be completely saved from sin. We will not only be declared innocent on the basis of Jesus' death, but we will also become truly innocent and pure, transformed by the very power of God that raised Jesus from the dead!

God Intends To Create A Loving Faith Community

In Romans 9–11 Paul pauses to answer objections that might be raised by Jewish critics or by uncertain Jewish believers. Again in these chapters Paul returns to the Old Testament to show that in universalizing the Gospel God has not acted inconsistently or unfairly. God has always been Sovereign, free to act as his nature dictates. With this established, Paul shares a vision of what God has for believers here and now.

Paul's focus in chapters 12–15 shifts from what God has for individual believers, to explore what the new relationship with Jesus means to believers living together as a community of faith. Again we need to remember that in the first century serious tensions existed between Jew and non-Jew, between members of different social classes, between men and women, between rich and poor. These same kinds of tensions exist today. There are racial tensions, radical differences between the generations, gender differences, and differences between rich and poor, the educated and the uneducated. Yet in Romans Paul gives us a vision of what God intends, and how it can be achieved. For God intends to create a healing community of love that will be a powerful witness to the world.

The principles of our life together as Jesus' own are again universal. They are intended to apply to all Christians, everywhere. They are especially intended to apply to us today, in our own churches and communities.

We are all to use our gifts to serve each other (Romans 12: 1–8). God has equipped each believer with a spiritual gift—a special God-given ability to contribute to the growth and well being of others. As we accept our roles as servants of God's people and use our gifts for their benefit, we help to build the loving community of faith that Christians are to establish here and now.

We are to humbly love one another (Romans 12:9–21). A spirit of selflessness and a genuine concern for others is to characterize the Christian community. In a series of brief exhortations Paul gives us a picture of a people who are filled with God's Spirit living together as God intends.

We are to be good citizens and act in love toward all (Romans 13:1–14). God's people are to be responsive to secular authorities, and to use love as the standard by which we measure how to relate to our fellow citizens.

We are to maintain harmony within the community of faith (Romans 14:1–15:13). Disputable matters—matters about which the Bible remains silent and about which believers have differing convictions—are not to disrupt the harmony of the Christian community. We maintain harmony by acknowledging that Christ is Lord, and each individual believer is responsible to him. We maintain harmony by refraining from judging others whose convictions on disputable matters may differ from our own. And we maintain harmony by quietly living by our own convictions, not flaunting them, yet remaining sensitive to the feelings of others about them. Our goal is to welcome all who trust Jesus into our fellowship, to encourage them as they seek to grow in the faith, and "with one heart and mouth" to glorify the God and Father of our Lord Jesus Christ (Romans 15:6).

What Others
are Saying:

Saint Augustine: Paul says that we should receive the weak man in order that we might support his weakness by our strength. Neither should we criticize his opinions by daring to pass judgment on someone else's heart, which we do not see.[4]

Romans Packs A Punch

From the very beginning the Book of Romans has had an unmatched impact on Christianity. In the first century it defined the relationship between Jew and non-Jew, showing the universal application of the Gospel to all humankind.

Nearly every Christian writer before A.D. 200 alludes in his writings to the Book of Romans. The theologian Origen (A.D. 185–A.D. 254) wrote no fewer than fifteen books on this one epistle! In the course of following centuries other significant commentaries on Romans were written in both Greek and in Latin, the languages of the eastern and western churches. John Chrysostom (347–407), the famous preacher who became patriarch of Constantinople, left thirty-two homilies which constitute a verse-by-verse exposition of Romans. Perhaps most significantly, the thought of Saint Augustine, the greatest of the Latin church fathers, was shaped by his reading of Romans.

The greatest impact of Romans on Christianity today can be traced to its role in the conversion of Martin Luther. Luther was a

Catholic monk who struggled with a sense of his own sinfulness. Luther desperately tried to live up to the standard of righteousness that he found in Scripture. Driven to despair by the awareness of his failures, Luther found peace when he was gripped by the message of Romans 1:17: the just live by faith. Suddenly Luther realized that God freely gave his own righteousness to those who trust Jesus as Savior. Luther became the catalyst for the rediscovery of the doctrine of justification by faith alone, out of which the Protestant Reformation grew along with most Protestant churches existing today.

One of the best-known examples of the impact of Luther's rediscovery of Romans' teachings happened in London, England. There one evening a failed missionary to American Indians sat and listened as Luther's commentary on Romans 1:17 was read aloud. Later the missionary wrote that he felt his heart "strangely warmed." Transformed by the message of justification by faith alone, that man, John Wesley, began preaching in the villages and fields of England. Wesley stimulated a great revival, which historians credit for saving England from the anarchy and horrors that accompanied the French Revolution. During his fifty years of active ministry Wesley also founded societies of believers from which our Methodist and Wesleyan Methodist churches grew.

KEY POINT

Romans had a major impact on such central figures in Christian history as Origen, John Chrysostom, Saint Augustine, Martin Luther, and John Wesley.

Warren Wiersbe: Imagine! You and I can read and study the same inspired letter that brought life and power to Luther and Wesley! And the same Holy Spirit who taught them can teach us.[5]

What Others are Saying:

Remember This . . .

Of all the books of the Bible, and of all books ever written, the Book of Romans is arguably the most influential book in the Christian world. Most wonderful of all, Romans has opened the eyes of untold millions to the love and grace of a God who cares for sinners, and who invites all to find forgiveness and new life in Jesus Christ.

Study Questions

1. What two groups made up the Christian church shortly after Jesus' resurrection?
2. What are the three types of death in Scripture, and which one is Paul concerned with in Romans?
3. What has God always accepted as a substitute for the righteousness no human possesses?
4. What is the basis for our salvation?
5. Is righteousness something that we will enjoy only in heaven?

- God's offer of salvation by grace through faith in Jesus Christ is universal. No one is left out.

- All humans fall short of their own standards for perfection, let alone God's. We are all sinners.

- God is not God of the Jews only. He is God of all, and he has always revealed himself to everyone.

- Every human who puts his or her faith in Christ is one of God's own and will one day enjoy the full presence of God for eternity. Furthermore, God grants believers the Holy Spirit whose instruction and strength will make righteousness not only a future promise but a present reality.

- The Book of Romans is very likely the most influential book in all of Christian history. It has inspired such spiritual notables as Luther and Augustine.

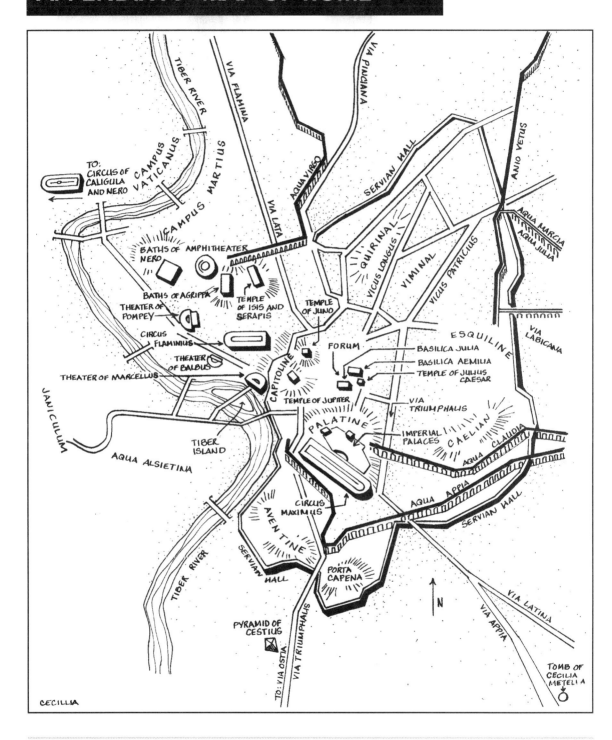

APPENDIX B—PAUL'S DOCTRINES

Doctrine	References
The Inspiration of Scripture	Galatians 1:11–12; 2 Timothy 3:14–17
Divine Election	Romans 8:29–30; 9:6–33; Ephesians 1:3–14
God's Plan for Israel	Romans 11:1–32
The Universality of Human Sinfulness	Romans 1:18–3:20; 3:23; Titus 3:3
Victory over Sin and Satan	Romans 6:11–7:6; 8:31–39; Ephesians 6:10–18
The Twofold Nature of Jesus Christ	Romans 1:3–4; Philippians 2:5–11
The Sacrificial Atonement of Christ	Romans 3:25–26; 5:6–10; Galatians 3:10–14
Reconciliation between Human Beings and God	Romans 5:10–11; 2 Corinthians 5:16–21; Colossians 1:19–23
Christ as the Second Adam	Romans 5:12–21; 1 Corinthians 15:20–22, 42–49
The Supreme Lordship of Jesus Christ	Romans 10:9–13; Ephesians 1:15–23; Philippians 2:9–11; Colossians 1:15–20; 2:6–15
The Old and New Covenant	2 Corinthians 3:1–18; Galatians 3:15–4:7; 4:21–31
Justification by God's Grace through Faith	Romans 1:16–17; 3:21–4:25; Galatians 2:16–3:14; Ephesians 2:1–10; Philippians 3:7–11; 1 Timothy 1:12–16; Titus 3:4–8
Life through the Holy Spirit	Romans 8:1–17, 26–27; Galatians 5:16–26
The Christian's Life of Love	Romans 12:9–21; 13:8–10; 1 Corinthians 13; Galatians 5:13–15; Colossians 3:12–14
The Gifts of the Holy Spirit	Romans 12:3–8; 1 Corinthians 12:1–11, 27–31; 14:1–40; Ephesians 4:7–12
Marriage in Christ	1 Corinthians 7:1–40; Ephesians 5:22–33; Colossians 3:18–19
Christian Freedom	Romans 14:1–15:13; 1 Corinthians 8:1–13; 10:23–33; Galatians 5:1–12; Colossians 3:16–23
Unity in the Church	1 Corinthians 1:10–17; Ephesians 2:11–21; 4:1–16
Baptism	Romans 6:1–10; 1 Corinthians 12:12–13; Colossians 2:11–12
Lord's Supper	1 Corinthians 10:14–22; 11:17–34
Death for Believers	2 Corinthians 5:1–8; Philippians 1:19–26
The Resurrection	1 Corinthians 15; Philippians 3:20–21
The End of History	1 Corinthians 15:23–29; 2 Corinthians 5:10; 1 Thessalonians 5:1–11; 2 Thessalonians 1:5–2:12; 2 Timothy 3:1–9
The Second Coming of Jesus Christ	1 Corinthians 15:51–57; Philippians 3:20–21; 1 Thessalonians 4:13–18; Titus 2:11–14

SOURCE: Kenneth L. Barker and John R. Kohlenberger III, eds., *Zondervan NIV Commentary, Volume 2: New Testament* (Grand Rapids: Zondervan, 1984), 549.

APPENDIX C—THE OLD TESTAMENT IN ROMANS

Romans Text	Old Testament Text	Subject
Romans 1:17	Habakkuk 2:4	The righteous live by faith
Romans 2:6	Psalm 62:12; Proverbs 24:12	God's fair judgment
Romans 2:24	Isaiah 52:5; Ezekiel 36:22	God's name cursed among Gentiles
Romans 3:4	Psalm 51:4	God's righteous judgment
Romans 3:10–18	Psalm 5:9; 10:7; 14:1–3; 36:1; 53:1–3; 140:3; Ecclesiastes 7:20; Isaiah 59:7–8	Sin of humanity
Romans 4:3, 9	Genesis 15:6	Faith of Abraham
Romans 4:7–8	Psalm 32:1–2	Blessings of forgiveness
Romans 4:17	Genesis 17:5	Abraham as a father of many
Romans 4:18	Genesis 15:5	Offspring of Abraham
Romans 4:22	Genesis 15:6	Faith of Abraham
Romans 7:7	Exodus 20:17; Deuteronomy 5:21	Tenth commandment
Romans 8:36	Psalm 44:22	Sheep for the slaughter
Romans 9:7	Genesis 21:12	God's choice of Isaac
Romans 9:9	Genesis 18:10, 14	Promise for Sarah
Romans 9:12	Genesis 25:23	God's choice of Jacob
Romans 9:13	Malachi 1:2–3	Love for Jacob, not Esau
Romans 9:15	Exodus 33:19	Mercy of God
Romans 9:17	Exodus 9:16	Purpose of Moses
Romans 9:20	Isaiah 29:16; 45:9	Potter and clay
Romans 9:25–26	Hosea 1:10; 2:23	Now God's people
Romans 9:27–29	Isaiah 1:9; 10:22–23	The remnant
Romans 9:32–33	Isaiah 8:14	A stone on which people stumble
Romans 9:33	Isaiah 28:16	Trust in the cornerstone
Romans 10:5	Leviticus 18:5	Living by the law
Romans 10:6	Deuteronomy 30:12	The word not in heaven
Romans 10:7	Deuteronomy 30:13	The word not in the deep
Romans 10:8	Deuteronomy 30:14	The word near you
Romans 10:11	Isaiah 28:16	Trust in the cornerstone
Romans 10:13	Joel 2:32	Salvation in the Lord
Romans 10:15	Isaiah 52:7	Beautiful feet

Appendix C—The Old Testament in Romans (continued)

Romans Text	Old Testament Text	Subject
Romans 10:16	Isaiah 53:1	Unbelief of Israel
Romans 10:18	Psalm 19:4	General revelation
Romans 10:19	Deuteronomy 32:21	Making Israel envious
Romans 10:20	Isaiah 65:1	Salvation of the Gentiles
Romans 10:21	Isaiah 65:2	Obstinate Israel
Romans 11:3–4	1 Kings 19:10, 14, 18	A saved remnant
Romans 11:8	Deuteronomy 29:4	A misunderstanding mind
Romans 11:8	Isaiah 29:10	God seals the eyes
Romans 11:9–10	Psalm 69:22–23	Judgment on enemies
Romans 11:26–27	Isaiah 59:20–21	Deliverer from Zion
Romans 11:27	Isaiah 27:9	Full removal of sin
Romans 11:34	Isaiah 40:13	The mind of the Lord
Romans 11:35	Job 41:11	God owns all
Romans 12:19	Deuteronomy 32:35	God avenges sin
Romans 12:20–21	Proverbs 25:21–22	Treating one's enemies
Romans 13:9	Exodus 20:13; Deuteronomy 5:17	Sixth commandment
Romans 13:9	Exodus 20:14; Deuteronomy 5:18	Seventh commandment
Romans 13:9	Exodus 20:15; Deuteronomy 5:19	Eighth commandment
Romans 13:9	Exodus 20:17; Deuteronomy 5:21	Tenth commandment
Romans 13:9	Leviticus 19:18	Lover your neighbor as yourself
Romans 14:11	Isaiah 45:23	Every knee shall bow
Romans 15:3	Psalm 69:9	Insults on Christ
Romans 15:9	2 Samuel 22:50; Psalm 18:49	Praise among the nations
Romans 15:10	Deuteronomy 32:43	Rejoice, O nations
Romans 15:11	Psalm 117:1	Nations praising God
Romans 15:12	Isaiah 11:10	The root of Jesse
Romans 15:21	Isaiah 52:15	Gentiles hear the gospel

SOURCE: Kenneth L. Barker and John R. Kohlenberger III, eds., *Zondervan NIV Commentary, Volume 2: New Testament* (Grand Rapids: Zondervan, 1984), 604–605.

APPENDIX D—THE ANSWERS

ROMANS 1: A SERVANT'S LONGING

1. Paul's confirmation began with his encounter with Christ on the road to Damascus. God sent a disciple by the name of Ananias to confirm both Paul's salvation and his call as an apostle to take God's message of love to the Gentile world (Acts 9:3–16). We find him taking his first mission assignment in Acts 13. (Romans 1:1)

2. Paul built his identity on being a servant of Christ. (Romans 1:1)

3. Jesus' resurrection from the dead was the ultimate confirmation of the Lord's divinity. He was declared by the Holy Spirit to be the Son of God. (Romans 1:4)

4. The key to the greatness of Paul's powerful worldview and the authority with which he ministered was his belief in the Scriptures and his understanding of God's grace through the Gospel of Jesus Christ. (Romans 1:2–5)

5. Paul was not ashamed because he knew the Gospel was the power of God giving life to all who believe. It was the Gospel that brought transformation in his life, and so he was not ashamed of the truth it brought to him and to the whole world. (Romans 1:16–17)

6. It was the Fall in Genesis 3 that introduced man to sin. In Romans 1–3, Paul writes of God's indictment of the world, demonstrating why man needs the righteousness of God. The truth was given to men, but since the Fall they have continued to *suppress the truth by their wickedness.* (Romans 1:18–23; Revelation 20:11–15)

ROMANS 2: JUDGMENTALISM AND HYPOCRISY

1. God is concerned about judgmentalism because humankind's judgment is always based on partial truth. God is the only one who has all the facts all the time. So God says that when we continue pointing the finger at each other we are bringing more condemnation upon our own heads. (Romans 2:1–4)

2. God's kindness buys us time. If God were not as kind as he is, he might pour out his wrath on us as soon as we sinned, but he doesn't. He gives us time to come to repentance. (Romans 2:3–4)

3. Paul meant that though people weren't experiencing God's wrath at that moment, they shouldn't therefore sit back and think all is well. As long as they continued to look down on people and ignore their own faults, the lake of God's wrath was getting bigger and bigger. (Romans 2:5–7)

4. God has declared everyone a sinner regardless of race. Then he offers his hand of love to all who will receive it. To receive God's grace is an expression of faith on the part of humans. (Romans 2:9–11; John 1:10–14; Ephesians 2:8–10)

5. Man (male and female), who is created in the image of God, has been given the gift of conscience. We are aware of our sinfulness. We are conscious of our rebellion. We are internally aware that we do not meet the requirements of the law. (Romans 2:12–16)

ROMANS 3: IN SEARCH OF RIGHTEOUSNESS

1. The Jews had an advantage in the sense that God entrusted the Jews with his Word. They had a direct source of righteousness from the perspective of the Creator. In addition, the Word given to the Jews was validated by a multitude of miracles, interventions, and special revelations. (Romans 3:1–4)

2. Our unrighteousness causes God to judge us because of how serious God is about sin. Our God is a holy God and cannot allow any sin to go unpunished. God restored our righteousness through Jesus Christ, thereby making salvation a free gift to all who receive Jesus as Savior and Lord. (Romans 3:5–8)

3. God, through Paul, points out, *"There is no difference,*

for all have sinned and fall short of the glory of God."
The sin of Adam has polluted every generation since
Adam, and the sin of humankind throughout history
is evidence of this truth. (Romans 3:22–23; 5:12–19)

4. The law defines righteousness and thereby exposes
unrighteousness. It is this simple fact that makes a
consciousness of sin universal. (Romans 3:19–20)

5. There can be no boasting in our accomplishments,
in our works, in our gifts, for God is the author of
our salvation, which is through grace and by faith.
No one but Christ Jesus has ever kept the law completely. (Romans 3:27–28)

ROMANS 4: ABE'S FAITH

1. Faith. When God spoke to him, a totally new experience for Abraham, he believed God and the proof
of his faith was his obedience. He did what God told
him to do. (Romans 4:1–3; Genesis 12–22)

2. Circumcision followed the promise given to
Abraham. Getting circumcised did not make
Abraham righteous. He had faith when he was still
uncircumcised. Circumcision was a mark of God's
ownership and man's commitment to his God. It became a ritual under Mosaic law. (Romans 4:9–12)

3. Abraham believed he would have a son because God
promised him that he would. (Romans 4:13–17)

4. Because God is holy, he cannot allow unrighteousness
into his presence. Without righteousness, no one
would see God, ever! Righteousness is our bridge
back to God. (Romans 4:3, 22–25)

ROMANS 5: THE BENEFITS OF BELONGING TO CHRIST

1. Peace comes from justification by faith through Jesus
Christ. (Romans 5:1–2)

2. We can rejoice in suffering because we know that
suffering has meaning and purpose. Suffering produces perseverance, perseverance produces character, and character produces hope. (Romans 5:3–5)

3. The proof of God's love is that while we were sinners, Christ died for us. Our experience of God's love
may be subjective, but this historical fact gives us
unmistakable proof that God's love is not imagined.
It is real. (Romans 5:6–8)

4. God's grace is bigger than sin, and the final results of
grace will be far beyond the results of sin. (Romans
5:17).

5. God added the law to magnify the reality of the trespass. It gave definition to man's sin and thereby increased sin's transgression. (Romans 5:15, 20–21)

ROMANS 6: A LIFE OR DEATH SITUATION

1. It is true that where sin increased, *"grace increased
all the more"* (Romans 5:20), but sin does not cause
grace to abound! It is simply the nature of grace to
abound. In reality, it is God acting on behalf of sinful
man showing us over and over that Satan is a defeated foe and we have been set free to follow God.
(Romans 6:1–2)

2. When Paul speaks of believers being *"baptized into
[Christ's] death,"* he is referring to the end of the
believer's old life as governed by association with
Adam. Water baptism that follows conversion is an
outward symbol of an inward reality. (Romans 6:3–
4)

3. "To be united with Christ in resurrection" is to be
united with Christ in his victory over death. Christians begin experiencing this victory as soon as they
become Christians, and the consummation of the
victory comes when we die and go to heaven. (Romans 6:5–7; 1 Corinthians 15:51–58)

4. Our union with Christ Jesus assures us that the old
self, our sin nature, has been crucified. That's good
news! Now we are called to listen to the Holy Spirit
and not the cravings of the flesh. In truth, we are no
longer slaves to sin, even though we are still tempted
by sin. The same power that raised Jesus is available
to raise us out of our sinful ways. (Romans 6:6–12)

5. We're still getting used to our new captain. Evil habits often take years to overcome, so while God is doing the work of sanctification the tendency to sin
still raises its ugly head. If we don't repent and get
right with God, we will continue in our former sin
habits. (Romans 6:19–23)

ROMANS 7: THE TENSION OF TWO NATURES

1. The law was fulfilled in the life and the work of Jesus
Christ. We are no longer in bondage to the law because we *"died to the law through the body of Christ."*
We belong to Jesus Christ, who teaches us the *spirit*
of the law, not just the letter. (Romans 7:6–7)

2. The new nature is freed from obligation to the law
whereas the old nature is slave to it. The old nature
is stimulated by the law while the new nature is
prompted by the Holy Spirit. The old nature produces sin, acts unto death, whereas the new nature
produces fruit unto God.

3. Because the law sets the standard for what's right and
what's wrong, it shows us where we have failed. (Romans 7:7–12)

4. The law is spiritual in that it comes from God, who is Spirit. The law is a direct revelation sent from God through Moses. To be unspiritual means to be a slave to sin. (Romans 7:14–20)

5. He means he is caught between the tension of two forces within him. One part desperately wants to follow God, but the old nature is a slave to sin. He is trying to fulfill the law as a Christian, and the result is failure and anguish. (Romans 7:24–25).

ROMANS 8: THE TRIUMPH OF SPIRIT-GUIDED LIVING

1. For a person to be "saved by the law," that person must keep the law perfectly. It is impossible, however, for a fallen human to keep the law no matter how sincerely s/he may seek to keep it, and therefore, the law is powerless to save people. The law can only show us our need for salvation in Christ, who (1) kept the law perfectly, and (2) paid the just penalty for our failure to keep the law. (Romans 8:1–4)

2. The mind has significant control in the spiritual journey. If the mind is following the desires of the sinful nature, then pollution enters our journey with God, but if the mind is set on the desires of the Spirit—God's righteousness—then life is filled with contentment and freedom. (Romans 8:5–8)

3. When we are controlled by the Holy Spirit, we are then liberated from the limitations that sin puts on life. The Spirit's control brings us into God's joy and freedom. (Roman 8:9–11; Galatians 5:1)

4. We know that everything belongs to Christ, but because of the grace of God we share in what is his. By the sovereign will of God, we are coheirs with his Son, Jesus. (Romans 8:12–17; 1 John 3:1–3)

5. Two of the most immediate and significant matters to which the Holy Spirit attends are helping us to pray and supporting us in our weakness. (Romans 8:26–27)

ROMANS 9: GOD'S IN CHARGE

1. Paul knew the Romans might be tempted to think he was exaggerating, so he stresses that he is telling the truth. (Romans 9:1–3)

2. God had given the Jewish nation a rich heritage. He lists the following:
   a. Theirs is the adoption as sons.
   b. Theirs is the divine glory.
   c. Theirs are the covenants.
   d. Theirs is the receiving of the law.
   e. Theirs is the temple worship.
   f. Theirs are the promises.
   g. Theirs are the patriarchs. (Romans 9:4–5)

3. People are offended by the concept of election because from a finite perspective they think it makes God out to be unjust or unfair. But in fact, election is a demonstration of God's mercy and compassion. (Romans 9:6–16)

4. Paul chooses two very significant historical events to illustrate the doctrine of election: the first is the birth of Isaac as the child of promise and the second is the choice of Jacob over Esau. This had nothing at all to do with the character of the children, but it was such to establish *"that God's purpose in election might stand"* (Romans 9:11).

5. Paul speaks of a *"remnant chosen by grace"* (Roman 11:5) of which he was a part. A remnant is a portion of a larger group, so out of all the Israelites, the remnant to which Paul referred was the people who because of grace chose to follow Christ as the Son of God. (Romans 9:27–28)

ROMANS 10: FAITH AVENUE

1. The Jews were zealous for God in the sense that they were focused on following the law and their Rabbinic traditions. They knew little if anything about the righteousness that comes through faith in Christ, and thus they refused God's open invitation. Their traditions and their polluted leadership prevented them from receiving Jesus, the Christ of Israel, their long-awaited Messiah! He offered them the righteousness that comes from faith in God and his promises, but they failed as a nation to receive their king. (Romans 10:1–5)

2. The Jews were stuck in a mode of thinking, impure and incomplete, that gave them a sense of righteousness that came from keeping the law, a *"righteousness by law."* The *"righteousness by faith"* is by grace through faith. This righteousness is a gift of God to all who receive his Son as Savior. (Romans 10:3–8; Ephesians 2:8–10; Titus 2:11–14)

3. Paul repeats the way of salvation again and again in his epistles. It is grace that makes salvation available—the grace of God in the life, death, and resurrection of Jesus Christ as Lord. It is faith that enables fallen man to appropriate that grace and love into his heart and therein receive Jesus as Lord and Savior. It is by faith plus nothing. That is the nature of God's saving grace. (Romans 10:9–11)

4. When Paul says *"there is no difference between Jew and Gentile,"* he is saying there is only one way to God, regardless of one's ethnic or religious convictions. *"The same Lord is Lord of all and richly blesses all who call on him"* (Romans 10:12). So no one can improve on God's free gift in Jesus Christ. We are all sinners. (Romans 10:11–13)

5. The expression *"how beautiful are the feet of those who bring good news"* is in reference to those who respond to the call and will of God to go forth in faith proclaiming the message of the Gospel, regardless of difficulties and insults. (Romans 10:14–15)

ROMANS 11: ISRAEL'S DESTINY

1. Paul clearly understood there is only one way for men and women to be saved from the eternal wrath of a holy, righteous God, and Jesus, the Messiah of Israel, is that way. Because Israel had officially rejected Jesus, Paul knew that many would be eternally lost. This was a great and ongoing grief in the heart of this faithful servant of God. (Romans 11:1–6)

2. Because of Israel's stand against Jesus, the spiritual dullness of the Jews, which had continued from the days of Isaiah the prophet, was now upon this generation also. Because they refused the way of faith (Romans 9:31–32), God made them impervious to his ministry of grace. This was the *"spirit of stupor"* to which Paul referred. (Romans 11:7–10)

3. Israel's fall was not permanent. God's love for this people had not diminished, but his discipline had increased due to their rebellion against, and rejection of, his Son Jesus. Here we see God's sovereign power in full display. His righteous nature is inviolable. (Romans 11:11–12)

4. The "mystery" to which Paul referred was the salvation of the nation of Israel. Paul said, *"all Israel will be saved."* (Romans 11:25–32)

5. The unbelieving Israelites were God's enemies in the sense that they had rejected God's gift of righteousness by faith. They were still loved by God in the sense that ever since the faith of Abraham, God has loved his covenant people.

6. We should see mercy against the dark background of our sin because mercy is not necessary without sin. We must understand that our sin is what brought about our need for God's mercy.

ROMANS 12: HOW TO DO CHURCH

1. The ritual work of the Old Covenant had come to a complete end. Christ is the fulfillment of the law (Romans 10:5)! We are now "living sacrifices" in contrast to dead animal sacrifices. (Romans 12:1)

2. The health of our spirits is directly related to the health of our minds. When we renew our minds by reading scripture and praying, we are building healthy spirits. (Romans 12:2; Philippians 2:5; 2 Corinthians 10:5)

3. Because man is saved by grace, salvation is exclusively the work of our Creator. To elevate ourselves is to diminish the grace of God that brought us the gift of salvation. (Romans 12:3)

4. God has given the Body of Christ multiple gifts and callings. Each gift has a specific purpose in building up Christ's church to do the work of ministry and to exercise the practice of worship. No gift is insignificant and no gift is greater than another. All are given to exalt and bring glory to God. When this is happening, the church will grow in grace and in the knowledge of God. (Romans 12:6–8)

5. The tests of life are what prove your love sincere or false. If your love for someone falters and fails during difficult times, your love was never sincere. If your love continues through both thick and thin, your love is sincere. (Romans 12:9–13)

ROMANS 13: GOD AND COUNTRY

1. The Scriptures are very clear on the matter of submitting to governing authorities. Earthly authorities have been established by God and must be obeyed by everyone. There are no special exemptions. (Romans 13:1)

2. Some examples are family, politics, work, and church. (Romans 13:2–7)

3. By doing what is right, we will not need to fear those who rule over us. If their leadership transgresses our righteousness, we must do what is right and trust God to be our defender and hope. (Romans 13:3)

4. One's conscience is a very important part of one's spirituality. The conscience acts as an administrator who distinguishes between right and wrong as we do our best to make good decisions in a complicated world. The Holy Spirit will draw upon the conscience in order to guide us toward righteousness. If one ignores one's conscience, one might be ignoring the work of the Holy Spirit. Regardless, the conscience

is a gracious part of God's protection to assist believers in their walk. (Romans 13:5)

5. Taxes are always a test, especially when we are being overtaxed. Yet, we are to pay taxes to support those who engage in the work of governing full-time. (Romans 13:6–7)

6. God paid a *"debt of love"* when he sent Jesus to redeem a lost humanity. In like manner, we have a debt of love. As a part of God's redeemed, we are to extend love to one another; *"love is the fulfillment of the law."* (Romans 13:10)

7. To do away with darkness, we must *"clothe [ourselves] with the Lord Jesus Christ, and do not think about how to gratify the desires of the sinful nature"* (Romans 13:14). This is what Paul calls putting on *"the armor of light."* (Romans 13:11–14)

ROMANS 14: KEEPING PEACE

1. The term *disputable matters* refers to issues about which well-meaning, God-fearing Christians may differ because Scripture is unclear. In Romans 14, the disputable matters Paul addresses specifically are the matters of (1) clean and unclean foods, and (2) the observance of certain days. (Romans 14:1–4)

2. The "strong" believer is a person who has a grasp of his full liberty in Christ. Paul pointed out as an example that a strong believer's conscience is not plagued by doubts about whether it's morally right to eat meat. The strong believer knows, as Paul did, that *"no food is unclean"* (Romans 14:14), whereas the "weak" believer's conscience may not allow him or her to eat meat. The "weak" believer is weak in the sense that's s/he does not have a grasp of his or her full liberty in Christ. The "weak" believer is burdened by doubts about whether it's right to do things which the "strong" can do without any guilt at all. (Romans 14:5–8)

3. Judgment is a serious matter because it creates wounds in the Body of Christ that in turn create a spirit of separation and disunity. It creates a spirit of rejection while we are called to love and share the light of our Lord. (Matthew 7:1–6; Luke 6:27–31; 37–42; Romans 14:9–18)

4. We are to keep in mind that one day we will have to give an account to God for our own behavior. We are to remember that the *"kingdom of God is not a matter of eating and drinking, but of righteousness, peace and joy in the Holy Spirit"* (Romans 14:17). This is God's divine leverage against our tendency to judge instead

of being a brother or friend. It should be mentioned, however, that this does not preclude godly discussion about issues. (Romans 14:16–18)

5. One would prove to be a stumbling block to another if one chose to exercise one's freedom at the expense of another person's spiritual growth. (Romans 14:19–21)

6. The "good" referred to here is the liberty to eat because all foods are clean. This liberty, however, may be regarded as evil if it is flaunted in the face of those who do not feel free to eat certain foods. Paul is encouraging his listeners to use the liberty lovingly, not arrogantly. (Romans 14:16, 22–23)

ROMANS 15: COME TOGETHER

1. The strong should bear the shortcomings of the weak because though Christ was the only person with the right to serve himself, he served others. The strong ought to follow his example. (Romans 15:1–4)

2. Paul selects a group of Old Covenant Scriptures that elevate the place of the Gentile in the plan and purpose of God. These Scriptures picture the Gentiles praising the God who saved them. (Romans 15:7–13)

3. The apostle Paul gloried in Christ Jesus. The Messiah was his focus in life and because of this, he was never distracted in his service to God. The immediacy of Christ's presence, both in Spirit and in power, helped to make Paul's service a glory to God and a blessing to the many churches he served. The same help is available to every succeeding generation. (Romans 15:17–22)

4. First we should remember that God knows our longings and will fulfill them if it is the best thing for us and the whole universe. Secondly, we ought to remember that no matter what suffering unfulfilled longings cause us here on earth, heaven will more than make up for it. (Romans 15:23–24)

5. Paul said that because the Gentiles were recipients of spiritual blessings from the Jews, it was appropriate for them to respond by giving giving back a material blessing. (Romans 15:25–29)

ROMANS 16: A FOND FAREWELL

1. Paul was a servant to the servants. He valued every person who gave of him- or herself for the work of God's Kingdom. Phoebe was that kind of person. She had helped many and had been "a great help" to Paul as well. It was by serving Paul and receiving service from Paul that Phoebe knew Paul on such a personal level. (Romans 16:1–2)

2. Priscilla and Aquila were in the city of Corinth where they practiced the trade of tentmaking. Paul was proficient in this skill as well, and in God's providence the three of them partnered in tentmaking and sharing the Gospel (see Acts 18:1–4). In this context they forged a fruitful friendship and ministry. (Romans 16:33–34)

3. It is beautiful to read Paul's greeting to his many friends and fellow workers. He held them all in high esteem in the Lord. His fellow servants loved him deeply and to have heard a word from him that was affirming would no doubt have brought joy to their hearts. (Romans 16:5–16)

4. False teachers create division and competition in the Body of Christ by being insincere and using *"smooth talk and flattery"* to deceive the minds of the faithful. They teach what is contrary to the Word of God. They follow their own passions. (Romans 16:17–19)

5. The Gospel renders Satan powerless so he seeks to confuse, clutter, and create tension in the church. But the Gospel brings peace, and God's peace is a crushing blow to the work of our Enemy. God promises that if we resist Satan, he will flee! We are also to put on the full armor of God mentioned in Ephesians 6:10–19. (Romans 16:20; James 4:7)

THE ROMANS RECAP

1. The two groups that made up the first Christians were Jews and Gentile God-fearers. The latter group was Gentiles who went to Jewish synagogue because they were interested in the Jewish God and in Jewish moral teachings.

2. The 3 types of death in Scripture are biological death, spiritual death, and eternal death. Biological death is when our bodies die, spiritual death is the state of being spiritually separated from God because of sin, and eternal death is the state of being spiritually separated from God forever. Paul is mainly concerned with spiritual death in Romans.

3. From Old Testament times until now God has always accepted faith in his promises as a substitute for the righteousness no human possesses.

4. The basis for salvation is the death and resurrection of Jesus Christ, the atoning sacrifice that God made for the sins of humans.

5. God starts the process of developing righteousness within believers as soon as they believe. He does this by giving us his spirit, the Holy Spirit, which resides in the hearts of all Christians.

APPENDIX E—THE EXPERTS

Sir Robert Anderson (1841–1918)—Foremost British barrister and extensive world traveler, head of the Criminal Investigation Department of Scotland Yard, Political Crime Advisor to the British Home Office, and author of numerous books on prophecy.

Apollinaris of Laodicea (*circa* 310–390)—Syrian prelate and theologian, bishop of Laodicea (Syria), and Greek biblical commentator.

Saint Augustine (354–430)—Early Christian church father and philosopher, also known as Saint Augustine of Hippo.

William Barclay—Internationally recognized scholar, teacher, author, and pastor, and the editor of the *Daily Study Bible* series of books.

Kenneth L. Barker—Executive Director of the NIV Translation Center of the International Bible Society, member of the NIV Translation Committee, and editor of the *NIV Study Bible*.

Karl Barth—Honorary professor of Reformed Theology, Gettingen, Germany, 1921–25; professor of Dogmatics and New Testament Exegesis, Munster, 1925–30; professor of Systematic Theology in Bonn, 1930–35; and author of more than a dozen books.

Robert Benson—Freelance writer. Author of *Between the Dreaming and the Coming True* and *Living Prayer.* Leads retreats and workshops on spirituality and writing.

James Montgomery Boice—Pastor of historic Tenth Presbyterian Church, Philadelphia; speaker on *The Bible Study Hour*; president of Evangelical Ministries; editor of *Eternity Magazine*; and author of more than a dozen books.

Dietrich Bonhoeffer—Author, teacher, and theologian, executed by the Nazis for his role in the German Resistance Movement.

Frederick Buechner—Presbyterian minister and author of over twenty fiction and nonfiction books.

John Calvin—French theologian, author, pastor, and reformer; founder of the Reformed church and a theocratic government in Geneva, Switzerland, which served as a focal point for defense of Protestantism throughout Europe. His famous *Institutes of the Christian Religion* were published in 1536.

Oswald Chambers (1874–1917)—A Bible teacher, conference leader, and YMCA chaplain. His writing, compiled after his death by his widow, is available in devotional books, including the popular *My Utmost for His Highest*.

John Chrysostom (347–407)—Syrian prelate, preacher, and archbishop of Constantinople, exiled and banished for his boldness.

Samuel Taylor Coleridge (1772–1834)—English poet and critic, Unitarian preacher, founder of the liberal journal *Watchman*, and coauthor with William Wordsworth of the *Lyrical Ballads*.

Mark Driscoll—Founder and pastor of Mars Hill Fellowship, Seattle, Washington, and church planting coordinator with Acts 29, headquartered in Boca Raton, Florida.

James D. G. Dunn—Professor of Divinity, University of Durham, England, and author of many publications, including *The Evidence for Jesus* and *The Living Word*.

James R. Edwards—Professor of Religion, Whitworth College; frequent contributor to scholarly journals; and coauthor of *The Layman's Overview of the Bible*.

Eusebius of Emesa (*circa* 300–359)—Greek prelate, theologian, and ecclesiastic writer of the Alexandrian school.

F. L. Godet (1812–1900)—Influential Swiss Protestant Reformed scholar and professor of biblical exegesis and critical theology, Theological School of the National Swiss Church of the Canton.

Billy Graham—World famous evangelist and author. (Billy Graham Evangelistic Association, 1300 Harmon Place, P.O. Box 779, Minneapolis, MN 56440-0779)

Robert Haldane (1764–1842)—Evangelist, writer, founder of *Society for Propagating the Gospel at Home* (1797), and instigator of *Haldane's Revival* in Geneva, Switzerland, and southern France.

Matthew Henry (1662–1714)—English scholar, pastor, and Bible expositor, best known for his 1704 detailed commentary on the Bible.

Charles Hodge—Author, lecturer, theologian, professor of Original Languages of Scripture at Princeton Theological Seminary in 1820, and also professor of Oriental and Biblical Literatures.

Saint Jerome (*circa* 347–420)—Latin church father who published the Latin version of the Bible, known as the Vulgate.

Craig S. Keener—Professor of New Testament, Hood Theological Seminary, Salisbury, North Carolina; ordained minister in the National Baptist Convention USA; contributor to such journals as *The Expositor Times* and *Christianity Today*; and author of *Paul, Woman and Wives*.

John R. Kohlenberger III—Author of the *NIV Interlinear Hebrew-English Old Testament* and the *NRSV Unabridged Concordance*.

C. S. Lewis (1898–1963)—English scholar and writer, fellow and tutor at Oxford (1925–54), professor of English at Cambridge (1954–63), and author of literary studies, fantasy tales for children, and many works of Christian apologetics.

D. Martyn Lloyd-Jones—Author, physician, and Presbyterian minister.

Martin Luther (1483–1546)—German religious reformer and founder of Protestantism and the Reformation; professor of biblical exegesis, Wittenberg (1512–46); known for his ninety-five theses nailed to the church door at Wittenberg; translator of the Old and New Testaments from Greek into German; and author of many commentaries, catechisms, sermons, and hymns.

Brennan Manning—Speaker, lecturer, and spiritual retreat facilitator.

Douglas J. Moo—Professor at Trinity Evangelical Divinity School, Deerfield, Illinois, and editor of *Trinity Journal*.

John Murray (1898–1975)—Professor of Systematic Theology at Westminster Theological Seminary, Philadelphia, Pennsylvania, and author of several books, including *Principles of Conduct: Aspects of Biblical Ethics and Redemption—Accomplished and Applied*.

Henri Nouwen—Netherlands born and educated author, priest, psychologist, and theologian; former professor at Notre Dame, Yale Divinity School, and Harvard; and pastor of Daybreak, a worldwide ministry for the mentally and physically handicapped.

Elizabeth O'Connor—Teacher, consultant, counselor, author, and support minister at The Church of the Saviour, Washington, D.C.

Origen (*circa* 185–254)—Christian writer and teacher, one of the Greek fathers of the church, and author of fifteen books on Romans.

Pelagius (*circa* 354–418)—British monk, theologian, and author.

John Piper—Pastor of Bethlehem Baptist Church, Minneapolis, Minnesota, and author of several books, including *Desiring God* and *The Pleasures of God*.

William S. Plumer (1802–1880)—Professor of Didactic and Pastoral Theology, Western Theological Seminary; founder and editor of *Watchman of the South*; and author of several books, including *Commentary on Romans* (1870).

Larry Richards—Author of over 175 books and general editor of the *God's Word for the Biblically-Inept*™ series.

Francis A. Schaeffer—Philosopher, theologian, author of more than twenty books, and founder or L'Abri Fellowship international study and discipleship centers.

Adolf Schlatter (1852–1938)—Professor at Tubingen University, author of more than a hundred books, and arguably one of the most brilliant New Testament interpreters of the twentieth century.

Stanley K. Stowers—Professor of Religious Studies, Brown University, and author of several books.

Peter Stuhlmacher—Professor of New Testament, University of Tubingen, Germany, and author of several books on Paul.

Charles R. Swindoll—Popular Christian author of more than twenty best-selling books, featured daily on his worldwide broadcast *Insight for Living*, and president of Dallas Theological Seminary, Dallas, Texas.

Mother Teresa (1910–1997)—Nobel Peace Prize recipient in 1979, noted for helping the dying, the destitute, lepers, AIDS victims, orphans, and society's outcasts around the world.

Theodoret of Cyr (393–458)—Greek theologian at the school in Antioch, Bishop of Cyrrhus, affirmed by the Council of Chalcedon, and author of church history, commentaries, exegesis, and biographies.

A. W. Tozer (1897–1963)—Pastor with the Christian Missionary Alliance. Author of many books including *The Pursuit of God*.

John F. Walvoord—Chancellor and professor emeritus of Systematic Theology, Dallas Theological Seminary; author or editor of twenty-six books and dozens of articles for magazines and scholarly journals.

Warren Wiersbe—One of the evangelical world's most-respected Bible teachers, and author of more than one hundred books.

Philip Yancey—Editor-at-large for *Christianity Today* magazine and author of eight Gold Medallion award-winning books.

Ravi Zacharias—President of Ravi Zacharias International Ministries, internationally known lecturer, debater, author, Christian apologist, and host of the weekly radio program *Let My People Think*.

Roy B. Zuck—Department chair and professor of Bible Exposition, Dallas Theological Seminary; author or editor of numerous books and magazine and journal articles.

Note: To the best of our knowledge, all of the above information is accurate and up to date. In some cases we were unable to obtain biographical information.

—THE STARBURST EDITORS

ENDNOTES

Romans 1: A Servant's Longing

1. D. Martyn Lloyd-Jones, *Romans: An Exposition of Chapter One, The Gospel of God* (Edinburgh: The Banner of Truth Trust, 1985), 1.
2. Samuel Taylor Coleridge, quoted in *Man's Ruin* by Donald G. Barnhouse (Grand Rapids, MI: Eerdmans, 1955), 2.
3. Martin Luther, quoted in *Man's Ruin* by Donald G. Barnhouse (Grand Rapids, MI: Eerdmans, 1955), 2.
4. F. L. Godet, quoted in *Man's Ruin* by Donald G. Barnhouse (Grand Rapids, MI: Eerdmans, 1955), 2.
5. Francis A. Schaeffer, *The Finished Work of Christ* (Wheaton: Crossway Books, 1998), 16.
6. W. E. Vine, *An Expositionary Dictionary of New Testament Words* (London: Oliphants, 1959), 318.
7. Schaeffer, *The Finished Work of Christ*, 19.
8. Saint Augustine, *Ancient Christian Commentary on Scripture* (Downers Grove, IL: InterVarsity, 1998), 15.
9. Adolf Schlatter, *Romans: The Righteousness of God* (Peabody, MA: Hendrickson Publishers, 1995), 12.
10. John F. Walvoord and Roy B. Zuck, eds., *The Bible Knowledge Commentary* (Colorado Springs, CO: Chariot Victor, 1985), 440.
11. Pelagius, *Ancient Christian Commentary on Scripture* (Downers Grove, IL: InterVarsity, 1998), 22.
12. William S. Plumer, *Commentary on Romans* (Grand Rapids, MI: Kregel, 1971), 57–58.
13. Dietrich Bonhoeffer, *Letters and Papers from Prison* (New York: Macmillan, 1962), 221–222.
14. Mother Teresa, quoted from "Mother Teresa Memorial Page," http://home.pacbell.net/mandmcc/motherteresa.htm

15. Schaeffer, *The Finished Work of Christ*, 20.
16. Apollinaris of Laodicea, *Ancient Christian Commentary on Scripture* (Downers Grove, IL: InterVarsity, 1998), 29.
17. Karl Barth, *The Epistle to the Romans* (London: Oxford University Press, 1933), 35.
18. Lloyd-Jones, *Romans: An Exposition of Chapter One*, 311.
19. Barth, *Epistle to the Romans*, 42.
20. Barth, *Epistle to the Romans*, 49.
21. Schlatter, *Romans*, 42.
22. Pelagius, *Ancient Christian Commentary on Scripture*, 48.
23. Schaeffer, *The Finished Work of Christ*, 43.

Romans 2: Judgmentalism and Hypocrisy

1. Matthew Henry, *Commentary on the Whole Bible* (Grand Rapids, MI: Zondervan, 1961), 1757.
2. Ibid., 1757.
3. Martin Luther, *Luther: Lectures on Romans*, vol. 25 of *The Library of Christian Classics*, ed. Wilhelm Pauck (Philadelphia: Westminster Press, 1961), 3.
4. Schaeffer, *The Finished Work of Christ*, 62–63.

Romans 3: In Search of Righteousness

1. Eusebius of Emesa, *Ancient Christian Commentary on Scripture* (Downers Grove, IL: InterVarsity, 1998), 81.
2. James R. Edwards, *New International Biblical Commentary: Romans* (Peabody, MA: Hendrickson, 1992), 84–85.
3. Lloyd-Jones, *Romans: An Exposition of Chapter One*, 305.

4. Apollinaris of Laodicea, *Ancient Christian Commentary on Scripture* (Downers Grove, IL: InterVarsity, 1998), 83.
5. Sir Robert Anderson, *Redemption Truths* (Grand Rapids, MI: Kregel, 1980), 152.
6. Augustine, *Ancient Christian Commentary on Scripture*, 96.
7. Barth, *The Epistle to the Romans*, 85–86.
8. Manning, *The Ragamuffin Gospel* (Sisters, OR: Multnomah Publishers, 1990), 23.
9. Henry, *Commentary on the Whole Bible*, 1761.
10. Schaeffer, *The Finished Work of Christ*, 79–80.
11. Lawrence O. Richards, *The Victor Bible Background Commentary* (Wheaton, IL: Victor Books, 1994), 326.

Romans 4: Abe's Faith

1. James D. G. Dunn, *Romans 1–8*, vol. 38 of *Word Biblical Commentary* (Dallas: Word Books, 1988), 219.
2. Henry, *Commentary on the Whole Bible*, 1761.
3. Augustine, *Ancient Christian Commentary on Scripture*, 110.
4. Charles R. Swindoll, *The Grace Awakening* (Dallas: Word Publishing, 1990), 24.
5. Ibid., 25.
6. Schaeffer, *The Finished Work of Christ*, 92.
7. Augustine, *Ancient Christian Commentary on Scripture*, 112.
8. Lawrence O. Richards, *Complete Bible Handbook* (Waco, TX: Word Books, 1982), 611.
9. Luther, *Lectures on Romans,* 266.
10. John Piper, *Future Grace* (Sisters, OR: Multnomah Books, 1995), 190.
11. Henry, *Commentary on the Whole Bible*, 1762.
12. Edwards, *New International Biblical Commentary*, 118.
13. Piper, *Future Grace*, 189.
14. John Calvin, *Calvin's Commentaries* (Grand Rapids, MI: Eerdmans, 1973), 100.
15. Theodoret of Cyr, *Ancient Christian Commentary on Scripture* (Downers Grove, IL: InterVarsity, 1998), 122.
16. John Chrysostom, *Ancient Christian Commentary on Scripture*, 123.
17. Schaeffer, *The Finished Work of Christ*, 108.

Romans 5: The Benefits of Belonging to Christ

1. Calvin, *Calvin's Commentaries*, 104.
2. Joni Eareckson Tada, quoted in Dave Goetz, "Thriving with Limitations," *Leadership Magazine*, Winter 1996, 62–63.
3. Charles R. Swindoll, *Laugh Again* (Dallas: Word Publishing, 1991), 53.
4. Schaeffer, *The Finished Work of Christ*, 133.
5. Bonhoeffer, *Life Together*, 17–18.
6. Yancey, *The Bible Jesus Read*, 27–28.
7. Frederick Buechner, *Wishful Thinking* (New York: Harper & Row, 1973), 53–54.
8. Yancey, *The Bible Jesus Read*, 205.
9. Calvin, *Calvin's Commentaries*, 109–110.
10. Origen, *Ancient Christian Commentary on Scripture*, 135–136.
11. Mark Driscoll, "The Power of Grace: Revealing Our Slavery" (Seattle: Mars Hill Church sermon notes, December 13, 1998), 30.
12. Schaeffer, *The Finished Work of Christ*, 142.
13. Chrysostom, quoted in Luther, *Lectures on Romans,* 173.
14. Luther, *Lectures on Romans*, 310.

Romans 6: A Life-or-Death Situation

1. Edwards, *New International Biblical Commentary,* 158.
2. Chrysostom, *Ancient Christian Commentary on Scripture*, 153.
3. Ibid., 158.
4. Oswald Chambers, *My Utmost for His Highest*, ed. James Reimann (Grand Rapids, MI: Discovery House, 1992), March 8 and January 15.
5. Schaeffer, *The Finished Work of Christ*, 161–162.
6. Luther, *Lectures on Romans*, 315.
7. Dietrich Bonhoeffer, *The Cost of Discipleship* (New York: Macmillan, 1963), 258.
8. Haldor Lillenas, "Wonderful Grace of Jesus," quoted from *Hymns for the Family of God* (Nashville: Paragon Associates, 1976), 114.
9. Luther, *Lectures on Romans*, 319.
10. Calvin, *Calvin's Commentaries*, 133.
11. Charles Hodge, *Commentary on The Epistle to the Romans* (Grand Rapids, MI: Eerdmans, 1977), 211.

Romans 7: The Tension of Two Natures

1. William Barclay, quoted in Mark Driscoll, "The Power of Marriage: Revealing Our Union with Jesus" (Seattle: Mars Hill Church sermon notes, January 3, 1999), 32.
2. Matthew Henry, *Commentary on the Whole Bible*, 1768.
3. Schlatter, *Romans*, 154.
4. Plumer, *Commentary on Romans*, 318.
5. Schlatter, *Romans*, 158.
6. Luther, *Lectures on Romans*, 327.
7. Douglas J. Moo, *The Epistle to the Romans* (Grand Rapids, MI: Eerdmans, 1996), 469–470.
8. Augustine, *Ancient Christian Commentary on Scripture*, 187.
9. Plumer, *Commentary on Romans*, 326–327.
10. Kenneth L. Barker and John R. Kohlenberger III, *New Testament*, vol. 2 of *NIV Bible Commentary* (Grand Rapids, MI: Zondervan, 1994), 557.
11. Walvoord and Zuck, *The Bible Knowledge Commentary*, 467.
12. Lawrence O. Richards, *Illustrated Bible Handbook* (Nashville: Thomas Nelson, 1982), 616.
13. Martin Luther, *Lectures on Romans*, 339.
14. Plumer, *Commentary on Romans*, 338.
15. Richards, *Illustrated Bible Handbook*, 616.
16. Barker and Kohlenberger, *New Testament*, 559.
17. Augustine, *Ancient Christian Commentary on Scripture*, 199.

Romans 8: The Triumph of Spirit-Guided Living

1. Yancey, *What's So Amazing about Grace?* (Grand Rapids, MI: Zondervan, 1997), 106.
2. Edwards, *New International Biblical Commentary*, 203–204.
3. Luther, *Lectures on Romans*, 348.
4. Henry, *Commentary on the Whole Bible*, 1770.
5. Barker and Kohlenberger, *New Testament*, 561.
6. Schlatter, *Romans*, 180.
7. Edwards, *New International Biblical Commentary*, 205.
8. Philip Yancey, *What's So Amazing about Grace?*, 282.
9. Moo, *The Epistle to the Romans*, 485.
10. Yancey, *What's So Amazing about Grace?*, 157.

11. Esther K. Rusthoi, "When We See Christ," *Hymns for the Family of God* (Nashville: Paragon Associates, 1976), 129.
12. Chrysostom, *Ancient Christian Commentary on Scripture*, 221–222.
13. Saint Jerome, *Ancient Christian Commentary on Scripture* (Downers Grove, IL: InterVarsity, 1998), 225.
14. John Calvin, quoted in Plumer, *Commentary on Romans*, 420.
15. Barker and Kohlenberger, *New Testament*, 564.
16. Bonhoeffer, *Life Together*, 86.
17. Philip Yancey, *Reaching for the Invisible God* (Grand Rapids, MI: Zondervan, 2000), quoted in "Living with Furious Opposites," *Christianity Today*, September 4, 2000, 73.
18. Chambers, *My Utmost for His Highest*, March 7.

Romans 9: God's in Charge

1. Mark Driscoll, "The Power of Election: Revealing God's Compassion" (Seattle: Mars Hill Church sermon notes, February 14, 1999), 38.
2. James D. G. Dunn, *Word Biblical Commentary* (Dallas: Word Books, 1988), 531.
3. Augustine, *Ancient Christian Commentary on Scripture*, 255.
4. D. Martyn Lloyd-Jones, *Romans: An Exposition of Chapter 10, Saving Faith* (Edinburgh: The Banner of Truth Trust, 1997), 2.
5. Larry Richards, *The Bible Reader's Companion* (Wheaton, IL: Victor Books, 1991), 745.
6. Peter Stuhlmacher, *Paul's Letter to the Romans* (Louisville, KY: Westminster/John Knox Press, 1994), 147–148.
7. Edwards, *New International Biblical Commentary*, 237–238.
8. Luther, *Lectures on Romans*, 386.
9. Edwards, *New International Biblical Commentary*, 240–241.
10. Barker and Kohlenberger, *New Testament*, 573.

Romans 10: Faith Avenue

1. Lloyd-Jones, *Romans: An Exposition of Chapter 10*, 20–21.
2. Ibid., 27.
3. James Montgomery Boice, *Romans: Volume 3,*

God and History, Romans 9–11 (Grand Rapids, MI: Baker Books, 1993), 1159–1160.

4. Lloyd-Jones, *Romans: An Exposition of Chapter 10,* 87–88.

5. Edwards, *New International Biblical Commentary,* 253.

6. Hodge, *Commentary on The Epistle to the Romans,* 340.

7. Moo, *The Epistle to the Romans,* 644.

8. Schlatter, *Romans,* 215.

9. Lloyd-Jones, *Romans: An Exposition of Chapter 10,* 198.

10. Plumer, *Commentary on Romans,* 523.

11. Luther, *Lectures on Romans,* 410.

12. Augustine, *Ancient Christian Commentary on Scripture,* 279.

13. Hodge, *Commentary on The Epistle to the Romans,* 349.

Romans 11: Israel's Destiny

1. D. Martyn Lloyd-Jones, *Romans: An Exposition of Chapter 11, To God's Glory* (Edinburgh: The Banner of Truth Trust, 1998), 5.

2. Calvin, *Calvin's Commentaries,* 242.

3. Billy Graham, *Storm Warning* (Minneapolis: Grason, 1992), 57.

4. Luther, *Lectures on Romans,* 425.

5. Barker and Kohlenberger, *New Testament,* 579.

6. Schlatter, *Romans,* 220.

7. Lloyd-Jones, *Romans: An Exposition of Chapter 11,* 87.

8. Jerome, *Ancient Christian Commentary on Scripture,* 294.

9. Boice, *Romans: Volume 3,* 1402.

10. Edwards, *New International Biblical Commentary,* 277–278.

11. Boice, *Romans: Volume 3,* 1476.

Romans 12: How to Do Church

1. A. W. Tozer, *The Pursuit of God* (Camp Hill, PA and Bloomington, MN: Christian Publications and Garborg's Heart 'n Home, 1993), April 26.

2. Haldane, *Exposition of the Epistle of the Romans,* 557.

3. Schlatter, *Romans,* 230.

4. Yancey, *What's So Amazing about Grace?,* 233.

5. Chrysostom, *Ancient Christian Commentary on Scripture,* 310.

6. Lawrence O. Richards and Gib Martin, *A Theology of Personal Ministry* (Grand Rapids, MI: Zondervan, 1981), 119.

7. Mark Driscoll, "Romans: The Mission Heart of God" (Seattle: Mars Hill Church sermon notes, April 18, 1999), 47.

8. Edwards, *New International Biblical Commentary,* 287.

9. Bonhoeffer, *Life Together,* 97.

10. Billy Graham, quoted by William Griffin and Ruth Graham Dienert, *The Faithful Christian* (Minneapolis: Grason, 1994), 93.

11. Swindoll, *The Grace Awakening,* 303.

12. Richards, *The Bible Reader's Companion,* 748.

13. Edwards, *New International Biblical Commentary,* 298.

14. Luther, *Lectures on Romans,* 466.

15. Augustine, *Ancient Christian Commentary on Scripture,* 323.

Romans 13: God and Country

1. Luther, *Lectures on Romans,* 468–469.

2. James Montgomery Boice, *Romans, vol. 4* (Grand Rapids, MI: Baker Books, 1995), 1643.

3. Pelagius, *Ancient Christian Commentary on Scripture,* 325.

4. Edwards, *New International Biblical Commentary,* 308.

5. Calvin, *Commentaries on the Epistle of Paul,* 483.

6. Ravi Zacharias, *Can Man Live Without God?* (Dallas: Word Publishing, 1994), 134.

7. Graham, *Storm Warning,* 84–85.

8. Origen, *Ancient Christian Commentary on Scripture* (Downers Grove, IL: InterVarsity, 1998), 330.

9. Augustine, *Ancient Christian Commentary on Scripture,* 331.

10. Yancey, *The Bible Jesus Read,* 205.

11. Calvin, *Commentaries on the Epistle of Paul,* 490.

12. Robert Benson, *Living Prayer* (New York: Tarcher/Putnam, 1998), 191.

13. Augustine, *Ancient Christian Commentary on Scripture,* 336.

Romans 14: Keeping Peace

1. Lawrence O. Richards, *The Teachers Commentary* (Wheaton: Victor Books, 1987), 836.
2. John Calvin, quoted by William S. Plumer, *Commentary on Romans* (Grand Rapids, MI: Kregel, 1971), 604.
3. Plumer, *Commentary on Romans*, 606.
4. Stuhlmacher, *Paul's Letter to the Romans*, 223.
5. Chrysostom, *Ancient Christian Commentary on Scripture*, 345.
6. Swindoll, *The Grace Awakening*, 299.
7. Stanley K. Stowers, *A Re-Reading of Romans* (New Haven: Yale University Press, 1994), 323.
8. Barker and Kohlenberger, *New Testament*, 593.
9. Stuhlmacher, *Paul's Letter to the Romans*, 228.
10. Karl Barth, *The Epistle to the Romans* (London: Oxford University Press, 1933), 519.
11. Edwards, *New International Biblical Commentary*, 330.
12. Schlatter, *Romans*, 258.
13. Yancey, *What's So Amazing about Grace?*, 272.
14. Pelagius, *Ancient Christian Commentary on Scripture*, 348.
15. Plumer, *Commentary on Romans*, 607.
16. Luther, *Lectures on Romans*, 506.

Romans 15: Come Together

1. Henry, *Commentary on the Whole Bible*, 1793.
2. Chrysostom, *Ancient Christian Commentary on Scripture*, 353.
3. John Murray, *The Epistle to the Romans* (Grand Rapids, MI: Eerdmans, 1965), 200.
4. Henri Nouwen, *The Genesee Diary* (Garden City: Doubleday, 1966), 162.
5. C. S. Lewis, *Mere Christianity* (New York: Macmillan, 1958), 158.
6. Elizabeth O'Connor, *Call to Commitment* (New York: Harper & Row, 1963), 139.
7. Ibid., 162.
8. Nouwen, *The Genesee Diary*, 169.
9. Augustine, *Ancient Christian Commentary on Scripture*, 361.
10. Edwards, *New International Biblical Commentary*, 346.
11. Yancey, *What's So Amazing about Grace?*, 280.
12. O'Connor, *Call to Commitment*, 158.
13. Jerome, *Ancient Christian Commentary on Scripture*, 366.
14. James Montgomery Boice, *Romans*, vol. 4, 1871.
15. Barker and Kohlenberger III, *NIV Bible Commentary*, 599.
16. Theodoret of Cyr, *Ancient Christian Commentary on Scripture*, 368.

Romans 16: A Fond Farewell

1. Lawrence O. Richards, *The Revell Bible Dictionary*, 764–765.
2. Boice, *Romans*, vol. 4, 1911.
3. Chrysostom, *Ancient Christian Commentary on Scripture*, 369.
4. Craig S. Keener, *The IVP Bible Background Commentary*, New Testament (Downers Grove, IL: InterVarsity, 1993), 448.
5. Barker and Kohlenberger, *NIV Bible Commentary*, 601.
6. Manning, *The Ragamuffin Gospel*, 183.
7. Edwards, *New International Biblical Commentary*, 357.
8. Keener, *The IVP Bible Background Commentary*, 449.

The Romans Recap

1. Origen, quoted in *Ancient Christian Commentary on Scripture, Romans*, vol. 6 (Downers Grove, IL: InterVarsity Press, 1998), 106.
2. Chrysostom, quoted in *Ancient Christian Commentary on Scripture, Romans*, vol. 6 (Downers Grove, IL: InterVarsity Press, 1998), 31–32.
3. Cyril of Alexandria, quoted in *Ancient Christian Commentary on Scripture, Romans*, vol. 6 (Downers Grove, IL: InterVarsity Press, 1998), 157.
4. Augustine, quoted in *Ancient Christian Commentary on Scripture, Romans*, vol. 6 (Downers Grove, IL: InterVarsity Press, 1998), 340.
5. Warren Wiersbe, *The Bible Exposition Commentary* (Colorado Springs, CO: Chariot Victor, 1998), 514.

Excerpts from the following are used by permission with all rights reserved:

The Bible Jesus Read by Philip Yancey. Copyright © 1999 by Philip Yancey. Used by permission of Zondervan Publishing House.

Calvin's Commentaries by John Calvin. Copyright © 1973. Used by permission of Wm. B. Eerdmans Publishing, Grand Rapids, MI.

The Epistle to the Romans by Karl Barth, translated from the sixth edition by Edwyn C. Hoskyns. Copyright © 1933. Used by permission of Oxford University Press.

The Finished Work of Christ by Francis A. Schaeffer, copyright © 1998, pages 16, 19, 20, 43, 62–63, 79–80, 92, 108, 133, 142, 161–162. Used by permission of Crossway Books, a division of Good News Publishers, Wheaton, Illinois, 60187.

The Grace Awakening by Charles Swindoll. Copyright © 1990. Word Publishing, Nashville, Tennessee. All rights reserved.

Life Together by Dietrich Bonhoeffer, pages 14, 16, 21–22, 17–28, 24, 86, 97. English translation copyright © 1954 by Harper & Brothers, copyright renewed 1982 by Helen S. Doberstein. Reprinted by permission of HarperCollins Publishers, Inc., New York, New York.

Luther's Works Vol. 25, copyright © 1972 by Concordia Publishing House. Reproduced under license number 00: 4–18.

New International Biblical Commentary by James R. Edwards. Copyright © 1992. Used by permission of Hendrickson Publishers, Peabody, MA.

Romans (Ancient Christian Commentary of Scripture) edited by Gerald Bray. © 1998 by the Institute of Classical Christian Studies (ICCS), Thomas Oden and Gerald Bray. Used by permission of InterVarsity Press, P.O. Box 1400, Downers Grove, IL 50515.

Romans: An Exposition of Chapter 10, Saving Faith by D. Martyn Lloyd-Jones. Copyright © 1997. Used by permission of Banner of Truth, Carlisle, PA.

Romans: The Mission Heart of God by Mark Driscoll. Copyright © 1999. Mars Hill Church sermon notes, April 18, 1999, Seattle, WA. Used by permission of Mark Driscoll.

Romans: The Righteousness of God by A. Schlatter. Copyright © 1995. Used by permission of Hendrickson Publishers, Peabody, MA.

What's So Amazing about Grace? by Philip Yancey. Copyright © 1997 by Philip D. Yancey. Used by permission of Zondervan Publishing House.

The Zondervan NIV Bible Commentary, Vol. 2. Copyright © 1994 by The Zondervan Corporation. Used by permission of Zondervan Publishing House.

INDEX

Boldface numbers refer to defined (What?) terms in the sidebar.

Goodness, 227–228
Gospel of Jesus Christ:
  foundation of, 232
  Gentiles receiving (see Gentiles)
  God's way of reaching the world, 19, 24
  as good news, not law, 96
  Holy Spirit as communicating, 150
  hope as from, 67
  law vs., 94, 147–148
  as life-transforming energy, 151
  as Paul's deepest motivation, 24
  Paul's pride in, 67
  Paul as transformed by, 230–231
  role in salvation, 17
  Roman Empire as spreading, 9
  sharing news of, 150–151
  significance of, 10
  as for sinners, 43
  truth to the world, as bringing, 9, 18
  universalizing of, 265
Gossip, 209
Governing authority, secular:
  American government, 190–191
  Christian responsibility to, 26, 189–196
  civil disobedience, 193
  evil, 194
  God as establishing, 189–190
  God's law and, 192
  good purpose of, 194
  Jesus as respecting, 195
  law, two ways to uphold, 193
  New Covenant teaching on, 189
  obedience to, 201
Grace of God, 8, 19, 46–47, 86, 106
  Abraham, as given to, 52–53
  access to, 65
  being born again, 148 (see also Born again)
  as bigger than sin, 71–72
  eternal life and, 29 (see also Eternal life)
  faith enabling man to receive, 53, 61
  as by faith, not law, 58–59
  as gift from God, 72
  human effort and, 135
  in Jesus' life, death, and resurrection, 7
  judgment and, 21
  justification as by, 55
  and law, relationship between, 56, 86
  law as supplanted by, 45, 144
  and living in accordance with Spirit, 109
  and mercy, relationship between, 134

Reign of, through Christ, 70
  rejecting, 160
  result of, 97
  and righteousness, relationship between, 159
  sainthood and, 9
  salvation and, 158 (see also Salvation)
  significance of, 86
  sin as not causing, 78
  sin escaped through, 43, 86–89
  as undeserved, 132
  works vs., 158–159, 228
Graham, Billy, 148
  on Christian responsibility, 182–183
  on Christianity as daily decision, 196
  on spiritual renewal, 160
Gratitude, 11
  expressing to God, 236
  of Paul, 10–11
Great Commission, 250
Greece, 9
Greed, 23
Greek (language), xvii
Greeks, 16, 43
  attitudes prevalent among, 17
  Paul's obligation to, 16

H
Habakkuk, Book of, Paul as quoting, 20
Haldane, Robert, on Christians, changed hearts and minds, 177
Hardships (see Suffering)
Harmony, among believers, 183–185, 207–208, 227, 266
Hatred:
  of Christians, 17
  as evil, 245
Healing, grace as bringing, 86
Heart(s), 21, 27
  faith as effort of, 149
  hardening of, 134, 159
  Holy Spirit as touching, 150
  of Jews, as darkened, 144
Heaven, 54, 120
  eternal life and, 29
  grace and, 158
  Jews and Gentiles in, 137
  to make up for suffering, 235
Hebrews, Book of, 28
  as quoted, 51
Hell, 128, 136
Hendricks, Dr. Howard, 64
Henry, Matthew:
  on Abraham as spiritual father, 57
  on Abraham's faith, 53

on God's grace, 47
  on God's wrath, 28
  on good works, 94
  on Jesus, self-denial of, 222
  on justification of believers, 107
  on repentance, 27
Heralded, **151**
Hermas, 245
Hermes, 245
Herod, **183**
Herodian, 243–**244**
High Priest, **13**, **176**
  illustration of, 14
His will, **101**
Hodge, Charles:
  on God in nature, 153
  on grace and holiness, 89
  on salvation, 147–148
Holiness, **88**, 200
Holy City, Jerusalem as, 151, 246
Holy kiss, 246
Holy of Holies, 175–176
Holy Spirit, **xvi**, 108, 111, 148, 226
  as always in believers' hearts, 213
  body as temple of, 84, 105, 110–111
  confronting human disobedience, 32
  controlling believers, 108
  as counselor, 215, 223
  fruits of, 213
  gifts of, 179 (see also Gifts)
  helping and supporting us, 117, 119
  Jesus linked to believers through, 255, 263–265
  Jesus raised from dead by, 111
  life through, 109, 263
  listening to, 209
  our need for, 93
  Pentecost, 225
  role of in prayer, 13, 117
  as strengthening us, 227, 228
  in Trinity, 263–264
  zeal, as source of, true, 143
Homosexuality, 22–23
Hooker, Thomas, 149
Hope, 60, 181
  Gospel as source of, 64–65, 67
Hosea, Book of:
  Paul as quoting, 137
  as quoted, 72
Hospitality, 181–182, 240
House church, **241**
  illustration of, 242
Human nature:
  sinfulness as, 135, 258–259 (see also Sin nature)
  as unchanged since Paul's day, 199–200

Humility, 15, 135, 138, 179, 188, 207, 209
    of Paul, 227, 235
Hypocrisy, 32–33, 36, 146

I

Idols, Idolatry, 21
    in Athens, 45
    Baal, 156–157
    Israelite calf idol, illustration of, 205
    meat offered to, 204–205
Ignorance, 171
Impediment, **196**
Imperfect and aorist, **100**
Incarnation, the, **7**
Incarnational, **151**
Insults, on Christ, 220
Insurrection, **195**
Intercedes, **117**
Intercession, 118
Interpretation, **40**
Isaac, 32, 60, 129, 131–133
    as patriarch, 146
Isaiah, Book of, 137, 152, 168, 231
    Paul as quoting, 159, 170, 225
Ishmael, 60, 132
Israel, **130**
    blessings given to, 129–130
    destiny of, 155–156, 160–163, 165–
        168, 226
    fall of, 155–162, 171
    God's covenant people, 30, 129–130
    God's promises to, 226
    Jesus as Messiah of, 7
    Jesus rejected by, 128–130, 140–141,
        152, 155–159, 162, 164–168, 232
    the law as given to, 146
    legalism of, 4–5
    Old Covenant and, 127
    Paul's grief for, 138
    present-day, 186
    righteousness, as clinging to old
        ideas of, 139, 143–144, 259
    salvation of, future, 155–156, 160–
        163, 165–168, 226
    "spirit of stupor," 158–159
    zeal of for God, 141–144, 153
    (See also Jews)

J

Jacob, God's choice of, 32, 129, 131–
    133, 146
James, Book of, as quoted, 94, 187
James, son of Zebedee, 183
Jason, 248–249
Jenkins, Jerry, Tim LaHaye and, *Left
    Behind*, 35

Jeremiah, 8
Jerome, Saint:
    on glory, 115
    on the Gospel's rapid spread, 234
    on the olive tree, 165
Jerusalem, 231–232, 246
    early Christianity in, xvii, 7, 12
    as Holy City, 151
    Paul's journey to, 234–237
Jesse, Root of, 225
Jesus Christ:
    ancestral line of, 6–7, 131–133
    authority of, 224
    behavior of, 221–222
    believers in likeness of, 119–120
    Christians as coheirs with, 113–114
    compassion of, 88
    death of, significance, 46–48, 68, 74,
        106, 255, 263
    death, victory over, 82–84
    as divine and human, 7
    as end of the law, 144
    faith in, 46, 255 (*see also* Faith)
    God as in person of, 262
    God, relationship with, 6
    as God's gift, 226
    God's love expressed in, 253
    holiness of, 88
    interceding for us, 121
    Israel's rejection of (*see under*
        Israel)
    Jewish identity of, 34
    as keeping the law perfectly, 139
    Lamb of God, 47
    as Lord, xviii, 147
    love for us, 74, 121, 181, 224
    as Messiah, xvi (*see also* Messiah)
    ministry of, 224
    as mystery revealed, 250
    nature of, 6
    New Covenant of, 127
    Paul as compared to, 128–129
    personal relationship with, xviii, 200,
        263–264
    prayer, role of in, 13
    purpose of, 94
    resurrected, Paul's encounter with,
        41–42
    resurrection of, 6, 60, 82, 111, 263
    righteousness of, 19–20, 97
    sacrificial atonement of, 46–49, 120,
        261
    salvation as through, 34, 147, 224
        (*see also* Salvation)
    as Savior, 147
    as "Second Adam," 70–73, 77

Second Coming of (*see* Second
    Coming)
selflessness of, 222
as servant, 178, 219–222, 224
as sin offering, 106
sin's effect on, 224
as Son of God, 6
suffering of, 60, 224
Supreme Lordship of, xviii, 147
as Teacher, 200
in Trinity, 263–264
twofold nature of, 7
unbelievers to acknowledge, 147
union with, 79–83, 89, 92, 255, 262–
    264
    (*See also* Gospel; Messiah; New
    Covenant)
Jew(s), **32**
    Abraham as forefather of, 51–52,
        130–132, 155, 254
    ancestral line of, 32
    Christ as servant of, 224
    Christian converts from among (*see*
        Jewish Christians)
    Christianity as rejected by, 161–165
    circumcision of, 261
    David as forefather of, 55
    disobedience of, 155
    and Gentiles' salvation, 160–168
    as God's chosen people, 30, 128–
        130, 155–161, 167–168, 254, 260
    God's faithfulness to, 39–40
    God's promises to, 129
    God's relationship with, 137–138,
        255–256
    identity of, 260
    Israel as nation of, 30
    Jewish Christians (*see* Jewish
        Christians)
    Messiah as from, 34
    Old Covenant as ruling, 210
    Old Covenant vs. New Covenant, 127
    Patriarchs' importance to, 146, 168
    Paul as, 128, 141–142, 144
    Paul's concern for, 33–34
    Paul's ministry to, 162
    rich heritage of, 128–130
    Roman attitude toward, 253
    Rome, as expelled from, 3, 190
    salvation as from, 224
    salvation for, 138
    Savior as from, 43
    spiritual privileges of, 129–130
    the Sanhedrin (*see* Sanhedrin)
    value of being, 39–40
    (*See also* Israel; Jews and Gentiles)

Jewish Christians, **3**, 163
    Gentile Christians, relationship with
        (*see* Jews and Gentiles)
    in Rome, 7–8
    "the remnant" (*see* Remnant)
    special advantages of, 39–40
    (*See also* Gentiles; Jews; Jewish
        Christians)
Jews and Gentiles:
    Christian harmony among, 207–208
    commonality of, 43
    compared, 29–30, 35–36
    equality of, in Christ, 260, 262
    in God's kingdom, 137
    helping each other, 234
    Jews' advantages, 39–40
    Jews' attitude toward Gentiles, 17, 254
    mutual sharing of blessings, 234
    regarding sin, 36
    relationship in God's plan of
        redemption, 232
    righteousness offered to both, 152
    Roman Empire populations of, 253
    salvation for both, 149
    sharing blessings, 234
    significance of Romans (Book of) to,
        266
    as sinners alike, 255
Jezebel, 156
Job, Book of, Paul as quoting, 170
John, Book of, as quoted, 10, 17, 34, 51,
    121, 181, 263
1 John, Book of, as quoted, 29, 181
Joy, 170, 213, 226
Judah, xvii
Judaism:
    Christianity as supplanting, 161
    Gentile converts to, 18, 253
    Old Covenant rule in, 210
    the Torah, 40, 222
Jude, martyrdom of, 183
Judea:
    Herod as king of, 183
    unbelievers in, 235
Judge, **206**
Judgment (God's), **21**, 23, 134, 140, 159
    final, 198
    as God's job, 25–28, 208–209, 216
    original sin as bringing, 71
    standard of, 259
Judgment, of other people (*see*
    Judgmentalism)
Judgment day, 32, 55
Judgmentalism, avoiding, 16, 25–27, 30,
    203–211, 216
Judgments, **134**

Julia, 245
Junias, Andronicus and, 242
Justice, of God, 46, 49
Justification, **34**, 53, **105**
    of Abraham, 57
    benefits of, 64–65, 74
    forgiveness and, 61
    as by God's grace through faith, 53,
        55, 64, 106, 261–262
    Martin Luther rediscovering
        doctrine, 267
    and sanctification, 105
Justified, **47**, **51**
Justified by faith, **77**

K

Keener, Craig S.:
    on Satan's defeat, 248
    on Tryphaena and Tryphosa, 245
Kindness, 165–166
    to enemies, 186–187
    God's, 165–166
King Ahab, **156**
King, Martin Luther, 193
Kingdom, **5**
Kingdom of God, Jew and Gentiles in,
    137
1 Kings, Book of, as quoted, 156–157
Kinsman-redeemer, Jesus as, 72
Kiss, holy, 246
KJV, **40**
Knowledge:
    faith as depending on, 150
    as test of zeal, 143
Kohlenberger, John R., III (*see* Barker,
    Kenneth L., and John R.
    Kohlenberger III)
Kosher, 204

L

LaHaye, Tim, and Jerry Jenkins, *Left
    Behind*, 35
Lamb of God, **10**, 47
Lamb's Book of Life, 242
Laodicea, 18
Law (Old Testament), 30, **32**–33, 91–92,
    96, **159**
    as defining righteousness and sin,
        44–45, 97–98, 104, 143–145
    "dying to the law," 92–95
    fulfilled in life and work of Jesus, 144
    God's guidance vs., 93
    as God-given and holy, 91, 97, 99,
        104
    Jesus as end of bondage to, 53, 57–
        59, 92, 139, 144, 147–148

    Jewish trust in, 45
    knowing vs. doing, 30–36
    mistaken perception of, 259
    as not itself sin, 100
    old vs. new, 96
    Paul as well schooled in, 91
    purpose of, 49, 93, 98, 106
    salvation impossible through, 48–49,
        91–104, 106, 153
    as showing need for salvation, 44–
        45, 48
    and sin, relationship between, 92,
        95, 98
    standards as helpful, 98
Law (principle of sin nature), **101**
Law (Roman), 113
Law (secular) (*see* Governing authority)
Law of sin and death, **105**
Law of the Spirit of life, **105**
Lazarus, 184
Left Behind series, 35
Legalism, 4–5
Leviticus, **146**
Leviticus, Book of, as quoted, 259
Lewis, C. S., 179
    on perfection, 226
Libya, 246
Lies, Satan as father of, 22
Life, eternal (*see* Eternal life)
Life, living for glory of God, 99
Light (holy), 21, 51, 199–200
Light, armor of, 199–200
Lillenas, Haldor, 87
Lineage, **6**
Listening, value of, 182
Litmus test, **143**
Lloyd-Jones, D. Martyn:
    on faith, 41
    on faith, expression of, 149
    on future for Jews and Gentiles, 156
    on the heart of the Gospel, 19–20
    on intellectualism vs. the Gospel, 147
    on Jews and Gentiles, 131
    on Paul's letter to the Romans, 5
    on writing people off, 163
    on zeal, 142–143
Lord, in Old and New Testaments, xviii
Love, **67**, 68
    agape, 181, 197
    among believers, 182, 211–212, 221,
        245–246, 265
    brotherly, 245–246
    Christian's life of, 92, 181–182
    Christ's for us, 74, 121, 181, 224
    church problems, as solution to, 122
    debt of, 196–197

in Christian life, 213
with God, 64–65
God's, 109, 226
from justification by faith, 64–65
meaning of, 214
with others, 186
Paul's concern for, 237
proclamation of, 151
Pelagius:
on Christian freedom, responsibility of, 216
on God and government, 193
on God directing Paul, 13
on lust, 22
Pentecost, **225**
Perfection, 226, 254–255
serpent's promise of, 101
sinless, 101
Persecution, 183–184
of early Christians, 250–251
of early Christians, Paul's history of, 27
of Paul, 231
Perseverance, 65
Persis, 243–244
Peter, martyrdom of, 183
1 Peter, Book of, 137
as quoted, 88, 191
Peterson, Eugene, 179
Pharaoh (in time of Moses), 134
Pharisee(s), **xvi, xviii**, 60, 65, **193**
as focused on outward things, 97
Nicodemus as, 51
Paul as former, xvi, 13, 91, 97, 142, 222
Philadelphia (form of love), 181
Philip, **7**
martyrdom of, 183
Philippians, Book of, as quoted, 7, 109, 147, 178
Philippians, Paul's ministry to, 7
Philologus, 245
Phlegon, 245
Phoebe, 240–242
Phrygia, 63, 232
Piety, **11**
Piper, John:
on Abraham's faith, 57
on faith vs. law, 58–59
Plumer, William S.:
on Christian freedom, right use of, 208
on Christian struggle with sin, 101
on God's hand, 13
on law vs. gospel, 94
on law, purpose and uses for, 98

on levels of Christianity, 216
on preaching, 151
Politics, politicians:
religion and, 179
(*See also* Governing authority)
Pontius, 63
Potter and clay, 135–136
Power of God, 17
Praise, for God, 64, 68–69, 209, 236
Paul's doxologies, 169–170, 250
Prayer, 10–11, 13, 118, 181, 209
for each other, 227
formal, as ritual, 34
by the Holy Spirit, 117
intercession, 118
as key to faith, 24
Paul as requesting, 232, 235
of Paul for Romans, 10–12
Preaching, 151, 153
Gospel, sharing news of, 150–151
of Paul (*see* Paul's ministry and teaching)
(*See also* Evangelism; Witness)
Predestination (doctrine of), **133**, 144
Predestined, **119**
Prejudice, 16–17
of Greeks, 17
Jews vs. Gentiles, 17, 254
Pride:
destructiveness of, 178
God's mercy as counter to, 135
Paul's for the Gospel, 67
two kinds of, 35–36
Priestly duty, **228**
Priests, **176**
Christians as believer-priests, 175–176, 214, 228
Old Covenant, 175–176
Priscilla and Aquila, 241–242
Prison, Paul imprisoned in Rome, xvii, 235–236
Problems (*see* Suffering)
Promises, of God (*see* God's promises)
Prophesy (Old Testament), xvi, 6, 128
of Jeremiah, 8
promises of Messiah, 240, 253
Prophetic message, the, **128**
Prophetic writings, Jesus predicted by, 250
Prophets, **146**
as Jewish, 129
Prophets (writings), the, **46**, **159**
Propitiation, 47–49
Propitious, **13**
Protestant Reformation, 6, **55**, 144, 267 (*see also* Luther, Martin)

Proverbs, Book of, as quoted, 189
Psalms, Book of, 13, 20, 118, 159–160, 257
Paul as quoting, 41, 121, 159, 221, 225
as quoted, 102, 163, 191, 226
Punishment:
on judgment day, 32
for sin, 256
Put to death, **112**

Q

Quartus, 248–249

R

Rebekah, 131–133
Rebellion, against governing authority, 192–193
Reborn (*see* Born again; Salvation)
Recalcitrant, **144**
Reconciled, **16**, **68**
Reconciliation (between humans and God), 64, 68–69
Red Sea, 134
Redemption, 116
costliness of, 47
Old Covenant system of, 47
of our bodies, 111
Reformation (Protestant), 6, **55**, 144, 267 (*see also* Luther, Martin)
Reformers, the, 149
Reign, **92**
Relatives, **242**
Remnant, **138**, 140, 156–159, 161, 171
Repentance, 27
Resurrection (end-time, of Christians), 255, 264
Resurrection (of Jesus), 6, 60, 82, 111, 263
significance of, 89
union with Christ in (*See under* Jesus Christ)
Retribution, **21**
Revelation, Book of, as quoted, 242
Revenge, 186–187
Richards, Larry, 100–102
on differences among Christians, 206
on Esau, 132
on Jesus, costly death of, 48
on justification and righteousness, 55
on kindness to enemies, 186
Righteousness, 8, 140
of Abraham, 60
Christian community and, 256
in Christian life, 213

Books by Starburst Publishers®

(Partial listing—full list available on request)

The **God's Word for the Biblically-Inept™** series is already a best-seller with over 100,000 books sold! Designed to make reading the Bible easy, educational, and fun! This series of verse-by-verse Bible studies, topical studies, and overviews mixes scholarly information from experts with helpful icons, illustrations, sidebars, and time lines. It's the Bible made easy!

Romans—God's Word for the Biblically-Inept™
Gib Martin

The best-selling *God's Word for Biblically-Inept™* series continues to grow! Learn about the apostle Paul, living a righteous life, and more with help from graphics, icons, and chapter summaries.
(trade paper)   ISBN 1892016273   **$16.95**

The Bible—God's Word for the Biblically-Inept™
Larry Richards

An excellent book to start learning the entire Bible. Get the basics or the in-depth information you are seeking with this user-friendly overview. From Creation to Christ to the Millennium, learning the Bible has never been easier.
(trade paper)   ISBN 0914984551   **$16.95**

Daniel—God's Word for the Biblically-Inept™
Daymond R. Duck

Daniel is a book of prophecy and the key to understanding the mysteries of the Tribulation and end-time events. This verse-by-verse commentary combines humor and scholarship to get at the essentials of Scripture. Perfect for those who want to know the truth about the Antichrist.
(trade paper)   ISBN 0914984489   **$16.95**

Genesis—God's Word for the Biblically-Inept™
Joyce L. Gibson

Genesis is written to make understanding and learning the Word of God simple and fun! Like the other books in this series, the author breaks the Bible down into bite-sized pieces making it easy to understand and incorporate into your life. Readers will learn about Creation, Adam and Eve, the Flood, Abraham and Isaac, and more.
(trade paper)   ISBN 1892016125   **$16.95**

Health & Nutrition—God's Word for the Biblically-Inept™
Kathleen O'Bannon Baldinger

The Bible is full of God's rules for good health! Baldinger reveals scientific evidence that proves the diet and health principles outlined in the Bible are the best for total health.

Learn about the Bible diet, the food pyramid, and fruits and vegetables from the Bible! Experts include Pamela Smith, Julian Whitaker, Kenneth Cooper, and T. D. Jakes.
(trade paper)   ISBN 0914984055   **$16.95**

Life of Christ, Volume 1—God's Word for the Biblically-Inept™
Robert C. Girard

Girard takes the reader on an easy-to-understand journey through the Gospels of Matthew, Mark, Luke, and John, tracing the story of Jesus from his virgin birth to his revolutionary ministry. Learn about Jesus' baptism, the Sermon on the Mount, and his miracles and parables.
(trade paper)   ISBN 1892016230   **$16.95**

Life of Christ, Volume 2—God's Word for the Biblically-Inept™
Robert C. Girard

Life of Christ, Volume 2, begins with events recorded in Matthew 16. Read about Jesus' transfiguration, his miracles and parables, triumphal ride through Jerusalem, capture in the Garden of Gethsemane, and his trial, crucifixion, resurrection, and ascension. Find out how to be great in the kingdom of God, what Jesus meant when he called himself the light of the world, and what makes up real worship.
(trade paper)   ISBN 1892016397   **$16.95**

Men of the Bible—God's Word for the Biblically-Inept™
D. Larry Miller

Benefit from the life experiences of the powerful men of the Bible! Learn how the inspirational struggles of men such as Moses, Daniel, Paul, and David parallel the struggles of men today. It will inspire and build Christian character for any reader.
(trade paper)   ISBN 1892016079   **$16.95**

Prophecies of the Bible—God's Word for the Biblically-Inept™
Daymond R. Duck

God has a plan for this crazy planet, and now understanding it is easier than ever! Best-selling author and end-time prophecy expert Daymond R. Duck explains the complicated prophecies of the Bible in plain English. Duck shows you all there is to know about the end of the age, the New World Order, the Second Coming, and the coming world government. Find out what prophecies have already been fulfilled and what's in store for the future!
(trade paper)   ISBN 1892016222   **$16.95**

Revelation—God's Word for the Biblically-Inept™
Daymond R. Duck

End-time Bible prophecy expert Daymond R. Duck leads us verse by verse through one of the Bible's most confusing books. Follow the experts as they forge their way through the captivating prophecies of Revelation! (trade paper)   ISBN 0914984985   **$16.95**

Women of the Bible—God's Word for the Biblically-Inept™
Kathy Collard Miller

Finally, a Bible perspective just for women! Gain valuable insight from the successes and struggles of such women as Eve, Esther, Mary, Sarah, and Rebekah. Interesting icons like "Get Close to God," "Build Your Spirit," and "Grow Your Marriage" will make it easy to incorporate God's Word into your daily life. (trade paper)   ISBN 0914984063   **$16.95**

The ***What's in the Bible for . . .*™** series focuses on making the Bible applicable to everyday life. Whether you're a teenager or senior citizen, this series has the book for you! Each title is equipped with the same reader-friendly icons, callouts, tables, illustrations, questions, and chapter summaries that are used in the *God's Word for the Biblically-Inept™* series. It's another easy way to access God's Word!

What's in the Bible for . . .™ Couples
Larry and Kathy Miller

Restore love, unity, and commitment with internationally acclaimed relationship experts Larry and Kathy Miller as they explore God's Word on such topics as dating, sex, money, and trauma. Don't miss the "Take It from Them" feature, which offers wisdom from couples who have lived and learned, and the "Couples of the Bible" feature that spotlights the experiences of such couples as Adam and Eve, Abraham and Sarah, and Joseph and Mary. (Available Spring 2001.) (trade paper)   ISBN 1892016028   **$16.95**

What's in the Bible for . . .™ Mothers
Judy Bodmer

Is home schooling a good idea? Is it okay to work? At what age should I start treating my children like responsible adults? What is the most important thing I can teach my children? If you are asking these questions and need help answering them, *What's in the Bible for . . .™ Mothers* is especially for you! Simple and user-friendly, this motherhood manual offers hope and instruction for today's mothers by jumping into the lives of mothers in the Bible (e.g., Naomi, Elizabeth, and Mary) and by exploring biblical principles that are essential to being a nurturing mother. (trade paper)   ISBN 1892016265   **$16.95**

What's in the Bible for . . .™ Teens
Mark and Jeanette Littleton

This is a book that teens will love! *What's in the Bible for. . .™ Teens* contains topical Bible themes that parallel the challenges and pressures of today's adolescents. Learn about Bible prophecy, God's plan for relationships, and peer pressure in a conversational and fun tone. Helpful and eye-catching "WWJD?" icons, illustrations, and sidebars included. (trade paper)   ISBN 1892016052   **$16.95**

What's in the Bible for . . .™ Women
Georgia Curtis Ling

What does the Bible have to say to women? Women of all ages will find biblical insight on topics that are meaningful to them in four sections: Wisdom for the Journey; Family Ties; Bread, Breadwinners, and Bread Makers; and Fellowship and Community Involvement. This book uses illustrations, bullet points, chapter summaries, and icons to make understanding God's Word easier than ever! (trade paper)   ISBN 1892016109   **$16.95**

(see page 308 for purchasing information)

• **Learn more at www.biblicallyinept.com** •

God Things Come in Small Packages: Celebrating the Little Things in Life
Susan Duke, LeAnn Weiss, Caron Loveless, and Judith Carden

Enjoy touching reminders of God's simple yet generous gifts to brighten our days and gladden our hearts! Treasures like a sunset over a vast sparkling ocean, a child's trust, or the crystalline dew on a spider's web come to life in this elegant compilation. Such occasions should be celebrated as if gift wrapped from God; they're his hallmarks! Personalized Scripture is artfully combined with compelling stories and reflections. (cloth)   ISBN 1892016281   **$12.95**

God Things Come in Small Packages for Moms: Rejoicing in the Simple Pleasures of Motherhood
Susan Duke, LeAnn Weiss, Caron Loveless, and Judith Carden

The "small" treasures God plants in a mom's day shine in this delightful book. Savor priceless stories, which encourage us to value treasures like a shapeless, ceramic bowl presented with a toothy grin; a child's hand clinging to yours on a crowded bus; or a handful of wildflowers presented on a hectic day. Each story combines personalized Scripture with heartwarming vignettes and inspiring reflections. (cloth)   ISBN 189201629X   **$12.95**

The Weekly Feeder: A Revolutionary Shopping, Cooking, and Meal-Planning System
Cori Kirkpatrick

A revolutionary meal-planning system, here is a way to make preparing home-cooked dinners more convenient than ever. At the beginning of each week, simply choose one of the eight preplanned menus, tear out the corresponding grocery list, do your shopping, and whip up each fantastic meal in less than 45 minutes! The author's household management tips, equipment checklists, and nutrition information make this system a must for any busy family. Included with every recipe is a personal anecdote from the author emphasizing the importance of good food, a healthy family, and a well-balanced life.

(trade paper)   ISBN 1892016095 $16.95

God Stories: They're So Amazing, Only God Could Make Them Happen
Donna I. Douglas

Famous individuals share their personal, true-life experiences with God in this beautiful new book! Find out how God has touched the lives of top recording artists, professional athletes, and other newsmakers like Jessi Colter, Deana Carter, Ben Vereen, Stephanie Zimbalist, Cindy Morgan, Sheila E., Joe Jacoby, Cheryl Landon, Brett Butler, Clifton Taulbert, Babbie Mason, Michael Medved, Sandi Patty, Charlie Daniels, and more! Their stories are intimate, poignant, and sure to inspire and motivate you as you listen for God's message in your own life!

(cloth)   ISBN 1892016117 $18.95

God's Little Rule Book: Simple Rules to Bring Joy & Happiness to Your Life
Starburst Publishers

Let this little book of God's rules be your personal guide to a more joyful life. Brimming with easily applicable rules, this book is sure to inspire and motivate you! Each rule includes corresponding Scripture and a practical tip that will help to incorporate God's rules into everyday life. Simple enough to fit into a busy schedule, yet powerful enough to be life changing!

(trade paper)   ISBN 1892016168 $6.95

Life's Little Rule Book: Simple Rules to Bring Joy & Happiness to Your Life
Starburst Publishers

Let this little book inspire you to live a happier life! The pages are filled with timeless rules such as, "Learn to cook, you'll always be in demand!" and "Help something grow." Each rule is combined with a reflective quote and a simple suggestion to help the reader incorporate the rule into everyday life.

(trade paper)   ISBN 1892016176 $6.95

God's Abundance
Edited by Kathy Collard Miller

Over 100,000 sold! This day-by-day inspirational is a collection of thoughts by leading Christian writers such as Patsy Clairmont, Jill Briscoe, Liz Curtis Higgs, and Naomi Rhode. *God's Abundance* is based on God's Word for a simpler, yet more abundant life. Learn to make all aspects of your life—personal, business, financial, relationships, even housework—a "spiritual abundance of simplicity."

(cloth)   ISBN 0914984977 $19.95

Promises of God's Abundance
Edited by Kathy Collard Miller

Subtitled: *For a More Meaningful Life*. The Bible is filled with God's promises for an abundant life. *Promises of God's Abundance* is written in the same way as the best-selling *God's Abundance*. It will help you discover these promises and show you how simple obedience is the key to an abundant life. Scripture, questions for growth, and a simple thought for the day will guide you to a more meaningful life.

(trade paper)   ISBN 0914984098 $9.95

Stories of God's Abundance for a More Joyful Life
Compiled by Kathy Collard Miller

Like its successful predecessor, *God's Abundance*, this book is filled with beautiful, inspirational, real-life stories. Those telling their stories of God share Scriptures and insights that readers can apply to their daily lives. Renew your faith in life's small miracles and challenge yourself to allow God to lead the way as you find the source of abundant living for all your relationships.

(trade paper)   ISBN 1892016060 $12.95

Treasures of a Woman's Heart: A Daybook of Stories and Inspiration
Edited by Lynn D. Morrissey

Join the best-selling editor of *Seasons of a Woman's Heart* in this touching sequel where she unlocks the treasures of women and glorifies God with Scripture, reflections, and a compilation of stories. Explore heartfelt living with vignettes by Kay Arthur, Elisabeth Elliot, Emilie Barnes, Claire Cloninger, and more.

(cloth)   ISBN 1892016257 $18.95

Seasons of a Woman's Heart: A Daybook of Stories and Inspiration
Edited by Lynn D. Morrissey

A woman's heart is complex. This daybook of stories, quotes, Scriptures, and daily reflections will inspire and refresh. Christian women share their heartfelt thoughts on seasons of faith, growth, guidance, nurturing, and victory. Includes Christian writers Kay Arthur, Emilie Barnes, Luci Swindoll, Jill Briscoe, and Florence Littauer.

(cloth)   ISBN 1892016036 $18.95

Why Fret That God Stuff?

Compiled by Kathy Collard Miller

Subtitled: *Stories of Encouragement to Help You Let Go and Let God Take Control of All Things in Your Life.* Occasionally, we all become overwhelmed by the everyday challenges of our lives: hectic schedules, our loved ones' needs, unexpected expenses, a sagging devotional life. *Why Fret That God Stuff* is the perfect beginning to finding joy and peace for the real world! (trade paper)   ISBN 0914984500   **$12.95**

Allergy Cooking with Ease

Nicolette M. Dumke

Subtitled: *The No Wheat, Milk, Eggs, Corn, Soy, Yeast, Sugar, Grain, and Gluten Cookbook.*
A book designed to provide a wide variety of recipes to meet many different dietary and social needs, and whenever possible, save you time in food preparation. Includes recipes for foods that food allergy patients think they will never eat again, as well as time-saving tricks and an Allergen Avoidance index. (trade paper)   ISBN 091498442X   **$14.95**

Migraine—Winning the Fight of Your Life

Charles Theisler

This book describes the hurt, loneliness, and difficulty that migraine sufferers live with. It explains the different types of migraines and their symptoms, as well as the related health hazards. Gives 200 ways to help fight off migraines, and shows how to have fewer headaches, reduce their duration, and decrease the pain involved. (trade paper)   ISBN 0914984632   **$10.95**

More of Him, Less of Me

Jan Christiansen

Subtitled: *A Daybook of My Personal Insights, Inspirations & Meditations on the Weigh Down™ Diet.* The insight shared in this yearlong daybook of inspiration will encourage you on your weight-loss journey, bring you to a deeper relationship with God, and help you improve any facet of your life. Each page includes an essay, Scripture, and a tip-of-the-day that will encourage and uplift you as you trust God to help you achieve your proper weight. Perfect companion guide for anyone on the Weigh Down™ diet! (cloth)   ISBN 1892016001   **$17.95**

Desert Morsels: A Journal with Encouraging Tidbits from My Journey on the Weigh Down™ Diet

Jan Christiansen

When Jan Christiansen set out to lose weight on the Weigh Down™ diet she got more than she bargained for! In addition to *losing* over 35 pounds and *gaining* a closer relationship with God, Jan discovered a gift— her ability to entertain and comfort fellow dieters! Jan's inspiring website led to the release of her bestselling first book, *More of Him, Less of Me.* Now, Jan serves another helping of her wit and His wisdom in this lovely companion journal. Includes inspiring Scripture, insightful comments, stories from readers, room for the reader's personal reflection, and *Plenty of Attitude* (p-attitude). (cloth)   ISBN 1892016214   **$17.95**

Purchasing Information • www.starburstpublishers.com

Books are available from your favorite bookstore, either from current stock or special order. To assist bookstores in locating your selection, be sure to give title, author, and ISBN. If unable to purchase from a bookstore, you may order direct from STARBURST PUBLISHERS. When ordering please enclose full payment plus shipping and handling as follows:

Post Office (4th class)
$3.00 with a purchase of up to $20.00
$4.00 ($20.01–$50.00)
8% of purchase price for purchases of $50.01 and up

United Parcel Service (UPS)
$5.00 (up to $20.00)
$7.00 ($20.01–$50.00)
12% ($50.01 and up)

Canada
$5.00 (up to $35.00)
15% ($35.01 and up)

Overseas
$5.00 (up to $25.00)
20% ($25.01 and up)

Payment in U.S. funds only. Please allow two to four weeks minimum for delivery by USPS (longer for overseas and Canada). Allow two to seven working days for delivery by UPS. Make checks payable to and mail to:

Starburst Publishers®   •   P.O. Box 4123   •   Lancaster, PA 17604

Credit card orders may be placed by calling 1-800-441-1456, Mon–Fri, 8:30 A.M. to 5:30 P.M. Eastern Standard Time. Prices are subject to change without notice. Catalogs are available for a 9 x 12 self-addressed envelope with four first-class stamps.

NOTES

NOTES

NOTES

NOTES

NOTES

NOTES

NOTES

NOTES